THE DYNAMICS OF EUROPEAN UNION

The Dynamics of
EUROPEAN UNION

Edited by ROY PRYCE

CROOM HELM
London • New York • Sydney

© 1987 Trans-European Policy Studies Association
Croom Helm Ltd, Provident House, Burrell Row,
Beckenham, Kent, BR3 1AT
Croom Helm Australia, 44-50 Waterloo Road,
North Ryde, 2113, New South Wales

Published in the USA by
Croom Helm
in association with Methuen, Inc.
29 West 35th Street
New York, NY 10001

British Library Cataloguing in Publication Data
The Dynamics of European union.
 1. European federation 2. European
 Economic Community countries — Economic
 integration
 I. Pryce, Roy
 337.1'42   HC241.2
 ISBN 0-7099-4327-X

Library of Congress Cataloging in Publication Data
ISBN 0-7099-4327-X

Printed and bound in Great Britain by
Biddles Ltd, Guildford and King's Lynn

CONTENTS

PREFACE

This study, undertaken by the Trans-European Policy Studies Association, is concerned with the attempts of the member states of the European Community to achieve their declared aim of 'an ever closer union'. In pursuit of this goal they committed themselves in 1972 to transform the Community into a European Union. This has not yet been achieved, but the commitment has been regularly reaffirmed, and over the years much experience has been acquired about the nature of the obstacles to be overcome in the search for closer union, the conditions necessary to enable progress towards it to be made, and the strengths and weaknesses of different types of strategies intended to hasten its achievement. The central purpose of this study is to distil this experience and explore the lessons it offers.

The first chapter sets out a framework of analysis to enable a systematic comparison to be made of the main attempts undertaken to push the process of integration forward, and in particular to identify the most important factors contributing to their success or failure. The case studies which follow in Part II deal first with the emergence and experience of the six-member Community, including the early attempt to create a Political Community which is here given the importance it deserves. The successive attempts of the enlarged Community to move towards European Union are then examined, beginning with the Tindemans Report of 1975 and concluding with the most recent negotiations which produced the 'Single European Act' late in 1985. The final chapter assesses its significance, explores the obstacles in the way of further progress towards European Union, and suggests the strategies most likely to overcome them. We hope that our analysis will widen and deepen understanding of the dynamics of the process of integration on the part of policy-makers, opinion leaders, and students of the Community.

We are most grateful to the European Cultural Foundation whose financial assistance made the study possible, and for the cooperation we received from the European University Institute which provided an opportunity for an exchange of ideas at a conference organised by its European Policy Unit in Florence. For my own part, I would also like to thank the Nuffield Foundation for support through the European Centre for Political Studies which enabled me to follow the work of the European Parliament on European Union; Jacques Vandamme, the Chairman of TEPSA, for his sustained help as well as his hospitality; and - above all - the contributors from the member institutes and associations of TEPSA who bore patiently with editorial demands. The views expressed by those of them who work for European institutions are strictly personal.

Roy Pryce

NOTES ON CONTRIBUTORS

<u>Gianni Bonvicini</u> is Deputy Director of the Instituto Affari Internazionali, Rome.

<u>Rita Cardozo</u> is a member of the Secretariat of the European Parliament.

<u>Richard Corbett</u> is a member of the Secretariat of the European Parliament's Committee on Institutional Affairs.

<u>Christian Franck</u> is Chargé de Cours at the Facultés Universitaires of Namur and at the Catholic University of Leuven.

<u>Pierre Gerbet</u> is a Professor at the Institut d'Etudes Politiques, Paris.

<u>Patrick Keatinge</u> is Associate Professor in Political Science at Trinity College, Dublin.

<u>Hanns Jürgen Küsters</u> is a Lecturer at the Institute for Political Studies and European Issues at the University of Cologne.

<u>Ann Murphy</u> is a graduate of the National Institute of Higher Education, Limerick, and the College of Europe, Bruges.

<u>Roy Pryce</u> is Director of the Federal Trust for Education and Research, London, and a Visiting Professor at the European Institute of Public Administration, Maastricht.

<u>Otto Schmuck</u> is a Research Fellow at the Institut für Europäische Politik, Bonn.

<u>Jacques Vandamme</u> is Chairman of the Trans-European Policy Studies Association, Professor at the Catholic University of Leuven, and Visiting Professor at Université de Paris V.

<u>Wolfgang Wessels</u> is a Director of the Institut für Europäische Politik, Bonn, and Director of Administrative Studies at the College of Europe, Bruges.

Chapter One

THE SEARCH FOR AN EVER CLOSER UNION: A FRAMEWORK FOR ANALYSIS

Roy Pryce and Wolfgang Wessels

Since 1972 the member states of the European Community have been formally committed to the achievement of a European Union. This was conceived as the next phase in the search for that 'ever closer union among the European peoples' to which the preamble of the Rome treaties refers. But in spite of a spate of proposals and reports, an intergovernmental conference, and the intensive involvement of the leaders of the Community countries, little progress towards it has been made. A package of reforms was belatedly agreed, with much difficulty, at the end of 1985. But it fell far short of a Treaty establishing European Union for which some had hoped. Do we have to conclude - as others have long believed - that the commitment to European Union is mere rhetoric? And that the member states are either no longer interested in, or capable of achieving, a closer union?

These are two of the questions which this study sets out to answer. But its central purpose is to put this latest series of attempts to achieve a closer union in the context of the overall development of the process of integration in western Europe, and in particular to undertake a critical appraisal of the strategies which have been employed to further that process. Its aim is to distil the extensive body of experience accumulated over more than forty years of western Europe's sustained efforts to achieve greater unity, and to arrive at some general conclusions about the conditions necessary for successful forward movement. (1) We hope in this way not only to contribute to a better understanding of the process as a whole, but also to shed new light on the present state and prospects of the Community, and to offer some practical guidance for those involved in its day-to-day affairs.

In undertaking this work we are aware of the substantial body of academic literature focused on the dynamics of the process of integration to which the early years of the Community gave birth. But in more recent years academics have been wary of re-visiting an area of integration studies in which the neo-functionalists made so heavy and intensive an investment in the late 'fifties and 'sixties, but whose conclusions - unfairly in our view - have been consigned to the dustbin. (2) Attention has moved away from the dynamics of integration to individual policy areas or institutions, while at the same time there has been a general inclination to downgrade the nature of the Community, to cast doubt on its capacity to realise the ambitions of its founders and to assimilate it in a general category of 'international systems'. (3) Once bitten, twice shy: rather than suffer the same fate as the neo-functionalists who nurtured unduly optimistic hopes of the Community-building process academics have recently preferred to hedge their bets, and to concentrate on less problematic themes.

For their part, many politicians are also wary of reflections about the longer-term future of the Community. This is partly because - as Harold Wilson once remarked - even a week is a long time for those engaged in politics. But the result can be a very superficial approach to longer-term problems. It is, of course, generally accepted that progress towards a closer union will not take place automatically, and that if momentum is to be maintained initiatives will have to be taken. But, confronted by the difficulties of achieving forward movement, reflections on how they can be overcome often do not go beyond well-worn clichés which lament the lack of 'political will' on the part of the member governments, or their present preference for intergovernmental methods of cooperation rather than more Community or supranational approaches.

For our part, we accept that there are risks to be faced in trying to draw lessons from the Community's past experience. We are aware, in the first place, of the dangers inherent in the use of historical analogies. A strategy which worked in a given set of circumstances will not necessarily work on other occasions when circumstances are different. There is also the danger of erecting and perpetuating myths about the successes of the past which obscure reality, and present an easy target to 'revisionist' critics who all too often succumb to the temptation of over-stating a contrary thesis. (4)

Similarly, we have to be careful not to interpret history only from the point of view of the present, or to impose on it patterns and classifications which mislead rather than illuminate. (5) In analysing and addressing integration strategies we also have to avoid the twin dangers of, on the one hand, adopting so deterministic an approach that we allow no room at all for political action, or on the other believing that it is sufficient, after analysing the shortcomings of the world in which we live, to set out a vision of the future - a sort of Holy Grail - in the belief that all reasonable people cannot fail to appreciate its virtues and work without more ado towards its achievement.

To stress the dangers inherent in the study of strategies of integration is not to argue that it should not be attempted. But it does mean that such a study should, in the first place, make careful use of the historical data on which it is based. From Popper we know that a verification of causal theories in a complex social world is impossible: what we can do, however, is to test theories against the historical record and reject those which manifestly fail to provide a satisfactory explanation of events. This is the approach adopted in this study, with the modest ambition not of finding and asserting the one and only 'truth' to explain why strategies aimed at achieving a closer union have succeeded or failed, but to clear away some oversimplifications, to point towards some probabilities, and to identify a number of factors as likely to be crucial for success.

In the evaluation of any strategy what has to be taken into account are not only the goals, content and methods of a given initiative, but also the actors promoting it, and the circumstances (environment) in which the initiative is taken. These three sets of factors need to be considered together, for it is their interaction as well as their individual characteristics which account for the success or failure of attempts to move towards closer union.

ENVIRONMENTS

We begin with a series of considerations about the changing nature of the environment in which the process of integration in western Europe has developed since the end of the Second World War. That process can only be understood as a response to pressures generated within European society partly as a result of indigenous political, economic and social factors, and partly as a result of external factors. As the process itself has developed a third set of factors has also come into play: those generated by the dynamics of the process itself. All three sources have given rise to sets of rather contradictory pressures, some helpful to, and others creating obstacles in the way of, the search for closer union. We first need to identify the major sources and changing configuration of these pressures before analysing the reactions to them of Community elites and the strategies they have pursued in search of their goal.

National Environments

The process of integration in western Europe was initiated at a moment of weakness of its original member states. Badly shaken by the experience of the Second World War they were still involved in a difficult process of economic and political reconstruction. The creation of the Coal and Steel Community was part of that process. From the beginning, however, there were different views about the nature and purpose of the process of integration. Some argued that the division of the region into nation states was the fundamental cause of the repeated catastrophes which had overtaken it. According to this view what was needed was a new political framework equipped with a strong common authority in which the component nation states would have a diminished role. Others on the contrary saw the Community essentially as an instrument to help its member states recover their economic and political strength: a means to enable them to take collective action without undermining their autonomy and individuality.

In practice, it is the second view which has prevailed. Over the past forty years the nation state in western Europe, far from withering away, has acquired a far greater range of responsibilities and obligations than ever before. In the first place its economic functions have vastly increased. In many cases it has assumed not only much more extensive and intensive supervisory and regulatory functions, but has also undertaken direct ownership of substantial sectors of the economy. At the same time, its welfare functions have also been enormously extended. National governments have become responsible for services designed to nurture and protect the citizen from the cradle to the grave: the cost of these now absorbs up to half the gross national product, and their management has made national governments loom larger than ever in the life of each of its citizens. For the overwhelming mass of them the nation state remains the primary focus of their political loyalty. And in a society subjected to many technological and cultural pressures tending in the direction of uniformity, the deeply-felt need of Europeans to maintain diversity has even strengthened this attachment.

These factors have operated as basic parameters for the development of the European Community. At the same time, however, these same nation states have also had to recognise that they are unable by themselves to deal with many of the problems they now face. In terms of their two basic functions - welfare and security - the members of the Community are all acutely aware of the need to cooperate with their neighbours, and not merely sporadically, but regularly and intensively. The pressures impelling them to do so have grown steadily over the years. One important source of these are powerful economic interests, both public and private, which have seen the need for a large and secure European market not only as an outlet for their products and services, but also as a base to enable them to compete effectively in wider international markets. Those same interests have also generated strong pressures for the Community to develop policies to defend and promote European interests in negotiations with other countries and regions of the world. At the same time common strategic and defence interests have also persuaded most of the states in western Europe of the need for close cooperation in these policy areas also.

It has, nevertheless, always been difficult to reach agreement on how to respond to these pressures. A fundamental reason for this is that each nation state has its own national interests and its own concept of the common interest arising out of individual national histories, cultures and geographical situations. In the case of the Community this is reflected in the particular importance attached by successive French governments to their relations with the Federal Republic; the continuing concern in the United Kingdom to maintain a special relationship with the United States; Danish sensitivity about relations with other Scandinavian countries, and so on. These individual national concerns impinge directly both on individual fields

5

of policy (agriculture, energy and fisheries are three examples of sharply conflicting rather than complementary interests) and also on attitudes and policies to the overall development of the Community.

Although there have been some important permanent elements in the interests pursued by individual member states, their evaluation of these interests is constantly changing, as are the politics by which they are pursued. This process of adjustment is part of the normal daily activity of any government, though sometimes major changes of direction are preceded by a formal examination of alternative strategies – as was the case, for instance, with the original British decision to seek entry into the Community. (6) But however the process is carried out, it always involves the need to reconcile different interests within each individual country – a function performed by the leading figures in the government of the day, with a special role frequently being played by the prime minister (or, in France, by the president). In determining policies towards the development of the Community, too, such leaders play a key role, and the success or failure of projects for closer union has always rested firmly in their hands.

It has frequently been difficult, however, to ensure political support in several major member states at the same time for an initiative. One reason for this is the continued high degree of autonomy of each individual political system. National elections occur at different times, and with them changes of leadership. Party political trends, too, only occasionally follow similar directions in different member countries. So 'windows of opportunity' when the leaders of a significant group of member states are able to agree on a project for forward movement, and feel themselves in a strong enough position to push it to a conclusion, arise mainly in a haphazard and unpredictable way – and can easily and swiftly disappear again before a particular project has been decided.

All this means that chance and accident continue to play a large part in the dynamics of the process of integration, and in the search for closer union. But the conflicting pressures to which the members of the Community are subjected also means that moves towards closer union have to be very carefully designed to appeal to national interests, and to provide a point of convergence for them so that they can be harnessed to the achievement of a common goal.

The International Context

In the development of the Community an important but fluctuating and frequently unpredictable role has been played by external forces. The simple-minded view that the stronger the external challenges the easier it is to achieve closer union is not borne out by the record: the relationship between the Community and its international environment has been far more complex.

Throughout the process the fundamental feature of that environment has been the continued division of Europe into rival spheres of interest dominated by the two Super Powers, and the dependence of western Europe on the United States for its security and defence. The relationship however has been far from static, and its successive phases have had significantly different consequences for the development of the Community.

There is no doubt that intially the support of the United States was a critical factor in the successful launching of the Community. This not only guaranteed support against any Soviet attempt to intervene against it, but also neutralized British opposition. And in the period 1950-54 the United States also, though with some reluctance, threw its weight behind the attempt of the Six to create a Defence Union. This support reached its peak in December 1953 when the American Secretary of State, John Foster Dulles, threatened an 'agonising reappraisal' of the US commitment to the defence of western Europe if the French allowed the project for a European Defence Community to fail.

At this point the support of the would-be external federator proved counter-productive: it helped to fuel the nationalist reaction against the EDC project. But in the following years quieter US support, skilfully nurtured and mobilised by Monnet in particular at the highest levels of successive administrations, helped to re-launch the process of economic integration, fend off British attempts to dilute the EEC in a wider Free Trade Area, and subsequently in 1960 encouraged the Six to accelerate the timetable for the achievement of their customs union. (7) Under Kennedy hopes were also nurtured of a more equal Atlantic partnership being developed with an enlarged and strengthened European Community.

The change in the relationship since the mid-sixties has been gradual but profound. It has been characterised by an increasingly hard-nosed attitude on both sides of the Atlantic, and the emergence of a growing number of points of friction. But while the Community has acquired considerable clout in trade matters, it remains weak and divided on international monetary affairs, and as dependent as ever on the United States for its security. These asymmetrical aspects of the relationship have had a significant impact on the way the Community itself has developed. Friction on commercial issues, while sometimes - as in the case of steel - creating significant tensions between the members of the Community, has on the whole impelled them more firmly towards a common posture. But in the fields of foreign, defence and security policy worries about disturbing transatlantic relationships have dictated much prudence. Cooperation on general foreign policy issues ('political cooperation' in EC jargon) was begun in 1970 and has subsequently developed in a very low-key and pragmatic fashion; (8) and even those states which are members of NATO have been very cautious about developing a European caucus within it. Fear of giving offence and of weakening the US commitment to the defence of western Europe are at the root of this, together with divisions among the Europeans themselves on substantive issues of policy. So today the United States plays a far more ambiguous role than it did in the early days of the Community.

The Soviet Union, for its part, has played a far less direct and less significant role in the process of Community-building in western Europe. (9) This is true of each of the successive phases in its post-war relations with the United States, though there have been moments when Soviet policies and action have acted as a specific spur to the countries of western Europe to unite. This was undoubtedly true, for instance, at the time of the initiation of the process when the outbreak of the Korean War - perceived at the time in the West as signalling a more general threat - was used as an argument in favour of the urgency to take action on the Schuman Plan proposals. When, however, the same arguments were used by the United States to urge the need for German rearmament, followed by the proposal for a European Defence Community, powerful counter pressures were activated not only by the Communist parties of western Europe but also by right-wing nationalists. Together with the relaxation of tension which followed of death of Stalin in the Spring of 1953 they were sufficient to abort the project.

The period of detente which followed allowed the Six to refocus their attention on more pacific goals, and to relaunch their programme of economic integration. Soviet intervention to quell the Hungarian rising in 1956 was nevertheless a sufficient reminder of its strength to serve as an added argument for hastening the conclusion of the negotiations for the Rome treaties, while the disarray in western Communist parties which followed the criticism of Stalin by Kruschev at the 20th Party Congress in 1956, also weakened domestic opposition to their ratification, especially in Italy. The subsequent support given by the Italian Communist party to the new programme of economic integration, and the development of similar more independent Eurocommunist parties in several other countries both left the French party substantially isolated in its opposition to the Community, and also greatly reduced the leverage which Moscow could exert on the process. Without this, its own policy of continued hostility to, and non-recognition of, the Community had no significant effect on its development in the following years. The relative detente in its relations with the United States, on the other hand, enabled the process to proceed under its own dynamic.

While it is these relationships which have had the most important impact on the development of the Community, the high level of dependence of its members on trade with the rest of the world has made it also very vulnerable to stresses in the international economy. Whereas the initial establishment of the Community was facilitated by an environment which was favourable to economic growth in western Europe, the abrupt changes in that environment after 1973 initially had a series of negative consequences for its subsequent development. Both the collapse in 1970 of the post-war international monetary system established at Bretton Woods and the subsequent oil crisis following the Middle East war of 1973 had serious consequences for the economies of the member states. The initial quadrupling of the oil prices, and the rise which occurred later in the decade, contributed significantly to the inflation and recession which followed in their train. But their impact varied from country to country, as did the measures taken to combat them by individual national governments. (10) Severe strains were placed on Community solidarity, as was painfully apparent at the time of the threatened Arab oil embargo in 1973. At the same time a series of difficult new problems were thrust onto the Community agenda. All of this contributed to the developing sense of malaise which fuelled the atmosphere of 'Euro-pessimism' so apparent at the beginning of the 'eighties. It is only in more recent years that collective frustration has created a more positive thrust. But while this has become a noticeable element in the developing discussion of European Union it has not led - as its more ardent protagonists might have hoped - to a willingness to abandon the gradual development of collective action in favour of a major leap forward.

While the recent experience of the Community therefore confirms the general proposition that external pressures (of both a negative and positive sort) have been generally favourable to its development, it also lends weight to the view that these pressures by themselves have not been of decisive importance. There have nevertheless been some constellations of external circumstances which have been particularly favourable for progress towards closer union, and others which have impeded its achievement. Both in their structural and purely accidental aspects external factors have also played a significant part in determining the outcome of the successive phases of this search, as the individual studies in Part II will demonstrate.

The Community Environment

Just as both the national and international environments have generated sets of conflicting pressures - some helpful and others inimical to further development of the Community - so, too, has the process of Community-building itself.

This is in spite of the fact that the longer the process has continued, the greater has become the degree of mutual interdependence. By the early 1980s, for instance, intra-Community trade accounted for over half the total exports generated by its members: for over 70% in the case of the Benelux countries and Ireland; and over 40% for all the other member countries. This is but one, if the most striking, aspect of a de facto solidarity which has developed over the years as a result of the process of economic integration. But although this has certainly engendered pressures to go further, there have been other aspects of the process which have at the same time created new difficulties for those seeking an ever closer union.

The most important of these have arisen from the succession of requests for membership, and the subsequent successive enlargements. In the first place, negotiations with the candidate countries have proved a lengthy, time-consuming, and divisive process. It took almost twelve years for Britain, Denmark and Ireland to gain admission, during which time the original Six were subjected to considerable strains, and reduced for several years to virtual paralysis. (11) In comparison Greek membership was achieved in a flash: a mere six years from its request to join (1975) and entry (January 1981). Portugal and Spain took longer, over eight years; their requests to join were presented respectively in March and July 1977, and they only became members in January 1986.

In several cases - and no doubt this will also be true of the more recent members - entry then proved to be merely the beginning of further difficulties. In 1974 the British Labour government formally requested a re-negotiation of the terms of entry. This was a largely cosmetic and relatively speedy operation which was concluded at the Dublin Summit in December 1974 and then followed by a referendum in Britain in June 1975 which confirmed membership by a substantial majority. But Mr Wilson's attempt to find a formula to keep the British budgetary contribution within acceptable grounds failed to operate satisfactorily; Mr Callaghan, his successor, began to make disgruntled noises about it, and when Mrs Thatcher came to power in June 1979 she launched a full-scale assault on the issue, with typical forcefulness. A series of bad-tempered annual arguments then followed: a longer-term, but still temporary arrangement, was not found until the Fontainebleau European Council meeting in June 1984. In the meantime, the arrival in power in Greece of Mr Papandreou also led to what was originally announced as a demand for renegotiation of the terms of his country's membership, and which in practice amounted to a shopping list of additional concessions and financial help.

Enlargement has also meant the need to adapt the policies and instruments of the Community to the needs of its members. It was not at all surprising, for instance, that following the first enlargement which displaced its geographical centre of gravity towards the north-west seaboard, that fisheries policy became a major as well as a highly contentious issue. Similarly, with the more recent addition of new Mediterranean members, policies relating to wine, olive oil and citrus fruits have had to be revised. This second trio of new members has also raised in a much more acute way issues of redistributive justice: how far are the richer members of the group willing to go in helping the poorer?

But enlargement has not only added more sensitive and difficult issues to the agenda: it has also created conditions in which their resolution is more difficult. It has not only added to the numbers around the table of the various institutions - and in particular that of the Council of Ministers and the European Council; it has at the same time entailed successive disturbances to the balance of power within them. The entry of the United Kingdom in particular introduced another major partner, with important consequences for the Franco-German relationship. What had been a virtual duopoly was now converted into an uncertain triangle. (12) This weakened the original driving force behind the Community without creating a new one - especially as the British spent much of their time in the early years of membership playing a spoiling game. Nor did the new constellation do anything to provide a more certain role for Italy. Now the entry of Spain has created a further complication about the membership of the top table in Community affairs. It is a country which is not likely to be willing to accept a subordinate or minor role, yet Paris, Bonn and London may not view Spanish ambitions with great favour.

The earlier phases of enlargement also introduced into the Community countries which were either hesitant about, or quite firmly opposed to, the greater use of majority voting and the abolition of the veto. They therefore consolidated the abuses of the treaty rules at which the Five themselves connived in the 'Luxembourg Compromise' of 1966. The engine of the Community has been weakened by recourse to consensus politics while the braking power in the hands of the member states has been much increased by the use - or threatened use - of the veto.

In all these ways enlargement, while extending the geographical scope of the Community, has proved to be a positive hindrance to the achievement of a closer union in terms of a higher level of integration. At the same time, to the extent that the process has become more intensive - for instance, in the field of monetary policy cooperation through the creation of the European Monetary System - it has impinged more closely on the heartland of national sovereignty, and met with considerable resistance. It was only due to the strenuous efforts of Chancellor Schmidt that the opposition of the Bundesbank was overcome to enable the system to be set up in the first place. There is still very strong

opposition from the same source against embarking on
the promised second stage of the System, which would
involve a much more extensive pooling of reserves
through the creation of a European Monetary Fund and
further loss of national autonomy. Similarly
successive British governments, while formally
joining the EMS, have been anxious to maintain as
much authority as possible in their own hands, and
have not yet taken part in its most crucial element,
the exchange rate mechanism. The same sort of
reactions have also been painfully evident in
national reactions to the Commission's detailed
proposals on the completion of the internal market:
even from those - like the British - who have urged
their partners to make this the top priority for the
Community.

Alongside these factors is also another: a new
type of inertia induced by participation in the
Community and familiarity with its present ways of
doing business. What has now developed is a pooling
or mixing of national sovereignties with Community
competences to produce a new type of system which we
may call 'cooperative federalism'. (13) In contrast
to traditional federalist doctrine, which prescribes
that different levels of government, each
responsible for the matters under its own
jurisdiction, should be clearly separate in their
spheres of activity, what has now developed in the
Community is a system in which both levels of
authority (national and Community) share in the
responsibility for problem solving. Neither by
itself has either the material instruments or the
legal competence to deal adequately with a range of
problems: they each supplement the other. One of the
major consequences of this process is that
governments have gained power at the expense of their
national parliaments - and gained power over all the
major functions of government: policy determination,
policy execution, and policy control. Governments
and their bureaucracies are now involved in a
permanent process of transnational negotiation, the
outcome of which cannot normally be overruled by the
national or the European Parliament without
endangering the whole compromise. This is a major
advantage seen from the viewpoint of national
ministers and their civil servants, and not one that
they are at all anxious to surrender.

This is one of the reasons why there is now
resistance to changing the new status quo. An
additional reason is provided by the growth,
alongside those policy areas covered by Community

13

procedures, of an increasing number of others where the dominant mode of interaction is that of intergovernmental cooperation. This is true of foreign policy issues, of many educational and cultural matters, as well as the expanding field of legal cooperation. There is no doubt that most ministers and their civil servants feel much more at ease in this type of arena: essentially they feel much freer to agree or disagree, to undertake or refuse collective action. There are few of the constraints attached to the Community mode of working together - though the frustration related to the frequently-meagre outcomes are higher.

It is in fact frustration arising from the need for a consensus both in this type of cooperation and in the Community as it operates at present that has provided much of the fuel for recent attempts at reform. To an increasing number of the actors involved this now seems to be the only way to achieve more and better results from the effort deployed. And the more general this recognition of low efficiency of the system as it at present operates has become, the stronger the pressure has also become to do something about it. So, paradoxically, it is as much the failures as the success of the Community which have recently supplied the incentive to make progress towards a closer, and more effective union.

ACTORS

The initial creation by the Six of the European Community was both a response to a widely felt need in post-war western Europe for a new economic and political framework for the relations between its nation states, and a reaction against what many in those countries felt to be the inadequacies of the first generation of organisations created to foster cooperation between them. (See Chapter 2). But both the founding and the subsequent development of the Community have been essentially the work of elites: it is they who have taken the lead in devising strategies and projects to push the process forward, in mobilising support for their initiatives, and in persuading governments to take action.

The role and relative importance of different groups within these elites continues to be a source of lively debate both among historians and those involved in the process. Some, for instance, argue that national governments and parties have been the main source of opposition to the process of integration, being committed to the defence of national interests and national power structures. (14) National civil servants are sometimes accused of being the main villains in this context. Those who take this view emphasise, on the contrary, the positive role played by those individuals and movements which have promoted the cause of European unity: in their analysis it is the pressures generated from these sources which have provided the essential motive power for the creation and subsequent development of the Community.

Others, however, take the view that such pressures have played only a marginal role in the process. A recent powerful statement of this case flatly contradicts the view that the movement towards integration should be attributed to 'human idealism triumphing at specific moments over the narrow, anachronistic realism of national governments', and argues that as far as the period 1945-50 was concerned 'The very limited degree of integration that was achieved came about through the pursuit of narrow self-interest of what were still powerful nation states'. (15) Furthermore, according to this view, national bureaucrats were the real architects of what was achieved, rather than their political masters.

In our opinion, neither of these views does full justice to the complexity of the process they seek to explain. In the first place, there have been - and still are - marked differences in the attitudes and policies of the various national governments involved, some having been consistently favourable to the construction of a strong Community, while others have at various times been either hesitant or hostile. To put them all in the same category is a gross over-simplification. The same applies to blanket statements about the role of national civil servants. While all are professionally committed to the defence of 'the national interest' this does not mean that in a given country at a given time they agree on where that interest lies, or how it should be promoted. Nor does the evidence support the view that collectively they have sought to do this in ways consistently inimical to the development of the Community or that, on the contrary, it is they alone who have been responsible for its forward movement. Apart from anything else, the latter assertion makes vast and unjustified assumptions about the relationship between civil servants and their political masters: it is simply not true that the latter are always pawns in the hands of their bureaucratic advisers. The nature of the relationship is a variable which has to be examined in each individual case. So, too, is the influence exerted at a given time and place, and with respect to defined groups and individuals, by the ideology of European unity and its protagonists.

While it is natural that a process of such historical importance should generate rival claims about who should be considered its heroes and villains, it is not in our view accurate to analyse it simply in terms of a conflict between protagonists of European unity and defenders of national sovereignty. Some of the important actors have indeed seen it in these terms, but it is by no means the whole story. Most of the key figures have occupied a middle ground, accepting (with greater or lesser enthusiasm) the need for the Community and being willing to push forward its development, but at the same time being acutely conscious of the need to be able to justify and defend this to their national constituencies. Successful forward movement has therefore depended in the first place on there being a widespread conviction, among both elites and the general public, of the need for the Community as an instrument for common action and a willingness to see it develop. Those who have argued the case for this, and maintained and propagated the ideology of closer union, have played an important part in the process. But forward movement has also required the identification of areas of convergence between different national interests; the formulation of projects to incorporate and exploit these opportunities; and the mobilisation of pressures to to convert such projects into action. A combined effort between different groups and individuals within the political and economic elites of the various member countries has been necessary to achieve success.

Propulsive and supportive elites

Among these elites we distinguish two groups which have played a particularly important role: we call these propulsive and supportive elites.

The propulsive elites consist of those who conceive, launch and take the lead in promoting initiatives designed to achieve closer union. This task has always been performed by a small group of people. (16) They include those who provide the ideas for strategies and projects designed to achieve forward movement, as well as those who launch and promote them. Both functions are important. And while those who are primarily involved once an initiative has been launched are the professional politicians, their supporting staff and senior civil servants, the preparatory phase has often involved a range of non-governmental actors, such as those in universities and research institutes, whose expertise and creativity is mobilised by individuals or groups seeking to launch an initiative or prepare the ground for one.

Such groups (which include, for instance, the European Movement and the Union of European Federalists) also play an important role as part of the wider supportive elites which consist of those individuals and organisations which rally behind an initiative, provide networks for its dissemination and discussion, and the mechanisms for the mobilisation of governmental, party, parliamentary and media support for it.

Motivation. The effectiveness of both these elites has been dependent in the first place on the strength of their motivation. In the immediate post-war years there were two overriding motives for closer unity: the need to banish the threat of another conflict between France and Germany, and - with the onset of the Cold War in 1947 - the need for solidarity in the face of the perceived threat from the Soviet Union. Powerful additional reasons were provided by the wish of those countries which had been defeated to be readmitted to international society and to be freed of post-war restrictions; and - on the part of all the countries of the region - to restore war-torn economies, bring down barriers to trade, and to promote sustained economic growth. Together these provided a very powerful impetus. But, in many ways, the situation today is very different. Relations between Paris and Bonn have been so radically transformed that the possibility of renewed conflict has now become literally unthinkable. External pressures remain, but they are no longer exclusively associated with the risk of an attack by the Soviet Union. And although there is no lack of arguments about the need for closer unity, the original sense of urgency has faded. At the same time, and associated with it, there has also been even among the propulsive elites themselves a noticeable slackening of ambition, and a shortening of time horizons. With the exception of a few groups, like the Federalists, even the most dedicated supporters of the Community now limit their proposals to quite modest steps forward. The contrast in this respect with the 'fifties is quite striking, as the recent negotiations plainly demonstrated.

These negotiations also sharply underline the importance of another factor in determining the effectiveness of the propulsive and supportive elites: their capacity to agree among themselves on a strategy for the future of the Community. The lack of a consensus about this has been painfully evident throughout the long years of discussion about European Union. And although in retrospect the six-member Community is now sometimes presented as the golden age of integration, that too witnessed very sharp clashes between de Gaulle and his partners about how the Community should develop, and in particular about the exercise of authority within it. This ideological conflict about the role of the nation state was a major reason for the repeated failure of the Six to include defence and foreign policy as part of the process of integration, as well as the immediate cause of the crisis in the Community in the mid-sixties. But since the departure of de Gaulle his mantle has been assumed by the British, the Danes and the Greeks. It is their combined opposition which proved a major factor in thwarting the ambitions of those who sought to achieve European Union by a qualitative leap forward.

National Leadership. Another major factor in determining the strength and effectiveness of these elites has been the extent to which their ranks have included national political leaders. The strength of the support for the Community in its original member countries can be judged by the active part played in its initial creation and early development by those occupying the highest offices of state. The roll call of such names is both long and impressive, including Konrad Adenauer, Johan Beyen, Alcide De Gasperi, Guy Mollet, René Pleven, Robert Schuman and Paul-Henri Spaak. Those occupying such positions have always provided the crucial hinge between reflection and action, sometimes initiating projects themselves but more frequently sponsoring or supporting initiatives proposed by others. The importance of top leaders was symbolised, confirmed and enhanced by the creation of the European Council in 1974. Significantly, this body has in recent years devoted more and more of its time to discussing projects related to European Union. It has become not only the most desirable forum for the launching of such projects but also the most important for their discussion, and the only one at which final and binding decisions can effectively be taken.

The successive enlargements of the Community between 1973 and 1981 did not, however, significantly increase the number of Community leaders who could be counted among its propulsive elites. With the exception of Edward Heath, successive British prime ministers have acted as a brake rather than a spur to closer union, and although since 1984 Mrs Thatcher has made some attempts to be more positive, in Britain there is still little credit to be derived by politicians from identification with the Community. Danish governments have been even more firmly opposed to any than other purely economic extensions of the work of the Community, and in Greece Mr Papandreou has also been hostile to moves towards European Union. It is these persistent cleavages between national attitudes to the Community rather than generational changes which have weakened the promotional elites – though it is noticeable how in the moves leading up to the 1985 negotiations two of the most prominent roles were played by Mitterand and Spinelli, both of whom had been active in European affairs throughout the past forty years, and belong firmly to its first generation.

Their contribution also underlined the fact that it is still the elites in the original six member countries which in recent years have supplied the major motive force for the Community. Throughout its history a particularly important role has been played by those in France and Germany: just as it was a Franco-German agreement which made the creation of the Community possible in the first place, it is their new relationship which has underpinned and been an essential pre-condition for its subsequent development. The availability (or otherwise) of their support for projects designed to achieve closer union has always been of critical importance, just as their capacity to resolve their differences and strike bargains within a Community context has been essential for the conduct of its day-to-day business.

There have been many occasions, however, when one or the other has taken an initiative without the full support of the other, (17) and the occasions when they have jointly sponsored a project designed to achieve closer union have been rare. One recent notable case was the Schmidt-Giscard initiative which led to the creation of the European Monetary System in 1979. (18) Even then they were not in a position to dictate to the others. Both within the original Six and subsequently, the initiatives taken by Italy and the Benelux countries and the steady support they have given throughout the years to the Community-building process have also been of great importance. In the case of Italy De Gasperi made a major contribution in the early days, and although domestic party in-fighting has often subsequently reduced the Italian capacity for leadership, many Italians have nevertheless played prominent roles among the propulsive elites, and its own political class is firmly committed to closer union. The Benelux countries have also made a major contribution to the strength of the propulsive elites in the Community. The pressures exerted by their leaders and the initiatives they took were particularly important in the moves leading to the commitment to a common market; it was they who first proposed European Union as a further objective (see Chapter 6); and - in spite of their own disagreements on certain issues - it is these countries which have also played a consistently positive role in the discussions and negotiations about it.

Parties, Groups and the General Public

Many of the initiatives designed to achieve closer union have been the work of individuals and small groups within the propulsive elites. Most political parties have played a supportive rather than an initiatory role. One important reason for this is that such parties are primarily interested in winning prizes at the national level: it is success in national elections which offers the key to preferment and power. This does not mean that such parties are uninterested in European issues, but everywhere in the Community these are usually given only a minor role in national election campaigns. It may also be - and this certainly is the case for some parties - that a development of closer unity is seen as implying a further shift away from national centres of power and authority contrary to the interests of the parties themselves. So while most parties, their leaders and the national parliamentarians never fail to profess their dedication to a more closely united Europe, and a stronger Community, it is not difficult to detect - or explain - a certain dissonance between words and deeds. It is for similar reasons that the trans-national party groupings which have come into existence on a Community-wide basis have remained for the most part fragile and weak bodies, much stronger

20

in European rhetoric than European deeds. (19)

Nationally-based interest groups have been even less concerned about the further development of the Community, other than with respect to the specific policy sectors which impinge on their own activities. Many of the Community-wide associations also limit their sights and activities in a similar (and quite understandable) fashion: they have not become the great promoters of further integration which some of the early neo-functionalists expected would be the case. Those umbrella associations at the Community level such as UNICE, COPA and ETUC which have a wider remit do from time to time make statements on more general issues such as European Union. But it cannot be said that they have either singly or collectively sought to exert any sustained pressure designed to achieve a closer union.

The same is also true of the public in general: as a driving force the will of the citizens of the Community has been of secondary importance. This means that those strategies which have relied essentially on the mobilisation of the general public have not succeeded. This does not mean, however, that the attitudes of political parties, interest groups and the general public towards the Community and the process of integration have been of no importance. The widespread and high levels of support in favour of moves towards European unity in the immediate post-war period were a very important element in sustaining and encouraging the elites who were actively working for the objective. This same passive consensus was also an important background element in the launching and development of the six-member Community. While there has subsequently been some decline of popular support in one or two of the original member states, recent polls show that over 70% of the population in Italy, the Netherlands and Luxembourg consider membership to be 'a good thing', that there has been a recovery to well over 60% holding the same view in France and Belgium, and to 61% in the Federal Republic where in the Spring of 1985 only 54% took this view. (20)

But in the four countries which joined between 1973 and 1981 (Britain, Denmark, Ireland, and Greece) the level of support has been generally lower than in the original member countries, and very markedly so in the cases of Denmark and Britain. This is one aspect of the much more heterogeneous character of the present Community, and one which has had important political consequences, not least in the configuration and levels of support for moves designed to achieve closer union. As the table shows, in June 1985 not only was a substantial segment of the public in each member country indifferent about the issue of European Union but support for it was at particularly low levels in Denmark and Britain. The highest positive score was, on the other hand, recorded in Italy. In each of these three countries there was a close correlation between public attitudes and the policy being followed by its government. The availability or otherwise of general public support for the further development of the Community is therefore a factor which the propulsive and supportive elites have to take into account, even if the general public itself is not a prime mover in their strategies.

STRATEGIES OF UNION

As the foregoing analysis has made clear, although the protagonists of closer union have never lacked arguments or sources of support, they have at each stage of the history of the Community been confronted by serious obstacles. There has been no automaticity about the process of integration. Each forward step has required not only an effort of will, but careful consideration of the objectives to be sought, and the means to be employed to reach them. It has also required the mobilisation of support sufficient not only to persuade the member governments to give serious attention to the proposals being advanced by including them on their agenda of current business, but also to create a coalition of sufficient strength to bring them to a point of decision - and subsequent ratification (in those cases where the chosen legal instrument has required this). The purpose of the following analysis is to identify the main lessons which can be drawn from the experience acquired over the years about different types of strategies and the conditions required for success.

Types of Strategy

Throughout the history of the Community there have been marked divergencies about the most effective type of strategy to achieve closer union. These have again been in evidence during the long years of attempts to move towards European Union. Two of the most important areas of dispute have been the rival merits of elitist and populist strategies, and of big leaps forward compared with more modest advances.

Table 1.1: Attitudes to European Union, Spring 1985

	B %	DK %	D %	F %	IRL %	I %	L %	NL %	UK %	GR %	EC(1) %
1. Of every 100 interviewed											
For – very much	17	4	12	15	13	27	21	17	9	26	16
For – to some extent	34	12	30	35	25	29	31	34	14	20	27
Against – to some extent	5	14	9	9	6	5	7	8	11	5	9
Against – very much	2	33	4	3	4	1	5	6	11	6	5
Indifferent or no opinion	42	37	45	38	52	38	36	35	55	43	43
Total	100	100	100	100	100	100	100	100	100	100	100
Index (2)	3.15	1.78	2.92	3.02	2.97	3.31	3.06	2.94	2.48	3.15	2.95
2. Of every 100 with an opinion											
For – very much	29	5	22	24	27	43	33	26	20	45	28
For – to some extent	59	20	55	57	51	46	49	53	32	36	48
Against – to some extent	9	22	17	15	13	9	11	12	24	8	15
Against – very much	3	53	6	4	9	2	7	9	24	11	9
Total	100	100	100	100	100	100	100	100	100	100	100
N	584	643	549	628	487	705	191	637	658	568	5616

1. Weighted average.
2. "For – very much" = 4, "against – very much" = 1; non-answers excluded. Any figure over 2.5 reflects a positive attitude and any lower figure a rather negative attitude.

Source: Eurobarometer no. 23, June 1985. Table 28. p.51.

Elitist v Populist. As far as the first area of dispute is concerned, those favouring elitist strategies have taken the view that the crucial actors are those in positions of authority, and that projects designed to achieve closer union can only succeed if they are sponsored by important national leaders and capable of attracting the support of their colleagues and their supporting elites. This was the strategy consistently followed by Monnet, exemplified in the tactics he used to launch the Coal and Steel Community, which he repeated at the time of the project for a Defence Community and subsequently in the moves which led to the Rome treaties. His Action Committee for a United States of Europe, consisting of the leaders of the major parties and trade unions of the member states, was also characteristic of this elitist approach. (21)

Another major protagonist of successive attempts to achieve similar objectives, Altiero Spinelli, on the other hand followed with equal consistency a quite different strategy. He always took the view that national administrations are bound to defend the status quo, but that there is a large reservoir of popular support for closer unity among the public at large, and that the key to successful forward movement is to find ways of bringing this pressure to bear. At the beginning of the fifties his attempt to do so took the form of a Campaign for a European Constituent Assembly, launched with a petition which collected 600,000 signatures in Italy. He was subsequently instrumental in persuading De Gasperi to insert into the EDC Treaty an article giving the task of drawing up proposals for a Political Community to a parliamentary Assembly. (See Chapter 3). Undeterred by the failure of this, his efforts after 1955 were then directed at mobilising support for a Congress of European People, intended as an alternative route to a Constituent Assembly. His later activity as a member of the European Parliament in initiating the moves which led to its Draft Treaty of European Union (see Chapter 9) were also consistent with the same basic strategy. (22)

While no one could fail to admire his tenacity and courage, it is elitist strategies which have consistently proved more effective. They have not sought to challenge the control of national authorities over the process of integration: they have concentrated on finding allies among those in power, and on building up coalitions of interests sufficiently strong to drive through proposals for change. Individual projects have not always succeeded - the most notable failure being that of the EDC - but all the forward steps which have been taken have resulted from this type of strategy.

Has one therefore to conclude that Spinelli was wasting his time? And that his strategy was a complete failure? Not in our view. His approach provided a rallying point for those among the propulsive elites who sought faster progress towards closer union; it stimulated reflection about the future development of the Community and set up beacons to illuminate the way towards its further peaks; on several occasions - most notably in 1953 and 1984 - it helped to goad the governments into action; and in recent years it also succeeded in making the European Parliament a significant new actor in the struggle for European Union. By any standard, these were significant and substantial achievements. Without the pressures generated by this strategy and Spinelli himself, the thrust towards closer union would have been significantly weaker.

Transformation v Accretion. Another major set of issues in the choice of a strategy concerns the goals at which it aims. One aspect of this is the choice between strategies of transformation, which aim at big leaps forward, and strategies of accretion which incorporate a more gradualist and step-by-step approach.

Both types have had their successes. Transformation strategies were used to create all three of the founding Communities, and their success on these occasions has made this type of approach especially attractive to those who wish to emulate the achievements of the founding fathers. There were strong echoes of this when in 1972 the leaders of the enlarged Community adopted European Union as their goal and described it as involving a transformation of the whole complex of the relations between the member states. In subsequent negotiations in the early eighties a majority of the member states appeared to support a big leap forward as the most appropriate way of reaching this goal. (See Chapters 10 and 11). But in practice, since 1958, the Community has advanced by a process of gradual accretion, and the outcome of the 1985 negotiations provided yet another instance of this.

Some may be tempted to conclude from this that strategies should be adjusted to prevailing conditions, and that in particular bold strategies of transformation are inappropriate for times when caution is likely to prevail. Closer examination of the recent record, however, suggests that in such circumstances nothing is likely to happen unless some are willing to take a bold lead. So while prevailing circumstances may condition the outcome, the protagonists of closer union would be ill-advised to abandon attempts to force the pace.

Goal-definition: The Critical Factors

Whatever the chosen strategy, its chances of success are directly related to the degree to which its goals provide solutions for problems perceived as important and urgent by the leaders of the member states. It is this rather than the scope of a project which is of critical importance. It was the absence of clearly defined and relevant goals which for many years made it so difficult to make any progress towards European Union.

The ultimate objective of the process of integration was originally described in the Schuman Plan as a 'European federation', and in the early days there were frequent references to building a 'United States of Europe'. (23) But the Schuman Plan also emphasised that Europe would 'not be made all at once or according to a single general plan', and that what was needed was the gradual construction of a de facto solidarity. Most subsequent projects have been concerned with the successive stages of this process rather than with elaboration of a blueprint for a distant future. The bruising ideological conflict with de Gaulle about the ultimate aims of the Community and the continuing divergencies about these in the enlarged Community have been additional reasons for concentrating on more immediate goals. The essential problem has always been to identify short- or medium-term goals of a practical nature capable of gaining the support of a winning coalition of member states.

The preparatory phase of any project is therefore of great importance for it is then that its goals are determined, together with the methods to be used to achieve them. This phase, which leads to the drafting of a set of proposals ready for launching, is usually the work of a small group of people, and is quite frequently carried out outside formal governmental structures. Most of the fundamental and creative ideas which have later given rise to formal initiatives have been conceived in this way by those

working in private research institutes or
associations, groups set up by organisations such as
the European Movement or the European Union of
Federalists, or by the members of private 'think
tanks' set up around leading figures, such as Monnet.
(24) Governmental attempts undertaken in the 1970s to
create a more official Community think tank (of which
the Brookings Institute in the US was frequently
cited as a model) failed, and there is a good deal of
evidence to suggest that creative ideas flourish much
more readily in informal organisational frameworks
than within more structured and official
bureaucracies. (25)

Within such groups there have always been
differences about the best way forward at any
particular moment. Once, however, the decision had
been taken after the defeat of the EDC project to
revert to a strategy of economic integration the
achievement of a common market served as the central
objective throughout the period from the mid-fifties
to the late 'sixties. De Gaulle's attempt in the
early 'sixties to capture the process and also re-
direct it towards the more classic goals of a
political union (meaning essentially a common
foreign and defence policy) were rebuffed. (See
Chapter 5). Even after he had left power, only very
tentative steps in this direction were taken at the
Hague Summit in 1969. The main emphasis was still on
further instalments of economic integration, in the
form of steps towards the new goal of Economic and
Monetary Union. (See Chapter 6).

Although the initial attempt to move in this
direction soon foundered, the Six were anxious to try
to ensure that a wider Community did not mean an end
to their hopes of building a closer union. It was at
their suggestion that European Union was adopted as a
further goal at the Summit held on the eve of the
first enlargement. The intention was to provide a
coping stone for the twin pillars of Economic and
Monetary Union and Political Union. There were clear
parallels here with the earlier attempt in 1952-54 to
construct a Political Community to provide an over-
arching framework to contain the ECSC and the EDC.

As on that earlier occasion, however, the
governments provided few clues as to what they had in
mind. Their immediate purpose was essentially
declaratory. They suggested a procedure and a
timetable but neither agenda nor content. Initially
their silence on these critical issues was due to the
haste with which the new objective had been adopted.
But it soon became obvious that there were deep

disagreements not only about the substance of the proposed Union, but - more fundamentally - about whether or not to proceed in such a direction. So there was not only no specific project: there was not even a consensus that one should be constructed.

In the course of the many attempts to overcome these problems, another emerged. As long as the Community consisted of its original six members, the basic assumption was that all member states would advance together, and at the same pace, towards their declared goal of closer union. With the subsequent successive enlargements this assumption has not gone unquestioned. The treaties of accession themselves marked a first major breach by providing for transitional periods to enable the newcomers to catch up with obligations already assumed by the original members. These were based on the belief that once the period of apprenticeship was completed, all could then resume together the forward march. But both academic observers and practitioners began to question the continued validity of this assumption, both on theoretical and practical grounds. Theoretical explorations have subsequently led to a proliferation of alternative models of future development - all based on various types of differentiated, rather than uniform, advance. (26) In the meantime practice has also increasingly moved in the same direction. Not only have the treaties been applied in a more flexible way to accommodate the differing needs of a more heterogeneous Community, but major new developments have increasingly been taking place partially or wholly outside the Community framework, in ways which have accepted that not all Community members may wish - or be able - to participate fully in them, and that membership should not necessarily be limited strictly to members of the Community. The non-participation of several members, including Britain, in the exchange rate mechanism of the European Monetary System is one type of example: another is the Eureka high-technology initiative which has been organised outside the framework of the Community and includes several participating countries who are not members of it. But these are only two of an increasing number of such arrangements. (27)

These trends are another factor which have greatly increased the problem of goal-definition for those seeking to make progress towards European Union as they have cast doubt on the nature and boundaries of that Union. These uncertainties have also been reflected in the proliferation of alternative models of institutional development. Of these there are basically three types: those which propose to maintain decisive authority in the hands of the member states; those which aim to re-establish the equilibrium originally intended between institutions representing national interests and those represent- ing the common interest; and those which propose a decisive transfer of authority from national to Community institutions. (28) Cleavages in elite opinion across this spectrum of possibilities have impeded the creation of a strong consensus in favour of any single pattern. At the same time there has also been tension between those wishing to give priority to institutional reform and those who argue that this can only be achieved in the wake of changes in scope or substantive policies. The weight of experience lies with those who take the latter position, a further example having been provided by the 1985 agreements when institutional reform was only achieved when firmly embedded in a package of measures designed to achieve an effective internal market.

Negotiating a Deal

In addition to skilful targeting, careful presentation is also an important element in securing high-level sponsorship and a successful launch. Monnet in particular paid a great deal of attention to refining the texts both of the proposal which he put to the French government in 1950 and his subsequent initiatives. He also believed, and experience lends strong support to his view, that at this initial phase a proposal does not need to be elaborated in great detail: what is important is that its central idea and supporting arguments should be clearly and succinctly stated.

Once a project has been launched, its promoters must seek to bring it to the negotiating table as speedily as possible. One tactic used with great success in the moves which led up to the Rome treaties was the device of an Intergovernmental Committee to study issues related to the achievement of the goals agreed at the Messina conference, but without formal commitment. In practice under the powerful impetus of its chairman, Paul-Henri Spaak, the Committee successfully paved the way for the negotiation of the Rome treaties. More recent attempts to emulate this example, however, have served more to register disagreements than to overcome them. (See Chapters 8 and 10). The persistence of these disagreements has also made it far more difficult to bring a project to the point of a serious negotiation than was the case with the original Six. It is instructive in this context to compare the rapidity with which negotiations were successfully pursued on the basis of the Schuman Plan – and even the timetable of those leading up to the signature of the Rome treaties – with the prolonged failure, lasting more than a decade, to take any significant decisions in pursuit of European Union. Here is further evidence, if more is needed, of the current lack of relish for ambitious goals.

Changes in the nature of the Community have also had their impact on the way in which bargaining is conducted between the member states once serious negotiations are engaged. During those which led up to the conclusion of the basic treaties, a major role was ascribed to an authoritative figure charged to act in the general interest and to propel the negotiations forward by all possible means. Monnet fulfilled this role in the negotiation of the Paris Treaty, Paul-Henri Spaak in regard to the Treaties of Rome. Monnet also sought with some success to persuade all concerned in the Paris negotiations that they were engaged in a travail d'équipe rather than a classic negotiation, working hard with the heads of delegations to build up a sense of common purpose and determination to succeed. (29) It has however been increasingly difficult to create such an atmosphere as the members of the Community have become more numerous and more heterogeneous. It has also become more difficult to ensure the same type of dynamic chairmanship – not least because in a more settled and routinized system such as has grown up, rules relating to the six-monthly rotating presidency are now very difficult to breach – as the Germans discovered when they attempted to impose their own chairman of the Spaak II Committee during a period of the Irish presidency. The Irish successfully resisted, and Senator Dooge became chairman of the Committee. (See Chapter 10). Similarly, the Intergovernmental Conference which followed was chaired by Luxembourg, during the period of its presidency.

As far as the method of arriving at agreements is concerned, there has been much less change: the members of the enlarged Community have continued to behave in much the same way as the original Six. As the following chapters show, it has required very determined leadership and the exercise of the whole paraphernalia of diplomatic skills and artifice to achieve bargains acceptable to all concerned. The successful conclusion of such bargains has involved very detailed and complex negotiations: a great deal of horse-trading, log-rolling, side payments, the postponement of particularly difficult issues, procedural devices (including self-imposed time-tables) as a substitute for substantive agreements, and the judicious use of ambiguous language. All of these elements are to be found in the Single European Act in the same way that they figure largely in the Rome treaties. And they are to be expected when a serious attempt to made to find ways of reconciling the interests of any group of states.

There are, nevertheless, major differences in substance between the outcomes of the two negotiations. Without at this stage going into details of the 1985 agreements (see Chapters 11 and 12), it is sufficient to underline the scope and ambition of the Rome treaties compared with the modest - some would say insignificant - content of the Single European Act. The central provisions of the latter are also concerned with trying to remedy the failure to carry out effectively measures already agreed in 1957. Such comparisons are a sharp reminder of the realities underlying the rhetoric about progress towards European Union.

In Conclusion

The conduct and results of these negotiations, together with the preceding discussions about European Union, provide many insights into the nature of the Community in the latest phase of its evolution. They also invite comparisons with earlier phases of the search for closer union, which reveal both how much has changed and how much has remained the same in the Community over the years. These comparisons also provide a wealth of material about the different strategies which have been used in the search for a closer union, and the relevance and feasibility of these strategies in the enlarged Community. In the following chapters the different phases of this search are analysed to illustrate the propositions which have been advanced in this introduction. The concluding chapter will examine the implications of the outcome of the latest phase of this search, and the future prospects for the evolution of the Community.

Select Bibliography

Pierre Gerbet, La construction de l'Europe. Paris, 1983.

Max Jansen and Johan K De Vree, The ordeal of unity. Bilthoven, 1985.

Jean Lecerf, Histoire de l'unité européenne, 3 vols, Paris, 1965, 75, 84.

Walter Lipgens, A history of European integration, 1945-47, vol 1, vol 2, 1948-50, Oxford, 1982; 1986.

Alan S. Milward, The reconstruction of western Europe, 1945-51. London, 1984.

Hans von der Groeben, Aufbaujahre der Europäischen Gemeinschaft - Das Ringen um den Gemeinsamen Markt und die Politische Union (1958-1966), Baden-Baden 1982. (French ed., Combat pour l'Europe. La construction de la Communauté Européenne de 1958 à 1966. Brussels, 1984).

Paul Taylor, The limits of European integration. London, 1983.

Notes

1.   The analytical framework used in this chapter is based on a development of the ideas put forward in two papers presented at a seminar held at the European University Institute at Florence in October 1984: Wolfgang Wessels, Alternative strategies for institutional reform, EUI Working Paper No 85/184 July 1985, and Roy Pryce, 'European Union: some historical dimensions' (unpublished).

2.   For an evaluation by neo-functionalists of their own work, see Leon N. Lindberg and Stuart A. Scheingold (eds), Regional integration, theory and research, Harvard, 1971 and Ernst B. Haas, The obsolescence of regional integration theory, Berkeley 1975. For other comments see C. Pentland, International theory and the European Community, London, 1973; R. Harrison, Europe in question, London 1974; and Carole Webb, 'Theoretical perspectives and problems' in Helen Wallace, William Wallace and Carole Webb (eds), Policy making in the European Community, 2nd ed., Chichester, 1983.

3.   See, for instance, R. Keohane and J. Nye, Power and independence: world politics in transition, Boston, 1977.

4.   Alan Milward's recent book (see Select Bibliography) is a major work based on detailed study of newly-available archival material. Some of its conclusions, however, in our view fall into this revisionist trap. See, in particular, pp. 491-502. For a general discussion of this problem see Hans

Peter Schwarz, 'Europaische Integration als Zeitgescichtsforschung' in Vierteljahreshefte fur Zeitgeschichte, October, 1983, p. 569.
5. Notions such as 'second (or third or fourth) generation Europe' for instance are not very helpful unless very carefully defined. For a more elaborate and suggestive classification see Ralf Dahrendorf, Plaidoyer für eine Europäische Union, Munich 1973 and also his later A third Europe? Third Jean Monnet lecture, EUI, Florence, 29 November 1979. On the general issue of generational change, see Stephan F. Szabo (ed), The successor generation: International perspectives of postwar Europeans, London 1983.
6. See Miriam Camps, Britain and the European Community, 1955-63. London, 1964, ch. IX, and Michael Charlton, The price of victory, London 1983, ch. 8.
7. See, for instance, the testimony of E.H. van der Beugel in Charlton, op.cit., p.186.
8. See David Allen et al., European political cooperation: towards a foreign policy for western Europe, London, 1982; Pierre Hassner, 'Europe between the USA and the USSR' in Government and Opposition, Winter 1986; and William Wallace, 'Political cooperation: Integration through inter-governmentalism' in Wallace, Wallace and Webb, op.cit., ch. 13.
9. For a brief summary, and contrary view, see Jansen and De Vree, op.cit., pp.268-74. For a more detailed study, see Eberhard Schulz, Moskau und die Europäische Integration. Munich, 1975.
10. See Michael Hodges and William Wallace, Economic divergence in the European Community, London, 1983.
11. See Jansen and De Vree, op.cit., ch. 9 ('The chilling sixties').
12. Helen Wallace, with Adam Ridley, Europe: The challenge of diversity. London, 1985. pp. 29-31.
13. See Wolfgang Wessels, Alternative strategies, pp.60-64.
14. See, for instance, the historical works of Walter Lipgens, and the speeches and books of Altiero Spinelli.
15. Alan Milward, op.cit., p.492.
16. 'The first obstacle was the small number of people involved in this adventure. Very often the observation is made ... that Europe is an affair of the few ... The fact is incontestable'. Altiero Spinelli, The European adventure. London, 1972. p.5.
17. See Wessels, op.cit., pp.37-39.
18. See Peter Ludlow, The making of the

European Monetary System, London, 1982.
   19.   See D.L.   Seiler,   'Les fédérations de
partis au niveau communautaire' in R. Hrbek, J. Jamar
and W. Wessels (eds), The European Parliament on the
eve of the second direct election: Balance sheet and
prospects, Bruges, 1984.
   20.   Table 35, Eurobarometer No. 24, Brussels
(EC Commission) December 1985. For a general survey,
see David Handley,   'Public opinion and European
integration' in European Journal of Political
Research, vol. ix, 1981 pp.335-64. For British
attitudes, Roger Jowell and Gerald Hoinville (eds),
Britain into Europe: Public opinion and the EEC,
1961-75. London, 1976.
   21.   For a detailed account, see Pascal
Fontaine, Le Comité d'action pour les Etats-Unis
d'Europe de Jean Monnet, Lausanne, 1974.
   22.   For Spinelli's early life, see his own
account, Come ho tentato di diventare saggio. Io,
Ulisse. Bologna, 1984. Also Bernard Barthalay, Le
federalisme, Paris, 1981, pp.101-24, and Michael D.
Burgess, 'Federal ideas in the European Community:
Altiero Spinelli and European Union, 1981-84' in
Government and Opposition, Summer 1984, and 'Altiero
Spinelli, federalism and the European Union Treaty:
On the trail of a long progeniture' in Juliet Lodge
(ed), European Union: The European Community in
search of its future. London, 1986.
   23.   For instance, Jean Monnet, Les Etats-Unis
d'Europe ont commencé, Paris, 1955.
   24.   Monnet's Memoires contain many examples:
see, for instance, pp.341-353 for his account of the
group reflections which led up to the drafting of the
1950 proposals.
   25.   See, for instance, William Wallace, The
foreign policy process in Britain, London, 1976.
pp.77 et seq.
   26.   See Wessels, Alternative Strategies,
pp.18-21 and 70-75; and Helen Wallace, Europe: the
challenge of diversity, London 1985 for an extended
exploration of these issues.
   27.   See, for instance, Claus-Dieter Ehlermann,
'How flexible is Community law? An unusual approach
to the concept of "two speeds"'. Michigan Law Review,
April-May 1984.
   28.   See Wessels, Alternative Strategies,
pp.18-21.
   29.   See Monnet, Memoires, pp. 380-2.

Chapter Two

THE ORIGINS: EARLY ATTEMPTS AND THE EMERGENCE OF THE SIX (1945-52)

Pierre Gerbet

The problem of European Union has been posed since the end of the Second World War and has still not been solved in spite of many attempts to do so. Should co-operation be promoted between nation states retaining their sovereignty within the framework of alliances and associations, or should a European structure be created above or alongside the states, exercising power delegated to it by them? The organizations for co-operation set up immediately after the war in the economic and diplomatic/military spheres soon appeared to be inadequate to those who really wanted a United Europe. The Council of Europe, a political organ, was not capable of becoming a real European authority. A Federation was impossible and co-operation inadequate: hence the idea of setting up Communities between the six countries which wanted to move forward. These Communities established a centre of European authority, initally in economic and technical fields; but the question remained whether they could then move into the political field proper. They did not succeed in this and the problem of European Union is still with us.

THE ORGANIZATIONS FOR ECONOMIC AND MILITARY CO-OPERATION AND THEIR LIMITATIONS

The first European organizations were set up under the pressure of necessity. The governments of Western Europe were forced to draw closer together to try to find solutions for the problems of post-war reconstruction and of defence in the conditions of the Cold War. The United States, whose support proved to be indispensable, made its help conditional upon a joint effort on the part of the Europeans. The governments, however did not wish to go beyond cooperation between sovereign states.

So in order to benefit from the Marshall Plan the countries of Western Europe devised the Organization for European Economic Co-operation (OEEC) set up in Paris on the 16 April 1948. This organization was intended to play an important part in the use made of American aid by liberalizing intra-European trade (by the gradual reduction of quotas, but not of customs duties) and by setting up a European Payments Union to make possible multilateral settlement between currencies which were then inconvertible. However, owing to the opposition of the United Kingdom, the Scandinavian countries and Switzerland, the OEEC was not a strong organization enjoying any form of independence vis-à vis the governments. Decisions were taken by the Council of Ministers acting unanimously, though it was possible for a country disagreeing with a decision to abstain and not to apply it. Nevertheless, thanks to the part played by the Secretariat, the member states became used to co-operating and comparing their economic policies. The OEEC did not, however, have the power to harmonize the reconstruction plans which were implemented by each country independently from its partners. And the plans for a European Customs Union, already discussed in 1947, did not materialize. This was mainly because of opposition from the United Kingdom which did not wish to weaken its Imperial Preferences with the Commonwealth. Nor did attempts to achieve partial customs unions succeed except in the case of Benelux, decided upon as early as 1944. The European economy was therefore being reconstructed but without integration.

In the diplomatic/military sphere, the development of the cold war also led the countries of Western Europe to draw closer together in order to benefit from American protection. Ernest Bevin, the British Foreign Secretary, made a solemn appeal in his speech before the House of Commons on 22 January 1948. He denounced the menace of Soviet policy and stated that the free nations of Western Europe must now draw closely together. He used the term 'Western Union', but specified that it would not be a formal political union but a 'spiritual union' based on fundamental liberties and moral principles. He recommended a mechanism of mutual consultation, as within the Commonwealth, and a 'functional' approach: that is, pragmatic co-operation in each particular case in accordance with needs. The Brussels Pact of 17 March 1948, signed by the United

Kingdom, France, Belgium, the Netherlands and Luxembourg, chiefly entailed a promise of automatic mutual assistance should there be armed aggression in Europe; but, unlike traditional alliances, permanent structures were established. An Advisory Council of the five foreign ministers could be convened at the request of any one of them, or if the situation so demanded. To assist it, a permanent committee would meet in London every month. A standing military committee of civil servants was set up in order to work out defence plans and prepare the co-ordination of military machinery. Joint staff headquarters representing the Five were established at Fontainebleau and a defence plan was drawn up providing for integration of the air forces.

The Brussels Pact was not only a military alliance but also, at the request of Benelux, the embryo of a regional organization. Specialized committees were set up in the economic, social and cultural fields, with regular meetings attended by the ministers concerned. The Council of Ministers was only advisory, but the existence of a political authority of the Five, in which the governments could discuss among themselves European problems relating to all fields, was held to be a considerable step forward.

The Brussels Pact organization was described by the term 'Western Union' but this expression is not found in the text of the Treaty and it soon lost its importance since the armed forces of the Five proved to be very inadequate. American participation was indispensable: it was requested by France and the United Kingdom as soon as the Brussels Pact was signed. The Standing Committee prepared a preliminary draft treaty which was then discussed with the Americans. The Atlantic Alliance of the 4 April 1949 comprised, as well as the United States and Canada, not only the Five of the Brussels Pact but also Norway, Denmark, Iceland, Italy and Portugal. Greece and Turkey, already receiving aid from the Americans, joined in 1952. The implementation of the Alliance was achieved by the North Atlantic Treaty Organization with its Council, committees and integrated general staffs. From then on, European defence was organized within the Atlantic framework and had the benefit of massive American military and economic aid. Western Union was absorbed into this Atlantic context; henceforth, in the diplomatic and military spheres, everything would be done within the NATO framework. It was true that the promise of mutual assistance as between the

Five was still valid, whereas the Atlantic Pact was not automatic in nature, but in an effort to achieve simplification, the general staffs and military committee of the Brussels Pact disappeared, although they could have served as a basis for the construction of a 'European pillar' for the Atlantic Alliance. Western Union itself became dormant: in order to avoid duplication, its economic powers were transferred to the OEEC in which the Five, however, did not form a homogeneous group. Its few social and cultural activities were transferred to the Council of Europe.

After the abortive attempt to set up a European Defence Community, Western Union rediscovered a role. The Paris Agreements of 23 October 1954 re-established the sovereignty of Germany and admitted it to the Atlantic Alliance on an equal footing with that of the other members. However, in order to contain the new German national army, the Brussels Pact was revived: the Federal Republic of Germany and Italy were admitted alongside the Five. Western Union became Western European Union (and this time the title was included in the Treaty). Its governing body remained the Council of Foreign Ministers. They were to take decisions unanimously, except on questions concerning arms control for which majority voting was provided to avoid a veto by the country concerned. The member countries would thus supervise each other and this ensured that the Federal Republic of Germany would have equal rights. A parliamentary Assembly with a purely consultative function was instituted, as was an Arms Control Agency.

The WEU did not prove to be an effective European organization. It is true that the Council of Ministers had decision-making powers in regard to the military aspects of the Treaty (and was not merely consultative like the Council of the Brussels Pact) and could have served as a framework for political co-operation between the Seven. However, the Member States considered that the Atlantic Council, attended by the Americans, was the most appropriate body for discussing questions of diplomacy and defence. Besides this, the WEU did not have its own forces or its own high command. Its standing committee on armaments could only encourage agreements on standardization but, again, for this purpose, the Atlantic framework was considered to be preferable. WEU nevertheless remains a potentially useful framework.

Thus, the organizations set up in the immediate post-war years under the pressure of necessity to deal with the serious problems of economic reconstruction and defence in Western Europe did not produce any real European structures. These organizations relied essentially on intergovernment- al co-operation. The word 'union', the meaning of which was vague and which could be interpreted either as 'association' or 'unification', was used in fact to designate organizations bringing together states which had retained their sovereignty (European Payments Union, Western Union, Western European Union).

IN QUEST OF A EUROPEAN POLITICAL POWER: THE DEADLOCK OF THE COUNCIL OF EUROPE

While the governments set foot, with varying degrees of reluctance, on the road to co-operation, unofficial bodies were formed with the object of promoting the idea of a united Europe able to affirm its personality in all fields, to constitute an organic entity, to contain the recovery of Germany, to ensure peace between Europeans and to sustain economic growth by opening up a wide market. Among a wide segment of élites, European unification was now felt to be a necessity. There were, however, differences of opinion about the method of building this united Europe. The federalist movements held it to be indispensable to begin by giving Europe its own political structure, an authority over the nation- states, and wide powers. It was necessary to start by setting up a political authority in order to overcome the barriers to economic unification. Such a federal structure could be established either by means of a Constituent Assembly elected by the European peoples or by the conclusion between states of a Federal Pact with a transfer of jurisdiction and power. Europe should not be rebuilt within the confines of old structures but take advantage of the weakening of the latter in order to make a new start. Others refused to go so far: they recommended the development of co- operation through multilateral agreements and even common action without encroaching upon national sovereignty. For them it was much less a question of creating true European structures than of enabling the states to resolve their economic difficulties, to protect themselves against any external threat, and to safeguard democratic freedoms and institutions. In short, that would amount to strengthening the states while fostering a certain amount of solidarity. The protagonists of this method were called 'unionists' as opposed to the 'federalists'.

The opposition between these two concepts for the organization of Europe clearly became apparent at the Hague Congress (7-9 May 1948). The federalists, who were chiefly French, Belgians, Dutch and Italians, were in the minority compared with the unionists led by the British and Scandinavians. The differences over the structures of Europe continued. It is true that the final Resolution emphasised the pressing duty of the European nations to achieve economic and political union in order to ensure security and social progress and acknowledged that the measures for political and economic co-operation already adopted were inadequate. It recommended the setting of a 'Union or Federation', with no preference for either term, but asserted that 'the time has come for the nations of Europe to transfer some of their sovereign rights in order henceforth to exercise them jointly'. The declaration proposed the creation of a supreme court responsible for obliging the States to ensure respect for Human Rights. In the enthusiastic atmosphere of the Congress, the federalists obtained some satisfaction on matters of principle but as for concrete measures to be adopted in the immediate future, it was the unionists who won the day. With regard to the central issue of a European political power they turned down the federalists' proposal to set up a European Council consisting of national ministers with a special responsibility for European matters (rather than ministers for foreign affairs). As for the idea of setting up a European assembly to represent public opinion and to discuss European problems, they only accepted the principle of a consultative assembly, whereas some of the federalists would have liked it to be constituent. Finally, agreement was reached on the proposal for a European Assembly, consisting of delegates of the national parliaments, the function of which would be to advise the governments on how to achieve European unification, but with the governments retaining their freedom of decision. The federalists came round to supporting this as they considered it was an initial step forward and that, once the minimum number of institutions had been set up, their dynamism would enable progress to be made. The Assembly could then put forward federalist-inspired plans. In the economic sphere, the goal of economic union was approved by everyone but while the federalists in partnership with the socialists insisted on the need to have the trade unions participate in the economic management of Europe, the unionists showed that they were liberals above all else. The economic resolution stated as aims the free movement of persons, goods and capital, a customs union, monetary unification, co-ordination of budget policy and harmonization of social legislation as well as a joint equipment programme for energy production and key industries. The motion did not specify the link to be forged between economic and political organization although it recognized that economic unification would be effective only if measures of political unification were adopted simultaneously.

Twenty years later, Denis de Rougemont wrote 'With hindsight, I am inclined to think that really everything had its origin in the Hague Congress of May 1948: the first European parliamentary, legal, cultural and technical institutions, the general principles of the Common Market but, unfortunately also, the refusal to endow those institutions with a power of political decision-making required by popular enthusiasm which it was then felt possible to kindle'. That may be so. Nevertheless, it was a fact that the states did not intend to renounce their prerogatives and that it was necessary to have their agreement in order to create a new European institution.

While the co-ordination committee for the European Movements exerted strong pressure on the governments to urge them to take account of the Hague resolutions, it was the French Government which took the initiative. On 19 July 1948, Georges Bidault, Minister for Foreign Affairs, suggested that his colleagues of the Brussels Pact Advisory Council arrange for its Standing Committee to study the possibility of establishing a European Assembly and of setting up an economic and customs union between the Five and the other countries wishing to take part in it (a plan then being studied by the OEEC). On 18 August, the Co-ordination Committee emphasized, in a memorandum addressed to the Five, the need to convene a European Assembly which should 'give expression to the European peoples' desire for unity and peace', study the appropriate means of ensuring this unity at political and economic level and make recommendations to the governments 'until the nations decide to transfer some of their sovereign rights to a European authority ... The Assembly cannot have either legislative or executive power, but, on the other hand, it can play an important deliberative and advisory role'.

This point of view was shared by the French and

Benelux governments. Robert Schuman, who had succeeded Georges Bidault as Foreign Minister, considered it indispensable to set up a strong European organization to incorporate Western Germany which was soon to re-assume a political personality. Intergovernmental co-operation did not appear to him to be adequate. A European assembly of a political nature would make it possible to welcome German representatives and thus exert an effect on German public opinion. Moreover, it could strengthen the pro-European movements and create a momentum. This assembly would not be constituent or be given legislative powers, but it would discuss and propose measures to be taken by the governments in order progressively to ensure the economic and political integration of Europe, to study the constitutional problem which would arise from the creation of a European union and to define what a European authority could be. Nevertheless, if the assembly were to be able to address governments in an authoritative way and to be a fount of enthusiasm, it would be indispensable for it to be independent of them. The assembly's proposals about the economic and political integration of Europe would be studied by the governments which would decide the measures to be adopted and could arrange among themselves close co-operation for implementing them. However, the British Labour Government did not see it in the same way. Ernest Bevin, the Foreign Secretary, wished to maintain the intergovernmental method and, at the most, promote consultation in accordance with the Brussels Pact. The European Assembly, strongly advocated by Churchill and the Conservatives, looked dangerous to the members of the Labour Party. Even if it wielded no powers, the assembly might well embarrass the governments with its proposals. The Labour Government did not want to run the risk of being led astray by an assembly which it deemed to be 'irresponsible', especially as it was worried about the possibility of some transfer of sovereignty to a European authority. At most it would have accepted only an assembly consisting of national Members of Parliament nominated by the governments, grouped in national delegations under the authority of a minister and voting as delegations, in line with the practice of the General Assembly of the United Nations.

The differences were therefore considerable between the French and the Belgians on the one hand, and the British on the other. A compromise solution was suggested by the European Movement, then under the influence of the British Conservatives: the setting up of both a parliamentary assembly and a ministerial committee. The French and the Belgians, who wanted the Consultative Assembly to be independent, obtained the concession that its members could be elected by the Parliaments (or chosen by the governments that so wished, as was the case with the United Kingdom) and that their deliberations and voting should be free of any constraint. So it would not be a diplomatic conference but a genuine parliamentary assembly. However, they had to agree that this assembly should be placed under the control of a Committee of Ministers which would draw up its agenda, examine any resolutions it might adopt by a two-thirds majority, and decide <u>in camera</u> and by unanimous vote whether or not to communicate them to the governments which would remain absolutely free to take them into consideration or to ignore them. The Committee of Ministers was not to be vested with the powers of a true European executive: it was merely an organ to control the Assembly in which a State, even if it were outvoted, could block any initiative. Robert Schuman believed that these conditions had to be accepted in order not to alienate the United Kingdom and to be able to make a start with something, reliance being placed on a certain dynamic of the future institution. He would have liked to call it 'European Union', but the British insisted on Council of Europe, the term used by Churchill as long ago as 1943 which, in their view, also had the advantage of emphasizing its intergovernmental character.

The Statute of the Council of Europe was signed in London on 5 May 1949 by the Five of the Brussels Pact, plus Denmark, Norway, Sweden, Ireland and Italy. Its declared aim was 'to achieve a closer union between its members in order to protect and promote the ideals and principles which constitute their common heritage and to further their economic and social progress'. As far as its terms of reference were concerned, the Statute excluded defence - there were neutrals among the members and the others wished to reserve this field for the organisations of the Atlantic Alliance - and in practice foreign policy too. It listed economic, social, cultural, scientific, legal and administrative matters and also the protection and promotion of Human Rights and fundamental liberties. But there was to be no duplication with the work of the OEEC in economic affairs, and no timetable or any commitment to precise measures were specified. As for the means

to be used, there would be examination of questions
of common interest, the conclusion of agreements and
the taking of joint action - that is, diplomatic
procedures aiming at a convergence of the actions of
the various governments. Some nevertheless believed
that the Council of Europe was an important step
forward towards an eventual European Union.

When they met, full of enthusiasm, at Strasbourg
in August 1949 the members of the Assembly first of
all asserted their independence <u>vis-à-vis</u> the
Committee of Ministers. They took charge of their own
agenda and discussed all European problems including
those relating to defence. Nevertheless, the main
question remained that of the ultimate purpose of the
Council of Europe. The agenda of the first meeting
(which the Assembly had succeeded in extending)
included 'consideration of changes in the political
structure of Europe in order to achieve closer unity
between the Members of the Council of Europe and to
make European co-operation effective in the sphere
specified in Article 1 of the Statute'. This was the
continuation of the discussion at The Hague in which
many members of the Consultative Assembly had taken
part. As A.H. Robertson has observed, few delegates
were conscious of the difference between the Hague
appeal for a 'political and economic union' implying
a fusion of sovereignties, and the Statute of the
Council of Europe, aiming at closer union between the
Members to be achieved by the traditional methods of
'agreements and joint action'. Many delegates
considered their task was to be the creation of the
economic and political union which they had called
for at The Hague and that the function of the Council
of Europe was almost that of a constituent assembly.
The federalists in particular, who had made
concessions at The Hague, tried their utmost to have
the Assembly's role reinforced and for it to be
vested with real constituent powers. At first they
thought that the Council of Europe could evolve and
become the embryo of a federal Europe. But all the
plans for the reform of the Council came to nothing.

In the major political debate which took place
there was a clash between two fundamental tendencies.
The federalists advocated the rapid establishment of
political institutions by means of the 'constitutional' method. The unionists persisted in their
preference for the 'functional' method, leaving it to
the governments to solve practical problems and
postponing the institutional changes to the more or
less distant future. On 5 September, the British
federalist, Mr. Mackay, tabled an amendment to the

political report to the effect that 'The Assembly considers as the goal and purpose of the Council of Europe the creation of a European political authority endowed with limited functions but real powers'. Owing, no doubt, to the fatigue of the delegates towards the end of the meeting, the amendment was adopted without a division but subsequently it was found impossible to be more specific about its substance. Only the federalists considered themselves to be bound by this text, but they did not have a two-thirds majority in the Assembly. Even among the advocates of a real European authority, the Socialists were loath to differ too much from the Labour members who were completely opposed to it. In any case, it was impossible for the parliamentarians of the Consultative Assembly to overcome the opposition of the Committee of Ministers in which the British (both Conservative and Labour members) and Scandinavian governments vetoed any reform of the Statute. While the Council of Europe succeeded in establishing a European Court of Human Rights, it proved incapable of establishing a European political power or of going beyond the co-operative stage in legal, social and cultural matters.

THE COMMUNITY APPROACH OF THE SIX

The parting of the ways between those governments which tenaciously held to co-operation and those which wanted to move forwards by building European structures endowed with its own powers occurred with the institution of the European Communities by just six countries.

The system of intergovernmental co-operation appeared to be inadequate for practical action because decisions required unanimity (they could therefore be thwarted by a single Member State) and no organ existed to represent or safeguard the common interest. Federation appeared to be the most logical solution, but the governments were not ready to agree voluntarily to a surrender of their sovereign rights. A middle way had to be found: a more progressive system. As Robert Schuman was later to write: 'The organization of Europe in the sense of unification was indispensable. It could only be achieved within a new political structure. With this in view, the idea of a Federation sprang quite naturally to mind, but we did not think that we had to begin with such an ambitious legal construction. It was better to advance step by step in specific and practical areas'. In this way states would more readily agree to delegate some of their competence and powers in specific sectors. This was the solution chosen by Robert Schuman, Minister of Foreign Affairs, inspired by Jean Monnet, which he made public on behalf of the French Government on 9 May 1950. In his historic declaration, he maintained that 'Europe will not be made at once or according to a single overall plan. It will be built through concrete achievements which first create a de facto solidarity'.

He proposed to put 'the whole of Franco-German coal and steel production under a single joint High Authority in an organization open to the participation of the other countries of Europe. The pooling of coal and steel production will immediately guarantee the establishment of a common basis for economic development, as a first step in the federation of Europe'. This was a radical change in the method of building Europe. The common High Authority would truly constitute a European power, independent of the member states, but only in the fields subject to common action. This was the vital innovation and Robert Schuman made acceptance of the principle of supranationality the prior condition for the intergovernmental conference instructed to draft a treaty. Six countries signified their acceptance: France, the Federal Republic of Germany, Italy, Belgium, The Netherlands and Luxembourg. But the United Kingdom declined.

So it was a Community of Six which was established by the Treaty of Paris of 18 April 1951. The European Coal and Steel Community implemented the principle of supranationality thanks to an institutional system of a pre-federal nature. The central body was the High Authority, independent of the governments, instructed to implement the Treaty and directly wielding its powers over coal and steel undertakings. A Common Assembly, comprising members of the Parliaments of the member countries, exercised democratic control with the right to censure the High Authority. A Court of Justice ensured compliance with the Treaty and settled disputes. However, the States remained present on account of the existence of a special Council of Ministers instructed to see that contact was maintained between the two sectors of coal and steel entrusted to the High Authority and the remainder of the economic activities of the member countries. Its approval was necessary for the implementation of the most important decisions of the High Authority and it decided by unanimous or qualified majority, as the case required. This institutional system of the ECSC, balanced between supranational power and State powers, was with a few alterations to serve as a model for the other European Communities. Thus, there came to be established the 'hard core' of the Six, the driving force behind the progress of that European integration which the other countries refused.

However, the question still remained of the changeover from a sectoral authority to a real European political power with general jurisdiction. On this issue, attitudes diverged. In the opinion of Monnet and Schuman, the process was a progressive one: by creating de facto solidarities, sectoral integration would spread to an increasing number of economic and technical fields and would prepare the ground for the establishment of the future federation, but time would be needed to modify behaviour and change attitudes. Moreover, the ECSC Treaty, unlike the Declaration of 9 May 1950, no longer mentioned the term 'Federation'. Its preamble stated in a much less precise manner that by the creating of an economic community, it was to lay the foundations of a wider and deeper community.

In practice, events quickly put both methods to the test. The example of the ECSC encouraged plans for supranational authorities for other sectors, such as transport, agriculture and public health. But none of these came to anything. The federalists, for their part, appeared to be making more headway when the Consultative Assembly approved a resolution which they sponsored calling for the rapid conclusion of an agreement to establish a political authority subject to democratic control between those member states willing to take such a step. But the Committee of Ministers did not respond. And although the federalists seized the opportunity offered by the Defence Community project to push for a European Political Community, this also proved abortive when the French national assembly refused to ratify the EDC treaty. (See next chapter).

When the Six recovered from this failure, they returned to the economic sphere and to the functionalist method. The political objective remained, but it was expressed with extreme prudence: in the preambles to the Treaties of Rome setting up Euratom and the EEC, the intention was repeated of laying the foundations of 'an ever closer union between the European peoples' – but without specifying the form such a union could take.

It did not therefore prove possible to create a

European political structure in advance of the economic and technical integration of the Six; nor were the Six able to create it within a Community framework. De Gaulle attempted to fill the gap in his own way by means of an intergovernmental Union of States outside - and even opposed to - the Communities. He did not succeed in this either. It was only after him that attempts at political union could be resumed, this time in close association with the enlarged Communities.

Select Bibliography
Pierre Gerbet, La construction de l'Europe, Paris, 1983.
Henri Brugmans, L'idée européenne 1920-1970 Bruges, 1970.
A.H. Robertson, Le Conseil de l'Europe, Leyden, 1962.
Pierre Duclos, Le Conseil de l'Europe, Paris, 1970.
Jean Monnet, Mémoires, Paris, 1976.
Henri Rieben, Pierre Viansson-Ponte, Roger Massip, Pierre Gerbet, Francois Fontaine, La greffe européenne, Lausanne, 1973.
Histoire des débuts de la construction européenne, mai 1948-mai 1950. Actes du Colloque de Strasbourg (28-30 novembre 1984), Brussels, 1986.

Chapter Three

THE PROJECT FOR A POLITICAL COMMUNITY (1952-54)

Rita Cardozo

The project for a European Political Community (EPC),
though it is usually given only scant treatment in
the literature about the development of the
Communities, is of great interest in the context of
this study. The reasons for this are fourfold.

First, the EPC project was an attempt by the Six
to go beyond the sectoral preoccupations of the
treaties for the European Coal and Steel (ECSC) and
Defence (EDC) Communities and tackle their
underlying political aspects. In so doing, the
proposals which emerged provided for a Community
which was advanced in terms of its scope and the
structure of its institutions, but far less so in
terms of its powers. The proposed EPC was to embrace
such highly sensitive areas of national sovereignty
as foreign policy, defence and the establishment of a
common market. In the context of this study,
therefore, the project merits attention as an attempt
at a 'qualitative leap forward' over a very broad
front.

Second, the project marked a peak of federalist
endeavour. It was largely as a result of federalist
pressure that the project was initiated, and
federalist ideas also contributed a great deal to the
content of the proposals. The institutional
structure which was devised for EPC in the 1953 Draft
Treaty represented the most federal of the proposals
elaborated as a practical plan for adoption by
governments. But though the influence of federalist
ideas on the EPC project was great, the elaboration
stage was also to show the limits of that influence.

Third, the strategy followed for elaborating
the project was new. A parliamentary assembly was
given the role of working out the project rather than
a diplomatic conference. Like the European

Parliament's Draft Treaty on European Union some 30 years later, the Draft Treaty of 1953 was drawn up by parliamentarians in a public assembly rather than by diplomats working behind closed doors. The Draft Treaty succeeded in providing a definition of the concept of a European Political Authority and was a basis for subsequent governmental discussions. However, the experts' reports after two rounds of intergovernmental negotiations were to show the limits of this type of strategy and its disadvantages for achieving forward movement in the direction intended.

Fourth, a closer examination of the EPC project provides striking links with subsequent developments in European integration, though these are often forgotten. It was at this time that the groundwork was laid for subsequent developments, not least in that the first serious negotiations on economic integration, including the common market, took place alongside the political and institutional aspects. Other proposals relating to EPC also survived to subsequent stages of European integration while others still remain on the European agenda.

This chapter examines the initiation of the project, the strategy for elaborating the Draft Treaty in the Ad Hoc Assembly and the subsequent intergovernmental stage. In conclusion, the findings of the study are related to the European Parliament's initiative on European Union (1) and to the hypotheses advanced in the first chapter of the book.

INITIATION

Federalist demands for a European Political Authority echoed through all the early post-war plans for economic and defence cooperation. Government response to those demands went no further than the setting up of the Council of Europe (CE), a body which merely served to reaffirm the principle of intergovernmental 'cooperation' rather than 'integration'. The first ray of hope for federalists appeared in the form of the Schuman Declaration in May 1950 which promised that the Coal and Steel Community would be 'a first step in the federation of Europe'. Before federalists had time to react to this experiment, however, international events took matters further and forced defence into the foreground as the next sector for European integration.

The outbreak of the Korean war in June 1950

exposed the harsh reality that without a German military contribution, the combined forces of the Brussels Pact countries were inadequate in the event of Soviet aggression in western Europe. Moreover, the USA was insisting that its own contribution to Europe's defence was conditional upon German divisions being included in the NATO force. Thus the emotive question of German rearmament appeared at a time of fear of another European war. Europeans looked to Britain for a lead but the UK government failed to provide a proposal to counter American pressure. For its part, the French government had to contend with domestic alarm at the prospect of an independent German army re-emerging, and abroad with the risk of isolation from its allies if it continued to oppose the formation of a German army. At a difficult stage of negotiations with the US and Britain in October 1950, Monnet decided to take matters in hand.

One solution to France's dilemma already existed in the form of a Council of Europe resolution calling for the formation of a joint European army. (2) Monnet was to transform this idea into a plan of action. He elicited Prime Minister Pleven's support for a plan which underlined France's refusal to accept German rearmament on a national basis but suggested the formation of a European army in a European Defence Community in which German units would be integrated with those of other European nations. The 'Pleven Plan' was welcomed by the NATO Council on 28 October 1950 and Germany, Italy, Belgium and Luxembourg agreed to participate. A treaty-making diplomatic conference was eventually convened in Paris on 15 February 1951 and chaired by French diplomat Hervé Alphand. (3) The Netherlands delayed full participation until October 1951 which reflected that country's reluctance to take part without Britain and highlighted an underlying concern among the Six about Britain's absence from a European defence plan.

The plan for a joint European army clearly implied a measure of supranational authority and, therefore, a surrender of national sovereignty. Britain refused to countenance that. For their part the Six were still hesitant to go ahead without Britain. At a difficult stage in the negotiations in December 1951, Adenauer, De Gasperi, Schuman and Van Zeeland (Belgian Foreign Minister) appealed for support for EDC in the CE's Consultative Assembly. Britain's only response was to maintain her status as a 'supportive observer' at the EDC Conference. The following March Foreign Minister Eden presented an alternative plan to the Six. The essence of the 'Eden Plan' was to make the Council of Europe the parent body for the Coal and Steel and Defence Communities so that Britain could play a part in these latter communities but without being committed to the obligations of membership of supranational agencies. (4) Since the 'Eden Plan' was not accompanied by a British military commitment, the Six went no further than welcoming it as a first British initiative and treating it as a proposal for preserving links between the Six and the other countries in the Council of Europe. The decision to proceed without Britain did not, however, remove all difficulties.

For the Six the creation of a European Defence Community posed the problem of adequate democratic control. A political authority was seen by many as an essential accompaniment or pre-condition for a joint army. The Italian delegation at the EDC Conference became the chief advocate of a federalist model in which a European Political Authority would be democratically responsible through a directly-elected European Assembly and have powers of taxation and a joint decision-making structure. (5) Prime Minister De Gasperi lent full public support to this view and consistently advocated a federalist solution. Other governments showed less conviction, however, and the Conference could not decide whether the structure of the future permanent organisation should be 'federal' or 'confederal'. As agreement on this political dimension of EDC was lacking, the Italian delegation secured insertion of a special Article (38) in the EDC treaty which ensured that discussions on this aspect, although temporarily delayed, would ultimately have to be tackled.

Under Article 38 the temporary EDC Assembly was to examine the 'constitution' and 'powers' of a permanent and democratically-elected Assembly to take its place. This was to be 'so conceived as to be able to constitute one of the elements in a subsequent federal or confederal structure, based on the principle of the separation of powers and having, in particular, a two-chamber system of represent-ation.' The Assembly was also to examine 'problems arising from the co-existence of different agencies for European cooperation already established, or which might be established, with a view to ensuring coordination within the framework of the federal or confederal structure.' Paragraph 2 of Article 38 provided that the Assembly's proposals would be submitted to the Council within six months and, with its approval, they would be 'transmitted by the President of the Assembly to the Governments of the Member States' who would 'within three months ... convene a conference to consider the said proposals.' (6)

Article 38 met federalist aspirations insofar as it provided for an Assembly with limited but real constituent powers. But the immediate problem was that the constitutional procedure was subordinate to ratification by the six national parliaments of the EDC Treaty which had been signed on 27 May 1952. That process was likely to be lengthy. Federalists lost no time in securing adoption of a resolution in the CE's Consultative Assembly on 30 May 1952 which not only invited the six governments to implement Article 38 before the EDC treaty came into force but suggested going further. By means of a 'special agreement', distinct from the treaty itself, governments might instruct an assembly not merely to examine the political aspects described in Article 38 but to 'draft the Statute of a Political Community of a supranational character'. The resolution further suggested that the proposed assembly could be specially constituted either within the Council of Europe or the Assembly of the ECSC which was shortly to be convened. (7) The first choice was in line with the 'Eden Plan' which was discussed at the same session, but it was feared that Britain's influence could act as a brake on the project. On the other hand, the second choice would underline the determination of the Six to take the lead, while leaving the door open for Britain to join later.

The issue of speeding up convocation of the assembly was pursued by the Italian Prime Minister. At ministerial meetings of the Six De Gasperi elicited Schuman's support to entrust the tasks of Article 38 to the ECSC Assembly. While EDC negotiations were in progress, resolutions in the Italian, French and German parliaments had already demanded that creation of the political authority precede that of the European army and individual parliamentarians had expressed similar views in the other three countries. The climate of opinion in national arenas and in the CE's Consultative Assembly naturally lent weight to the Italian/French proposal and the other ECSC Ministers approved it at their meeting on 10 September 1952 in Luxembourg.

The 'Luxembourg Resolution' stated that the final aim of the six governments was still 'the establishment of as comprehensive a European Political Community as possible'. It took account of

the purpose of Article 38 of the EDC treaty and the
further scope offered by the resolution of the CE's
Consultative Assembly the previous May. A further
element of the bargain struck by the Ministers
provided the seed for expanding the scope of
negotiations still further by stating that 'the
constitution of a European Political Community ...
was bound up with the establishment of common bases
of economic development and a merging of the
essential interests of the Member States.' This was
in line with Dutch proposals for including a wider
economic dimension to the European edifice, a view
which was attracting German, Belgian and Luxembourg
support.

The 'Luxembourg Resolution' invited the Members
of the ECSC Assembly 'to draft a Treaty constituting
a European Political Authority' based on Article 38
and without prejudice to the provisions of the EDC
Treaty. Ministers left the Assembly to decide how
observers from non-ECSC member countries would be
associated with proceedings but required that work
should be 'undertaken and pursued in constant
cooperation with the organs of the Council of
Europe'. (8) The ECSC Assembly was given six months
to carry out its task and its proposals would then be
transmitted to the future EDC Assembly and to the six
Foreign Ministers. As President of the Council,
Adenauer presented the 'Luxembourg Resolution' to
the ECSC Common Assembly at its inaugural session on
10 September 1952.

NEGOTIATION - PARLIAMENTARY STAGE

The Common Assembly decided to accept the invitation,
and chose the title of 'Ad Hoc Assembly' (rather than
'Constituent Assembly' which some federalists would
have preferred) for its new task. Nine additional
members were coopted from the Council of Europe's
Assembly, as required by the 'Luxembourg Resolution'
so that its composition would correspond with that of
the proposed EDC Assembly. It then appointed the same
Bureau and Secretariat as that of the Coal and Steel
Assembly (9) and agreed that a 26 member committee
draw up a preliminary draft treaty for the Assembly's
consideration.

Round I – September 1952 to January 1953
The committee met in September and October 1952 to
agree its terms of reference and working procedures.

It decided to call itself the 'Constitutional Committee'; elected as its Chairman Heinrich Von Brentano (Chairman of the CDU Group in the Bundestag and a future Foreign Minister); and set up four sub-committees whose work was to be coordinated by a Working Party. (10)

In drawing up proposals these bodies did not have to start from scratch. The Ministers themselves had drawn up a list of questions about the scope of the EPC and the powers of its institutions as guidance. A group of jurists had submitted a report to the Council of Europe examining the various options and their implications, (11) and the European Movement submitted a report consisting of nine resolutions setting out a federalist approach to them. (12) Of the twelve leading lawyers and politicians who had drawn up this report, Becker, Benvenuti and Dehousse were also members and rapporteurs of the Constitutional Committee, while Pünder and Spaak were on the Bureau of the Ad Hoc Assembly. Though the Committee's own proposals were more cautious, there is little doubt of these members' strong influence on its work.

Interim Proposals. A set of interim proposals was agreed by the committee early in January 1953 by a vote of 13 to 0, (13) the low turnout reflecting disagreements in the committee. The intention of Guy Mollet (France SFIO) to abstain and of Michel Debré (France RPF) to vote against were recorded in the minutes. The latter put forward a counter project for a 'Pact for a Union of European States' (14) which subsequently formed the basis for the Fouchet negotiations in the early sixties. (See Chapter 5).

The interim proposals were discussed by the Ad Hoc Assembly later in January. They proposed that the future Political Community should not be a separate entity but should provide an over-arching framework for the ECSC and the EDC. The new entity would be 'supranational' and 'indissoluble'. It would inherit the competence and powers of the ECSC and EDC and in addition would have responsibility in the areas of foreign and economic policy. Although these new competences would be 'restrictively interpreted', the proposals envisaged wide-ranging powers in regard to trade liberalisation and the progressive establishment of a customs and monetary union, areas in which national ministers would have no veto. A majority in the committee felt that proposals relating to the economic sphere might be rejected and therefore favoured incorporating articles relating to them in a separate protocol. If this were rejected, it need not jeopardise adoption of the whole Statute. For its part, the Assembly referred all questions on economic powers to the committee for further study.

Proposals concerning institutional arrangements were also ambitious. The Parliament of the Community was to be bicameral, as requested by the governments, and composed of a directly-elected People's Chamber and a Senate elected by national parliaments to represent the states. Proposals provided for a weighted distribution of seats in both chambers, the method of weighting to be decided later. As in the ECSC and EDC, there would be a supranational element in the form of a European Executive Council but the new body would govern the Community and be responsible to its Parliament. A Council of National Ministers would represent national governments and have the same functions as the parallel institutions in the ECSC and EDC but with the addition of coordinating powers, especially in the field of foreign policy where decisions would be taken by unanimity.

Political Attitudes

As a nominated body, the Ad Hoc Assembly reflected the distribution of party political positions in national parliaments. The Constitutional Committee consisted of less than one-third of the Assembly's members (26 out of 87). It was representative in terms of nationality but in party terms the Christian Democrats were over-represented (13 out of 37) whilst the Socialists were grossly under-represented (only 5 out of 27). This was largely due to the decision of the German SPD to boycott the work of the Ad Hoc Assembly and its Constitutional Committee for fear that further European integration would jeopardise German reunification. However, even without their presence, attitudes towards European integration in the committee and the assembly were by no means cohesive. During discussions, divisions of opinion reflecting national differences towards European integration as well as party political attitudes had to be reconciled.

Generally, the Dutch and Italian members led a maximalist group favouring a broad interpretation of economic and political integration whilst French members led a minimalist group which wanted merely to coordinate the coal and steel and defence

Communities. In the course of discussions, however, a more complex picture emerged. Amongst the maximalists, the Benelux Christian Democrats pressed for national guarantees in the legislature and the executive. For the Senate this group advocated an equal distribution of seats rather than a weighted system, and a European government nominated by a Council of National Ministers, whose unanimous agreement would be necessary in all important matters. On the question of a directly-elected Chamber, Dutch members favoured a transitional period and were against its immediate creation. German members were in favour of harmonising different national economic policies whereas the Dutch envisaged voluntary coordination as practised in the OEEC or Benelux Customs Union. Italian members favoured the establishment of a supranational political authority with a less powerful Council of National Ministers and German Christian Democrats shared this view since it could achieve their primary goal of real economic integration.

Amongst the minimalists, the picture was no less complex. German Social Democrats and French Members of the Right (like Debré and Maroger) formed a curious alliance seeking to prevent any European achievement for the sake of their respective national preoccupations. French socialists demanded that the political authority be formed with no other function but to 'cap' the coal and steel and defence communities. By limiting the creation of new institutions among the Six, the SFIO hoped to keep the door open to a larger Europe. This official party view was advocated consistently by the SFIO party leader Guy Mollet but it masked positions within the party which ranged from opponents of European unification to convinced federalists like Gérard Jacquet. Other French Members were opposed to extending EPC's economic powers.

Round II - January to March 1953

During the final committee stage the Working Party of the Constitutional Committee met twice as a drafting committee to study the Assembly's directives and to turn the proposals into a legal text. This was put to the full committee meeting on 21-25 February, and the Preliminary Draft Treaty as a whole was agreed by 14 votes with Mr Debré voting against. At a session in Strasbourg from 6 to 10 March 1953 the Ad Hoc Assembly then adopted the Draft Treaty (with certain amendments of detail rather than substance) by 55 votes in favour and 5 abstentions (including three French Socialists).

Final Proposals. In line with the interim report, the 'Draft Treaty embodying the Statute of the European Community' (15) proposed that it should take over the functions of the ECSC and EDC, plus additional powers relating to foreign affairs and economic policy. The Community would be 'supranational' in character, 'founded upon a union of peoples and states' as in the ECSC and EDC treaties but, unlike them, it would be 'indissoluble'. National reservations on the latter question were to re-emerge in subsequent negotiations.

As in the ECSC Treaty, the institutional structure of the Community was dealt with in Part II of the Draft Treaty which reflected the importance accorded to institutional questions at this time. (16) It proposed a bi-cameral Parliament consisting of a People's Chamber and a Senate. The former would be directly-elected, its 268 seats distributed according to population but with a weighted system which ensured that any two large states could not dominate the Assembly. France would have 70 seats to take account of its overseas territories, Germany and Italy would have 63 seats each, Belgium and The Netherlands 30 each and Luxembourg 12 seats. The Senate would be elected by national parliaments and its 87 seats would be divided in the same proportions as in the lower chamber, except that France would only have the same number of seats as Germany and Italy (21 each); Belgium and The Netherlands being given 10 each, and Luxembourg 4.

A 'European Executive Council' was to 'undertake the general administration of the Community'. The methods agreed for its designation, however, indicated the underlying features of a European 'government' which was the term used in the French text. The President of the Executive Council would be elected by the Senate. He would appoint the other members (to be known as 'Ministers of the European Community') of whom not more than two would be of the same nationality. On its appointment the Executive Council would be obliged to seek a vote of confidence from both chambers of parliament. It would have to resign if the vote was negative or was refused. According to Article 31, a three-fifths majority of the People's Chamber would be required for a vote of no confidence. If this was not achieved the Executive Council would have the option of resigning or dissolving the chamber. The President of the Executive Council could dismiss or replace any of its members, subject to the approval of both chambers, and would represent the Community in international relations.

Alongside this body, a Council of National Ministers would represent the member governments. The tasks of this body, which were only briefly described, were 'to exchange information and consult' with the Executive Council, and to harmonise its action with that of the member states. Provision was also made for a Court of Justice, and a consultative Economic and Social Council.

Legislative proposals would need the approval of both Chambers, acting by simple majority. If one-quarter of the Members of the Senate requested it, a second reading of any bill would be held in both Chambers. In the absence of such request, the bill would become law and be promulgated by the President of the Executive Council unless the latter requested, within eight days, that Parliament hold a new debate. For its part, the European Executive Council could issue implementing regulations and, together with the authorities of Member States, would be entrusted with the execution of such laws and regulations.

The powers and competence of the Community were dealt with in Part III of the Draft Treaty. It was to have a 'general right of initiative' to make proposals to the member states through the Executive Council acting, either on its own initiative, or on the proposal of Parliament or one of its chambers. Such proposals would be made with the object of attaining the Community's general aims which embraced protection of human rights; cooperation with non-member states in security matters; coordination of the foreign policies of Member States in defence, security and economic matters; establishment of a common market; and cooperation with non-member states in achieving objectives laid down in the CE's Statute, the European Convention for Economic Cooperation and the North Atlantic Treaty.

The Community was to take over the powers and competence of the ECSC and EDC within a period of two years from the constitution of the People's Chamber. The Parliament and Council of National Ministers of the Community would replace the parallel institutions in the ECSC and EDC forthwith and judicial powers would be exercised by a single Court of Justice. The High Authority (ECSC) and Commissariat (EDC) would be subject to the 'supervision' and 'responsibility' of the European

Executive Council during a two-year transitional period, when their Presidents would be members of it and have voting rights. Thereafter, the High Authority alone would continue its existence as an 'administrative' board, with the effect of bringing its considerable powers under greater parliamentary control. The Commissariat, on the other hand, would have been replaced by a much more supranational institution than envisaged in the EDC Treaty.

But having endowed the Community with the institutions of a federal government, the Draft Treaty displayed extreme caution by limiting their powers. In the field of international relations, for instance, the Executive Council would act on behalf of the Member States but subject to the unanimous approval of the Council of National Ministers. Similarly, although treaty-making power was also vested in the Executive Council it could not ratify treaties or agreements without the consent of another organ of the Community.

Chapter IV provided for a Community budget to be submitted by the Executive Council to the Parliament which could amend it 'only within the limits of the overall total of the proposed expenditure.' It could not add new chapters involving additional expenditure. The financial resources of the Community would be derived from its own receipts, including taxes and loans, and the contributions of the Member States. The methods and rates for levying taxes were to be determined by the Executive Council with the unanimous approval of the Council of National Ministers. Similarly, the basis for determining contributions from Member States would be unanimously decided by the Council of National Ministers on the proposal of the European Executive Council.

The economic powers of the Community were incorporated in the Draft Treaty rather than in a separate protocol as envisaged by the interim proposals. Chapter V provided that, in accordance with its economic and social aims, including the promotion of economic expansion, development of employment, and improvement of the standard of living in Member States, the Community would 'establish progressively a common market among the Member States, based on the free movement of goods, capital and persons'. In order to achieve its aims the Community would 'foster the coordination of the policy of the Member States in monetary, credit and financial matters.' However, these powers would not apply for the first year of the Community's existence. During the following five years, economic powers would be given effect by means of proposals made by the Executive Council and approved by Parliament, but on condition that the unanimous approval of the Council of National Ministers, after consultation with national parliaments, was forthcoming. Subsequently, the 'concurrence' of the Council of National Ministers would be required before the Peoples Chamber voting by simple majority, and the Senate by a two-thirds majority, would approve the proposals of the Executive Council.

Provision was made for a 'European Re-adaptation Fund' to mitigate hardships caused to workers and enterprises by the creation of the common market. A further safeguard for member states was a right of appeal against any measures which they considered 'might cause fundamental and persistent disturbance to their economy'. But Member States would consult the European Executive Council before taking measures, particularly in monetary matters, which might affect the interests of other members or impede the free movement of labour and goods. In such cases the Executive Council could make proposals, with the agreement of the Council of National Ministers, to the member states concerned.

Provision was also made for associating the Community with the creation, sponsorship or supervision of 'specialised authorities' which were being proposed by governments at that time, such as the 'Green Pool' for agricultural markets, the 'White Pool' for health and medical services, the European Transport Authority and other more limited projects.

Other matters dealt with in the Draft Treaty included the association of other European states with the Community, relations with the Council of Europe, the automatic inclusion of East Germany in the Community in the event of reunification, and the procedure for amending the treaty.

Submission of Proposals. At a formal session on 10 January 1953, President Spaak officially handed over the Draft Treaty to the ECSC Ministers for Foreign Affairs represented by Bidault, who had replaced Schuman as Foreign Minister in January. As the new French government relied on Gaullist support, its attitude towards European integration was far more prudent than that of its predecessor. Bidault's speech was in line with this change: it did not invite optimism.

Another hurdle for the Draft Treaty was that,

according to the 'Luxembourg Resolution', the Assembly's proposals were to be 'transmitted to the future EDC Assembly and to the six Foreign Ministers'. Since the EDC Treaty was still in the process of ratification, this formula allowed ample scope for ministerial delay.

Under the circumstances, the Ad Hoc Assembly saw a need to maintain support for the project. It instructed the Constitutional Committee, in conjunction with the Assembly's Bureau, to take any necessary steps to enable the governments to benefit from the Assembly's experience in preparing the Draft Treaty. Though individual parliamentarians exerted pressure through national parliaments, political parties and the European Movement, and proposals were widely publicised by the Constitutional Committee, the latter's role was to be relegated to monitoring governmental action on the Draft Treaty. Nevertheless, it continued its activities and documented events until December 1954.

NEGOTIATION – GOVERNMENTAL STAGE

Even before work had been completed, it was becoming evident that in official circles the Ad Hoc Assembly's proposals were viewed as too audacious. Changes on the international scene also served to reinforce national reserves. In the United States the Eisenhower/John Foster Dulles administration replaced that of Truman/Acheson in January 1953 and in the USSR a new leadership took over after Stalin's death in March. Although there was little change in US encouragement for early ratification of EDC, Soviet statements were being received in Europe as signs of an easing of pressures in East-West relations and, particularly in France, a 'wait and see' attitude reigned for some time.

In these changed circumstances, ministers who had staked their political prestige on policies of European integration, especially De Gasperi and Adenauer, had to use all their influence to ensure that an early date be set for intergovernmental discussion of the draft Treaty. The ECSC Council of Ministers meeting in Paris on 12-13 May, invited members from the Ad Hoc Assembly to report on the implementation of the mandate they had been entrusted with. A deputation of leading members of the Constitutional Committee (Benvenuti, Blaisse, Dehousse, Teitgen and von Brentano) outlined the basic principles of the Draft Constitution to the

Ministers who made no comment. Despite these ominous signs, the Council did agree to hold an interim governmental conference in Rome from 12 June to 1 July, to be chaired by De Gasperi as President of the ECSC Council, and comprising Ministers or their substitutes and official experts, and to put the results to a meeting of ministers on 10 July in The Hague.

The governmental conference was postponed, however, as a result of a French ministerial crisis which lasted 40 days. This period brought other difficulties elsewhere. In Germany, Adenauer's government was soon to face elections and new initiatives were viewed with declining enthusiasm. Italy was also facing problems over Trieste and De Gasperi's new government fell in July 1953 after only a fortnight in office. Although the Pella government which replaced it maintained its support for the project, it had lost its foremost official leader at a crucial time.

The ECSC Council of Ministers next met on 7-8 August in Baden-Baden and reaffirmed the need to create a European Political Community, whilst maintaining close links with other European states and organisations. The Community should encompass the ECSC and EDC and lead to the creation of a common market and elimination of protectionist barriers. The Council statement, however, remained ambivalent on the form of such an entity which on the one hand would be 'a Community of sovereign states' and on the other 'would undertake its supranational functions based on the existing treaties or future treaties'. The institutions of the Community would be organised according to principles of democratic control over its executive organs, with a bicameral parliament including a directly-elected Chamber, but the Council of National Ministers would remain an essential element of the new Community. (17) Arrangements were made for detailed negotiations to open in Rome in September.

Meanwhile, the results of the German elections, contrary to many expectations, represented a vote of confidence for Adenauer's European and Atlanticist policies. In view of Germany's growing economic strength and its government's commitment to the West, Adenauer could have assumed a role of political leadership in Europe: but he was well aware of French and other European hostility to such a stance. Though most initiatives towards European integration up to 1952 had been French, the French government now appeared on the minimalist end of the spectrum and seemed likely to issue its delegation to the Rome Intergovernmental Conference with restrictive instructions which would have meant that the Ad Hoc Assembly draft could not serve as the basic text for negotiations. Prime Minister Laniel, in response to the urgings of French Ministers Paul Reynaud, Teitgen and Mutter (members of the Ad Hoc Assembly), finally succeeded in making the instructions to the French delegation more flexible although this stance held the threat of serious reservations by the Gaullists. Such was the atmosphere which prevailed at the beginning of the Rome Conference.

Round I - 22 September to 9 October 1953 in Rome

The Conference was made up of 64 individuals (11 for France, 15 for Germany, 14 for Italy, 10 each for Belgium and The Netherlands and 4 for Luxembourg). Ministers or senior diplomats presided over the national delegations, each of which included high ranking civil servants from Ministries of Foreign Affairs and Economics, legal experts and diplomats. (18)

An institutional committee, an economic committee, and a financial sub-committee were set up to study the problems of creating a European Political Community. They received instructions from the representatives and reported to them during the full sessions of the delegations. Although the Conference called upon the principal authors of the Ad Hoc Assembly's Draft Treaty to clarify certain points, it did not involve them in subsequent negotiations. Similarly, representation of the Council of Europe at the Rome Conference would seem to have been largely symbolic.

The form of the Rome report (19) reflected the fact that the Ad Hoc Assembly's Draft Treaty was an 'essential reference point'. However, the Rome meeting also had a number of other proposals before it, which suggested that some governments wanted to consider different starting points. Proposals tabled included a report of the Belgian 'Commission d'Etudes Européennes' a 'preliminary note' by the Italian government and a memorandum of the Dutch government entitled 'Le Projet des dispositions Economiques du Traité portant Statut de la Communauté Européenne' (also known as the Beyen proposals, see chapter 4 below).

The Rome report represented a basis for future negotiations. For each subject it recorded the Draft Treaty's proposal then enumerated the various national positions. On the question of powers, the French delegation at first envisaged only those contained in the ECSC and EDC treaties but later conceded that economic competences might be added in the future. By contrast, the Belgian, Dutch and Italian delegations insisted that economic powers be added and the German delegation went further still by advocating the transfer of general economic and monetary powers to the Community. This maximalist view provides a striking contrast with German attitudes some 30 years later when discussions in the Dooge Committee on the development of the EMS drew a German reservation (see chapter 10 below). In accordance with the Beyen proposals, the Dutch delegation advocated a customs union while the Belgians, in accordance with their document to the Conference, proposed a solution between the two by which the Community would be given wide economic powers but so precisely defined as to avoid excessive erosion of national sovereignty. In its report, the Conference left these matters open.

On the subject of institutions, the principle of a directly-elected People's Chamber was accepted by all delegations but the Dutch, in line with a similar view expressed in the Ad Hoc Assembly, (20) advocated a transition period of three years during which members would be appointed by national parliaments and a common electoral law would be enacted. As to the distribution of seats, the Belgian, French and Luxembourg delegations were reluctant to re-open questions on the system already agreed for the Assembly of the ECSC and EDC. This would have meant that the People's Chamber would have been reduced to one-third of the size envisaged in the Draft Treaty. The German delegation concurred, providing that the institutional structure envisaged by the Ad Hoc Assembly, or a close equivalent, would be retained. In line with reservations expressed in the Ad Hoc Assembly, the Italian delegation advocated a distribution of seats in proportion to population, with a minimum and maximum number of seats for smaller and larger states.

The Conference considered an alternative model for an upper chamber composed of national ministers. The French and Luxembourg delegations supported this as a means of strengthening national control over legislation (while maintaining a role for the Council of National Ministers at executive level) while the Germans saw it as a body modelled on the Bundesrat and quite consistent with a federal system. (21) The same proposal thus represented both minimalist and maximalist tendencies. On the contrary, the Belgian and Italian delegations opposed the idea of a Senate of national ministers which they considered to be a possible source of confusion between executive and legislative powers and instead supported the Ad Hoc Assembly's proposal for an elected Senate of MPs though with representation based on parity.

For the executive, the Conference agreed that there should be a balance between supranational and national elements and that a new supranational institution should be created. However, while France and Benelux envisaged a mixed organisation where national ministers would play an essential role the German delegation advocated a 'purely European executive', as envisaged in the Draft Treaty, which would be independent of national control but working with the Council of National Ministers.

The Conference agreed with the Ad Hoc Assembly's provisions for a single Court of Justice and proposed that a committee of legal experts be convened to examine legal questions on the basis of the Draft Treaty.

The Belgian delegation insisted on a right of secession in line with its national constitution. On other matters, the delegations at this stage supported the Draft Treaty's proposals on questions of accession of new states, association agreements, liaison with the Council of Europe and the procedure for revision of the statute.

At the ECSC Council of Ministers' meeting in The Hague on 26-28 November 1953, French attitudes dominated the debates. Bidault's appointment in January had already implied that France would adopt a more restrictive attitude towards European integration. An increase in nationalist tendencies since then had carried that minimalist tendency further. The French government now advocated merely a coordination of ECSC and EDC with much more limited democratic control than envisaged in the Draft Treaty or by other Member States. This did not augur well, and the communiqué reflected caution by other governments so as not to prejudice EDC ratification in France. Nevertheless, work on EPC was to continue.

In line with the conclusions of the Rome report, the Ministers approved the creation of a People's Chamber and an Upper Chamber (or other institution) which would represent the States. The People's Chamber would be directly-elected immediately on the entry into force of the EDC treaty – a concession by the Dutch. Questions relating to the Senate were referred back to the experts. The Executive would be composed of a European Executive Council, responsible to the Parliament, and a Committee of National Ministers. The Rome agreements on the Court of Justice and some other items were confirmed. Other questions which had been left open were referred back to the Conference which was asked to begin preparing the text of a treaty. The Conference was to meet in Paris and report to the Ministers by 15 March in preparation for their meeting on 30 March 1953. (22)

Round II: 12 December 1953 to 8 March 1954 in Paris

In the following round of negotiations, conducted by officials (23), institutional issues again occupied much attention. As far as the People's Chamber was concerned the most important were those related to its composition, method of election, and powers. The Italian delegation was alone in opposing the proposed distribution of seats: it argued in favour of a system of representation more proportionate to each country's population. It was, however, agreed that until Community legislation was enacted, the Chamber would be directly-elected each five years in accordance with national procedures, although certain common electoral principles were discussed. (24) The French delegation took a generally restrictive line with regard to the role of the Chamber, proposing that apart from two ordinary annual sessions, extraordinary sessions could only be convened under strict conditions. It also wished to give the Council of National Ministers the power in certain circumstances to terminate parliamentary sessions. Only the Dutch considered it unnecessary to impose any limits whatsoever on the duration of parliamentary sessions.

Details of the legislative process were left open at this stage, but it was agreed that in principle the People's Chamber would have rights of initiative and amendment. Contrary to the German and Italian views, the French and Benelux delegations considered the investiture of the Executive by the People's Chamber as unnecessary. It was agreed that it would have the right to force the resignation of the Executive by a vote of three-fifths of its members, but the French insisted that censure motions should only apply to administrative matters (excluding, for instance, budgetary issues).

In line with previous positions, opinions about the nature of the Upper Chamber were divided. A Franco/German proposal envisaged a Chamber of States composed of national ministers, while the Italians opted for a Senate elected by national parliaments as proposed by the Draft Treaty. With certain reservations the Franco/German camp was supported by Belgium and Luxembourg and the Italian camp by the Netherlands.

The first camp proposed equal representation, with each state having one vote. The new institution would share legislative power with the People's Chamber and inherit the same legislative competences and voting procedures as those given to the Council of National Ministers by the ECSC and EDC treaties. Other powers would be transferred to the Community's Council of Ministers. The Chamber of States would not have censure power over the European executive nor a right to ask questions. Rights of initiative would be granted only to the People's Chamber and executive institutions and the latter would have sole competence in respect of new expenditure. In principle the People's Chamber, by an absolute majority of its members, would have the last word on legislation, but it would not have the right to reject amendments by the Chamber of States if these concurred with Executive opinion, unless it did so by five-sixths of the vote at a second parliamentary reading. The Luxembourg delegation maintained a reservation on this possibility of overruling the Upper Chamber.

For the second camp this model of an Upper Chamber of States risked confusing executive and legislative power. They proposed a Senate elected by national parliaments with a weighted system of representation. However, if the People's Chamber were to be elected proportionately, then equal representation would be accepted. The Dutch delegation was against the Senate having a role in the investiture of the Executive but the Senate would have a right of initiative in legislation and the right to question the Executive. This group envisaged that the powers of the Council of National Ministers would be gradually transferred to the supranational Executive rather than to the Senate.

All the delegations agreed on the eventual creation of a 'Conciliation Committee' for resolving disagreements between the two chambers. Some advocated the right of the Executive to veto draft amendments to its proposals and envisaged the possibility of a framework law procedure.

On the question of liaison between the Community parliament and national parliaments, the Franco/German group proposed the compulsory election of a certain number of national parliamentarians to the

People's Chamber without prejudice to rules of incompatibility. The Italian group felt that their model of a Senate assured such liaison.

Positions concerning the Executive diverged just as widely. The Belgian, French and Luxembourg delegations proposed a two-tiered executive comprising supranational and intergovernmental elements. Opposing this view, the other delegations proposed that the Council of Ministers should be a _sui generis_ institution so as to reinforce the autonomy of the Community.

With regard to the supranational executive, only the Italian delegation supported the proposal in the Draft Treaty that it be designated by an elected Senate. The others advocated that this function be exercised by the Council of National Ministers voting unanimously, at least for the designation of the President. The Belgian, French and Luxembourg delegations proposed that this procedure apply to the designation of all members of the supranational executive while others envisaged the involvement of the President. Only the Dutch opposed the inclusion of ECSC and EDC Executive members or Presidents in the supranational executive on the grounds that this would risk confusing their respective responsibilities. Different proposals were made concerning the term of office of the European Executive but it was agreed that it would function as a college, its decisions would be taken by majority vote, and a censure motion would therefore imply the resignation of all its members.

The function of the Council of Ministers would be to assure liaison between the Community and Member States and play an essential role in the new institutional structure. By means of its opinions and directives, it would in effect be part of the executive. The French delegation, partially supported by the Luxembourg delegation, particularly insisted on the Council having power to intervene in all matters. The other delegations, however, considered that Council directives should be limited but that it should have a general right of initiative.

A significant part of the negotiations was devoted to the economic powers to be given to the new Community, and in particular to those related to the creation of a common market. Although no definitive conclusions were reached, these discussions prefigured and provided the groundwork for the later negotiations leading to the establishment of the European Economic Community.

Five delegations firmly supported the creation of a common market as an ultimate aim. The Italians proposed a framework treaty for its achievement; the Benelux countries jointly put forward a ten-year programme for the gradual liberalisation of trade; and the Germans, while stressing the importance of the coordination of economic discipline, said that their country was willing to accept its share of the costs of reducing trade barriers. The French, however, were reluctant to commit themselves to more than a general statement of intent, and argued for a strict definition and limitation of the Community's economic powers, and provisions to cover all foreseeable contingencies. They also proposed that at least for the first five years the Community should have a purely consultative role, and entered reservations on a range of detailed issues - such as the free movement of goods, services, people and capital; the coordination of economic, social, monetary and trade policies, and the establishment of readaptation funds - on which the other five were able to reach either common positions or a substantial measure of agreement.

A range of other issues was also discussed. It was agreed that after a transition period a single budget should be established, though this was to contain separate chapters for the expenditure of each of the three Communities, which would be subject to different procedures (as, incidentally, is still the case today for the ECSC budget). No decision was reached on the method of funding, though it was agreed that a choice would have to be made between the ECSC method of a Community tax and the system proposed for the EDC for national contributions.

Matters relating to the accession of new member states, association agreements and cooperation with other bodies were also discussed. It was agreed that membership would be open to all democratic states belonging to the Council of Europe, but that the unanimous agreement of the Council of National Ministers would be required. Unanimity would also be required for treaty revision. But while the other members were in favour of the creation of an 'indissoluble' Community, the French supported the Belgians in wishing to preserve a right of secession. There was also a continuing disagreement about the relationship to be established between the new Community and the ECSC and the projected EDC. Germany, Italy, Belgium and Luxembourg proposed immediate integration, coupled with a certain degree of administrative autonomy, while the Netherlands argued in favour of the maintenance of separate identities, though a sharing of some common institutions - including the People's Chamber (together with a single Court of Justice, on which agreement had already been reached at The Hague).

OUTCOME

The experts' report should have been considered by the ECSC Council of Ministers meeting in Brussels on 30 March 1954 but this was postponed because difficulties with the EDC treaty were becoming increasingly apparent. On 24 March the minister's representatives issued a communiqué stating that the various committees of experts would continue their work for review by the representatives' next meeting in May. On 4 May another communiqué, this time issued by the 'Comité Intérimaire' for the EDC, sounded a death knell for the EPC project. It stated that the foreign ministers had agreed in principle to strengthen democratic control over ECSC and EDC but it was to be understood that this did not imply any modifications to the treaties nor any extension of competence. However, this decision would not prejudice EPC negotiations. Once the EDC treaty had been ratified, governments would take necessary steps to implement Article 21 of the ECSC treaty so as to arrange for a directly-elected assembly, to which the High Authority and the EDC Commissariat would be responsible. According to national constitutional procedures, the assent of national parliaments would be required. (25) The experts' institutional committee continued work from 3 June until 2 July and the economic committee from 12 May until 6 July. Since March, however, progress had been dependent on the outcome of the EDC treaty, and when this foundered in the French National Assembly in August, work on the EPC project was shelved indefinitely.

Conclusions

This early attempt to create a Political Community illustrates a number of the propositions advanced in the introduction to this study, as well as providing insights into the attitudes and policies of the founding members of the Community at this early stage of its development.

In the first place, changes in national and international environments clearly had a major impact on the rise and fall of the EDC project and hence, indirectly, on that for the EPC which never acquired an independent status of its own. While it was the fear of a superpower conflict which originally triggered off the EDC proposals, it was equally changes in the international environment following the death of Stalin which greatly reduced the pressures in favour of the project and added decisively to the strength of its opponents.

At the national level, the EDC and EPC projects showed both the strength of the pressures operating to create a new political structure for western Europe and the nature of the obstacles to be overcome. In 1952 national positions miraculously coincided to produce a window of opportunity which allowed a qualitative leap forward to be achieved in the process of integration with the establishment of the ECSC, signature of the EDC treaty, and the initiation of the EPC project. During the subsequent EDC and EPC negotiations, however, short-term national considerations began to prevail over wider European interests. The assertion of the desire of national administrations to preserve their autonomy was obvious throughout the EPC process, and in particular at the governmental conference when divergencies between the Six came out most clearly into the open.

The most critical change between 1952 and 1954, however, was that in the French position: from having been the initiator and promoter of the Community-building process, it developed into the most difficult and reluctant partner. Those elites in France committed to the Community were no longer able to control the domestic situation, and this proved fatal.

The failure of the project did not, however, diminish the commitment of the propulsive elites to the process of integration. On the contrary the involvement of such figures as von Brentano, Benvenuti, Dehousse, Spaak and Hallstein made them more determined than ever, and helped to prepare them for subsequent - and more fruitful - negotiations. Others, who had also served as driving forces behind the project, such as those involved in the European Movement and its associated party and economic organisations, emerged from the experience shaken but no less convinced of the need to try again as soon as possible.

In terms of alternative strategies of integration, the EPC was the first major test of the populist or constituent method favoured by the federalists of giving a major role to a parliamentary assembly. But it sharply underlined the limitations of this approach which, in this instance, had left the critical decisions wholly in the hands of the member governments. Its failure nevertheless appeared to vindicate Monnet-type elitist strategies, and it was these which were used in the next stages of the process. This was not, however, the conclusion reached by Spinelli who remained convinced of the validity of the method if properly applied. He also drew on the experience of the Ad Hoc Assembly in devising the procedure he followed in piloting the project for a Draft Treaty for European Union through the European Parliament more than thirty years later. He opposed the creation of sub-committees which he believed had proved divisive, and also arranged for plenary sessions to consider work in progress before being asked to vote on a final set of proposals.

EPC was shelved but the issues it had raised were not to go away. The first to be tackled were those relating to the creation of a common market, which had been given a good airing. These were to provide a springboard for the relance which was speedily achieved in the mid-fifties. But other developments took much longer: a merger of the Executives of the Communities was not achieved until 1967, and direct elections only in 1979. And foreign policy coordination, together with security and defence issues have proved even more difficult: they remain major items of unfinished business on the European agenda.

Select Bibliography

1. **Primary Sources**. A substantial volume of published documents is available in the libraries of the European Parliament in Luxembourg and the Council of Europe in Strasbourg. This includes the documentation produced by the Ad Hoc Assembly itself, covering its plenary sessions, the work of the Constitutional Committee and its sub-committees, and information documents; Council of Europe reports and debates; the reports produced by the Intergovernmental Conference; and proposals put forward by the European Movement.

2. **Secondary Sources**.

(a) On EPC Project. A detailed history of the EPC project does not appear to exist in English but is provided in French by Rifflet. Other sources below give legal analyses of the Draft Treaty and federalist reactions.

Robert R. Bowie and Carl J. Friedrich, Statute of the European Community, European Union; A Survey of Progress, Vol. III, Aug. 1953, pp.22-28, (American Committee on United Europe: New York)

Guy Héraud, 'Chronique constitutionelle européenne: Nature juridique de la Communauté européenne d'après le projet de statut du 10 mars 1953', Revue du Droit Public et de la Science Politique en France et à l'étranger, No. 3, Paris, juillet-septembre 1953, pp. 581-607

Raymond Rifflet, La Communauté Politique Européenne, Conseil Belge du Mouvement Européen, Bruxelles, circa 1957

A.H. Robertson, Notes, The European Political Community, British Year Book of International Law 1952 (Oxford University Press: London 1953)

Altiero Spinelli, Lettera Federalista, Tempo di Scegliere, Europa Federata, Periodico del Movimento Federalista Europeo, Anno VI, n.1, gennaio 1953, pp.3-5

UEF, Communauté politique européenne et Union Francaise, Mémorandum de l'Union Européenne des Féderalistes, Paris, 24 october 1953

(b) Background. Histories on EDC and Memoirs of personalities of the time are a good source of background material. In addition, the following sources were illuminating:

Robert R. Bowie and Carl J. Friedrich, Etudes sur le Fédéralisme, première partie Tome III Paris, 1966

Henri Brugmans, L'idée Européenne 1920-70, Bruges, 1970

Miriam Camps, Britain and the European Community 1955-63, London, 1964

Fernand Dehousse, Recueil d'Etudes, de rapports et de discours 1945-1960, Paris, 1960

Richard Mayne, The Recovery of Europe - From Devastation to Unity, London, 1970

A. Nutting, Europe will not wait - a warning and a way out, London, 1960

Hans A. Schmitt, The Path to European Union - From the Marshall Plan to the Common Market. Louisiana State University Press, 1962

Altiero Spinelli, L'Europa non cade dal cielo, Bologna, 1960

Notes

1.   See Chapter 9 below. Also 'The Crocodile Initiative', by Cardozo and Corbett in Juliet Lodge (ed), European Union: the EC in search of a future,

London, 1986.

2.   CE Resolution on a European Army, 11 August 1950 by Winston Churchill with amendments by André Philip.

3.   See E. Fursdon, The European Defence Community: A History, London, 1980, pp.92-99.

4.   A. Nutting, Europe will not wait - a warning and a way out, London, 1960, pp.41-42.

5.   The delegation was led by Ivan Matteo Lombardo, a federalist of long standing and a member of the Movimento Federalista Europeo. MFE, headed by Altiero Spinelli during this period, succeeded in channelling the Italian government's support towards a federalist solution. See A. Spinelli, L'Europa non cade dal cielo, Bologna, 1960.

6.   Doc. 1, pp.21-22, Information and Official Documents of the Constitutional Committee, October 1952 - April 1953.

7.   Doc. 2, op.cit., pp. 23-25. Resolution 14, 30 May 1952 concerning the most appropriate means of drafting the Statute of the European Political Community. See also CE Documents 6 and 27, May 1952 - Margue report with counter resolutions by Spaak and Jacquet and amendment by Benvenuti.

8.   Doc 3, op.cit., pp.26-29.

9.   The Bureau of the Ad Hoc Assembly was made up as follows: President: Paul-Henri Spaak (Belgium - Socialist Party), Member of the House of representatives, Minister of State, former Prime Minister. Vice-Presidents: Herman Puender (Germany CDU) Deputy, former Secretary of State; Pierre-Henri Teitgen (France Popular Republican Movement, Deputy, former Minister; G. Vixseboxse (Netherlands - Historical Christian Union Party), Member of the Upper House of the States-General; Alessandro Casati (Italy - Liberal Party), Senator, former Minister; Jean Fohrmann (Luxembourg - Socialist Party), Deputy. M.F.F.A. De Nerée tot Babberich, (Bonn Member) Clerk of the Common Assembly of the ECSC was appointed Clerk of the Ad Hoc Assembly.

10.   The four sub-committees were set up as follows: Powers and Competence: chairman P.A. Blaisse (Netherlands) Christian Popular Party; rapporteur L. Benvenuti (Italy) Christian Democratic Party. Political Institutions: chairman Pierre-Henri Teitgen (France) M.R.P.; rapporteurs A. Azara (Italy) Christian Democratic Party and F. Dehousse (Belgium) Socialist Party. Jurisdictional Institutions: chairman G. Persico (Italy) Socialist Party; rapporteur H-J. Von Merkatz (Germany) Free German Party. Liaison: chairman M. Van Der Goes Van Naters

(Netherlands) Socialist party; rapporteurs J. Semler (Germany) C.D.U. and P.L. Wigny (Belgium) Christian Social Party. The Working Party consisted of the Committee's Bureau, together with the Chairmen and Rapporteurs of the sub-committee.

11. 'Introductory report by the Committee of Jurists on the problem of a European Political Community'. CE Doc (SG(52)2), 13 September 1952. The Committee consisted of Roberto Ago (Milan), Fernand Dehousse (Liege), Paul Reuter (Aix-Marseille), Helmut Ridder (Frankfurt) and Jean H.W. Verzijl (Utrecht and Leyden).

12. Projet de Statut de la Communauté Politique Européenne, Travaux préparatoires, Comité d'études pour la Constitution Européenne, Brussels November 1952. Altiero Spinelli was also a member of this special committee and Lucien Radoux, prominent member of the EP's Institutional Committee, was its Administrative Secretary.

13. Assembly Document 1.

14. Assembly Document 3, January 1953.

15. Assembly Document 15R, March 1953.

16. By contrast, institutional issues are relegated to Part 5 of the EEC Treaty: a reflection of a different negotiating strategy which put functions before institutions.

17. Communiqué de presse, Baden-Baden, 7-8 August 1953. Constitutional Committee Document d'Information AA/CC/Inf. 26.

18. The leaders of the national delegations were: André de Staercke (Belgium - permanent delegate to the NATO Council); Jacques Fouques-Duparc (France - Ambassador in Rome); Walter Hallstein (Germany - Secretary of State for Foreign Affairs); Lodovico Benvenuti (Italy - Under Secretary of State for Foreign Affairs, and member of the Ad Hoc Assembly and the Constitutional Committee); Pierre Majerus (Luxembourg - Plenipotentiary Minister); Jhr. A.W.L. Tjarda van Starkenborgh Stachouwer (Netherlands - Extraordinary and Plenipotentiary Ambassador).

In the second round of the negotiations the French delegation was headed by Alexandre Parodi (Secretary General at the Quai d'Orsay) and the Luxembourg delegation by Nicolas Hommel (Permanent Representative to the NATO Council).

19. Conférence pour la Communauté Politique Européenne, Rome 22 September - 9 October 1953, Rapport aux Ministres des Affaires Etrangères, 9 October 1953 Document CIR/15.

20. Dutch and Belgian members of the

Constitutional Committee Working Party, Van der Goes van Naters and Wigny had unsuccessfully introduced amendments for a transitional period.

21.   See R. Corbett, 'Reform of the Council: the Bundesrat Model', in <u>The Federalist</u>, Year XXVI No. 1, July 1984, Pavia.

22.   Communiqué, The Hague 26-28 November 1953. Committee Documents op.cit., AA/CC/Inf. 44.

23.   Conférence pour la Communauté Politique Européenne, Rapport aux Ministres des Affaires Etrangères, CCP/Doc. 6.

24.   These included proportional representation or adequate representation of parties, exclusion of by-elections and correspondence or proxy votes for residents living abroad.

25.   Committee Documents AA/CC/Inf. 73 and 88.

Chapter Four

THE TREATIES OF ROME (1955-57)

Hanns Jürgen Küsters

When the Treaties creating the European Economic Community and the European Atomic Energy Community came into force on January 1 1958, this marked the biggest success to date for the many attempts at the unification of western Europe. Barely three years previously, after the defeat of the EDC treaty in the French National Assembly on August 30 1954, it looked as if that might be the end of the political and military unification of Europe. We need therefore to explain how the process was successfully continued, particularly in view of the strength of the opposition in France to the idea of integration.

TRADITIONAL HYPOTHESES AND NEW LINES OF THOUGHT

Existing studies do not provide altogether satisfactory answers. Four kinds of explanation occur frequently:
1. After the failure of the EDC and the related deliberations concerning a European Political Community it was no longer possible to take the direct route to the political unification of Europe. Therefore people started to think back to the aims of the Schuman Plan that had begun the process of economic integration; thus the Economic Community was born.
2. Continued integration in the economic field had come about of its own accord, because here an attempt could be made to establish gradually those links that would have been created immediately without specific preparation if the EDC had succeeded. Further, economic development was in the interest of all concerned, because in the modern industrial state economic integration was bound to have a politically

unifying effect. (1)

3.   Unification in the economic field was easier than political integration, because on the one hand economic progress had already been made in the Coal and Steel Community and on the other hand economic questions caused less controversy in public debate than the political problems of integration. (2)

4.   It was in the common interest of the Six to remove the drawbacks of a division into a number of small or medium-sized national economies. The liberalisation of internal European trade and the mutual convertibility of European currencies could be achieved only by the creation of a larger economic entity on a par with the United States of America and the Soviet Union. (3)

These reasons may be convincing, but two questions that are important for the birth of the Economic Community are not taken into consideration:

1.   In view of the unfavourable attitude the French Parliament had shown towards the EDC treaty and the idea of integration, how was it possible to win the support of French Government for a new initiative to continue the process of unification?

2.   The Treaties of Paris in October 1954, that took care of West European/Atlantic security relationships, removed a substantial part of the momentum from the driving force of European unification. Why, therefore, did the Treaty of Rome not suffer the same fate as the EDC Treaty?

THE RE-ARRANGEMENT OF WEST EUROPEAN/ATLANTIC RELATIONS

The failure of the EDC Treaty in 1954 caused the simmering crisis in the movement for European unification to boil over and at the same time carried things further forward than ever before. The effects were far reaching. The European Defence Community and the European Political Community had been an attempt to bring about a supranational defence, security, political and economic integration of Western Europe, and these aspects were now separated out from one another and shifted on to different levels.

As far as the most important sector - security - was concerned, the Treaties of Paris made use of the classic type of alliance in the shape of NATO, together with West European Union (in which the Federal Republic of Germany had been included with the active support of Chancellor Adenauer) that had emerged from the Treaty of Brussels of 1948. An important pre-condition was the resolution of two differences of opinion between Germany and France – the question of the Saar and the conclusion of a bilateral economic agreement.

As far as the political and economic unification of Europe was concerned, these aspects were not touched upon in the Treaties of Paris. There were, however, various reasons in favour of pressing ahead with integration as soon as possible in these areas as well:

1. The political and economic pressures to which Western Europe might be subjected in future between the superpowers of the USA and the Soviet Union, plus Moscow's seemingly threatening stance in the political and ideological sphere, brought to the fore the questions of the further development of the existing European institutions and of a continued integration of the West European states.

2. Economic problems – partly resulting directly from the post-war era – remained to be solved. Protectionism and an economy based on currency restrictions were a hindrance to trade and the movement of capital. Apart from balance of payments problems, the European states had to contend with disruptions to their domestic economies. Only through closer co-operation between the West European states could the allocation and distribution of existing resources be improved, barriers to trade be removed and the productivity of individual economies be raised.

3. After the failure of the EDC the supporters of integration feared that the partially supranational institutions of the Coal and Steel Community might be swept away in the maelstrom of anti-integrationist tendencies. It was their intention to counteract this. What had already been achieved in the Coal and Steel Community was to be maintained at all costs and extended by means of additional integrationist measures that would as far as possible not run the risk of triggering off insuperable political opposition.

4. Leading politicians in Western Europe, such as Adenauer, Hallstein, Spaak, Beyen and Monnet, were convinced that time was against them and the European idea if they did not succeed without delay in giving unification a new impulse. They stuck as a matter of principle to the policy of integration.

A new démarche had basically to take account of two things. Firstly, there was no hope of bringing about a supranational federal state in the short term. Secondly, it had to be assumed that no West

European state would be in a position on its own in the long term to solve its political and economic problems effectively within the framework of the nation state.

As it was clear that a settlement of the security questions would smooth the way for new efforts to bring about economic unification, further formal steps in this direction could only be expected to succeed when the Treaties of Paris had finally entered into force.

THE SO—CALLED 'RELANCE EUROPÉENNE' (SEPTEMBER 1954 — JUNE 1955)

Three political personalities were behind the initiatives for the continuation of the discussion on integration. They pursued different aims and methods but were in agreement on the urgency of a new European step forward.

One of the driving forces was Jean Monnet. Together with his staff he had worked out a plan that envisaged extending unification to the field of atomic energy and placing it under the High Authority. (4) This idea of involving the new technology of the time in the process of integration was of great interest to the Six because with the exception of France and Belgium they did not exchange any information regarding nuclear research. In addition, research on the peaceful use of atomic energy was still in its infancy and hardly a subject of political controversy. (5) Monnet, who had declined to renew his candidacy for the office of President in November 1954 - out of disappointment at the failure of the EDC - put the governments on the horns of a dilemma with his proposition; they could not simply decide on a successor for him without having first responded to his plan.

The deliberations of the Belgian, Dutch and also the German Governments were quite different. Here the debate concentrated on progress towards unification in the economic field. Taking up the work of the experts on the European Political Community, the governments in Brussels and The Hague intended developing the plan for a European Customs Union put forward by Beyen, the Dutch Foreign Minister, in 1953 which had originally been intended as the economic supporting structure for a political community. (6)

After the Treaties of Paris (integration of the Federal Republic in NATO, foundation of WEU) had entered into force on May 5, 1955, it was possible to

81

start a new European initiative. Most important of all was to avoid another EDC type of dilemma. Spaak succeeded in the course of extensive talks with Monnet and Beyen in bringing their diametrically opposed ideas (on the one hand Atomic Energy Community, on the other hand Customs Union) together in a single memorandum. Consequently on May 20, 1955, the Benelux countries proposed to the other members of the Coal and Steel Community to create on the one hand a European atomic organisation, on the other hand a customs union; the national economies were gradually to be merged with one another and common institutions with powers of decision established. (7)

At the same time, in March and April 1955, further deliberations were taking place in The Schuman Plan Department of the West German Ministry of Economic Affairs. Under the direction of Hans von der Groeben the plan for a customs union was further elaborated. The most important point in the German memorandum, which was then put forward at the Messina Conference, was the removal of all barriers to trade within the area of the Coal and Steel Community. In other words the movement of goods and capital was to be liberalised, the mobility of persons and services within the Community to be established and rules of competition binding on all members to be drawn up.

Even at the stage of discussion in the German Government considerable opposition became apparent. The Minister of Economic Affairs, Ludwig Erhard, emphatically rejected the integration of the Six because he believed that in this way a closed trading area would be created in Western Europe, encouraging regional protectionism. Erhard spoke out in favour of co-operation on the basis of global free trade. (8)

The attitude of the French Government, however, was an even greater headache for the supporters of the idea of European integration. After the experience of the EDC it hardly seemed likely that France's centre-right government under the leadership of Edgar Faure (Radical Socialist) would be prepared to make its restrictive attitude towards European policy more flexible. In particular the opposition to be expected from the Gaullists meant that the Government was not especially keen on continuing the talks about progress towards European unification in the framework of the Coal and Steel Community countries. The defence guarantees accorded by France's partners in the Treaties of Paris, the setbacks in French-Soviet relations and the difficult economic situation of the Fourth Republic put the Faure government in a difficult position. (9) On the one hand it did not want to revive a discussion in the National Assembly about European integration again; on the other hand it could not as a matter of course reject all the attempts of the other Coal and Steel Community countries at a continuation of the process of unification.

Only politicians of the Mouvement Républicain Populaire (MRP) and the Foreign Minister, Antoine Pinay (Independent Republican), showed an interest in a new European initiative. A decisive incentive for the French government to take part in a further attempt at integration was the wish to develop research on the use of nuclear technology and share financial or technological responsibility. So in order to get the French to the negotiating table it was necessary to include Monnet's Euratom project in the discussions. This became a condition <u>sine qua non</u> for developing the process of integration along with the interest of the other five to extend economic integration – where French interests coincided with those of the other Five. For either of the projects to be successful both had to be integrated in the new initiative. So the link between the common market and Euratom was born.

Only in the Benelux countries and in Italy was there no serious opposition to the project.

The conference of foreign ministers at Messina began in unfavourable circumstances. On the evening of June 2, 1955, more questions remained open than had been settled: Walter Hallstein, leading the Federal Republic's delegation, expressed his doubts as to whether people wanted to make any progress at all. The positions were too divergent, with Spaak and Beyen pleading for partial integration in the realms of atomic energy and a customs union, while the German side sought comprehensive economic integration. At the beginning of the negotiations Pinay rejected all the propositions but then let his own Government's interest in a common programme of nuclear research become evident. He refused, however, to transfer responsibility in this field to the High Authority of the Coal and Steel Community.

It was due mainly to the concessions made by France's partners that the foreign ministers finally reached a positive conclusion after all. They agreed to the French delegation's demand that an intergovernmental committee be formed which would have as its task not, for the time being, to draft any treaties but only to examine what might be technically possible. In the main it was here a question of whether European unification could be carried forward and extended by creating two new organisations, namely an atomic community (Euratom) and a Common Market. Once again the Six had reached agreement at the lowest common denominator; the 'Messina Resolution' tried to do justice to all the strands of integration but it could not eliminate the real differences of opinion and interest regarding further steps towards integration. (10)

At the end of the conference there was no time to decide about a political personality who should lead the inter-governmental committee. Four names were considered: the former president of the High Authority, Jean Monnet; Paul van Zeeland, Belgium's foreign secretary until April 1954, a convinced European; the former Italian Prime Minister, Giuseppe Pella, who followed Alcide De Gasperi as the president of the ECSC-Assembly; and last but not least Paul-Henri Spaak, who had been engaged in the integration process since the end of the war. The six governments finally chose Spaak for he was an acting Foreign Minister and one of the initiators of the Messina approach together with Monnet and Beyen.

THE WORK OF THE INTERGOVERNMENTAL COMMITTEE (JULY – OCTOBER 1955)

It was Spaak who had a decisive influence on the course of the further talks in Brussels attended by experts and officials from the six member states, the High Authority, and the United Kingdom from July to October 1955. Although he did not understand a great deal about the technicalities of the complex subject matter, he chaired the conference very energetically and put all his political weight behind the continuation of the process of unification. (11) Added to this, the governments had nominated a number of officials who identified with and were deeply committed to the idea of integration.

The heads of delegation set up five committees and four sub-committees. The central body was the Steering Committee, or Committee of the Heads of Delegation. Its task was to play a 'stimulating, directing, co-ordinating and observing' role vis-à-vis the work of the committees of experts. Its main duty was to formulate guidelines for further exploratory talks and to receive the progress reports on the work of the committees. In addition it was for the heads of delegation to keep an eye on those problem areas that did not feature in the work of other committees.

In their research the experts built up a picture of the technical problems connected with economic integration. But as a result of the differences of approach that seemed virtually insuperable, no agreement was reached during the first three months on the measures to be taken. The reports of the four Committees at the end of October 1955 contained a mixture of various considerations and pointers to possible solutions to the individual matters concerned but no clear-cut plan that could be taken as the basis for intergovernmental negotiations.

THE SPAAK REPORT (NOVEMBER 1955 — APRIL 1956)

The decisive move was then made by Spaak who declared himself dissatisfied with the technical remit of the Messina Conference. Exercising his political responsibility, Spaak brought together a small group of experts, in which Hans von der Groeben and Pierre Uri played a leading part, to work out an overall plan. In spite of the continuing differences of opinion and interest among the governments of the Six, it was this which was accepted as the basis for treaty negotiations at the conference of foreign ministers in Venice at the end of May 1956. So what had originally been intended as a technical report became a political plan of action which for the governments was no longer completely without obligation but nevertheless permitted them at any time to distance themselves from any unacceptable proposals.

The guiding principle behind the Spaak Report (12) was to answer the simple question of what the member states should do to promote European economic integration. The experts succeeded in providing theoretically simple answers that were above all capable of being put into practice. The Report set out a comprehensive structure of aims and means that was based only to a limited extent on theories of integration. Instead, it relied more on the practical experience of international co-operation and generally recognised values and principles of economic practice. It proposed that an overall integration of the economy should be the aim with the exception of the atomic energy sector, for which a separate organisation was to be created. The experience of the Coal and Steel Community showed that the process of partial integration had already reached the limits of its possibilities within only a few years and could therefore no longer provide a new impetus for the aim of overall integration. Economic integration would only hold promise for the future if it were not just individual sectors but the whole of the economy that was included.

The decisive impulses for progress towards further integration came through the instruments and methods that were to make the Common Market and its customs union capable of functioning. The debate about which economic framework was to be used started from different basic postures. The representatives of the market economy theory - particularly the officials of the West German Ministry of Economic Affairs and, to a lesser degree, the Benelux countries - regarded the Common Market as a suitable instrument for creating an extended West European economic region. At the same time this was to be the preliminary stage of a more far-reaching political grouping, although there were no clear ideas about its extent or final shape. On the other hand the advocates of the more dirigiste school - among them the French and Italians - pressed for a closer grouping but with the retention of their traditional protectionism in the interest of their agriculture and of their industries that were not geared to an extended regional economy. The Common Market for them was seen as a means to an end, namely the continuation of their national policy in the wider framework of Europe. Both camps used the rules of GATT in defence of their arguments. The one regarded the customs union as a means, justified by the GATT Treaty, of continuing to act to the disadvantage of third countries, while the other interpreted the customs union as a temporary regional preferential zone which as integration progressed would work to the advantage of all concerned, member states and non-member states alike. This latter train of thought was the one adopted in the Spaak Report.

As the majority of the experts had come out in favour of a market economy structure for the Common Market, the German negotiators, supported by the representatives of the Benelux countries, were able in the inner circle of experts to insert the relevant principles in the Report. Accordingly the customs union was to form the nucleus of the Common Market, around which an internal market would be created. And wider economic integration was intended in turn to lead to further political unification.

As far as the institutional form of the new economic organisation was concerned, the Coal and Steel Community Treaty served as a model. It was, however, significant not so much that the basic institutions were retained but rather more that, barely two years after the failure of the supranational European Defence Community and in the face of continued opposition in national government circles, the proposition that a federal institution be built into the decision-making structure of the new Community was accepted in principle by the governments of the Six.

Getting the Spaak Report accepted was by no means an easy matter of course. In Bonn it was the Ministry of Foreign Affairs and the Federal Chancellor, Adenauer, who defended it against its critics in the Federal Ministries of Economic Affairs, Atomic Energy, and Agriculture. The Chancellor wanted to push European unification forward, even if this were limited at first to the economic field. Admittedly his guideline decision of January 19, 1956, (13) did not persuade Erhard, Strauss and Blücher to abandon their objections. Adenauer was, though, always in a position to put his policy into practice. He did not see in their reservations any reason why he should withhold his support for the Report. On the contrary, he hoped that integration would bring him new links with France.

Forces favourable to the European idea may have prevailed in the Federal Republic, the Benelux countries and Italy, but in France the situation was just the reverse. After the general election at the beginning of January 1956 brought the Socialists to power under the leadership of Guy Mollet, (14) a more open-minded approach to European policy was expected of France. The political personalities did in fact change, but the administration - and with it its extremely anti-European stance - remained. In the short term the change of Government in Paris hardly had any effect on the talks in Brussels: during the first few months the pro-Europeans did not at any rate receive the support they had hoped for from the new head of government, although the press credited him with favouring a distinctly pro-European policy.

A gradual change of opinion did not begin to appear until the spring of 1956. This process was initiated by just a few European-minded officials close to Mollet who were convinced of the long-term benefit to France of participation in the Common Market. They effected the change of course from their key positions in the government machine. Nevertheless it was only with a great deal of effort that they were able to get the Government to accept the Spaak Report and achieve a moderate French line at the Venice Conference.

THE INTERGOVERNMENTAL NEGOTIATIONS (JULY 1956 – MARCH 1957)

The intergovernmental negotiations were officially opened on June 26, 1956, in Brussels under the chairmanship of Foreign Minister Spaak. Below the decision making level of the foreign ministers a central role was played by the Heads of Delegation Committee. Chaired by Spaak, it conducted the negotiations, agreed the texts of the draft treaties, and was also 'court of appeal' for the subordinate working parties in so far as particular questions could not be resolved in the ad hoc groups of experts or in the Editorial Group. In addition the Heads of Delegation prepared the decisions to be taken by the Foreign Ministers and, under the guidance of the latter, assured the formulation of these decisions in the treaties.

The negotiations themselves gained momentum only slowly. The substantive negotiations started only at the beginning of September after the summer break, by which time France had put aside its misgivings and the various governments were clear in their minds about their conditions for entering the Common Market.

The crucial points were set by the debate on Euratom in the French National Assembly in July 1956. In view of the criticism expressed in bureaucratic and party quarters Mollet needed the support of Parliament in order to be able to stay on the course towards integration taken in Brussels. A defeat in the vote, which was a real possibility, would have bound the Government's hands and probably brought the Brussels negotiations to an abrupt end. If the deputies were to be won over at all to new initiatives, then this would only be by virtue of France's considerable interest in extending the use of nuclear energy.

In the debate the government was forced to make some important concessions. (15) For instance, the Foreign Minister, Pinay, promised to retain France's right to participate in the work of the International Atomic Energy Agency. Until then it had in fact been envisaged that France would be represented in this organisation by the Community. Further, he promised the Gaullists that the proposed Common Assembly and the Court of Justice of the European Atomic Community would not be merged with the institutions of the Coal and Steel Community as the Spaak Report had envisaged. In order not to make a victory in Parliament impossible from the start, Mollet gave way to Gaullist pressure and made two further concessions. Firstly, he gave an assurance that research, already begun in France, on the military use of atomic energy would be continued; France would not renounce the right to produce atomic weapons. Secondly, he removed the whips from the vote, making it a free vote for each individual deputy; this raised the Gaullists' hopes of additional support from the ranks of the Government camp.

Nevertheless the vote on July 11, 1956, resulted in a victory for the Government. With votes from among the Socialists (SFIO), the left-wing Liberals (UDSR-RDA), the Popular Republicans (MRP), the left-wing Republicans (RGR), sections of the Gaullist party and the Independents Mollet received the required support for the Euratom negotiations. Indirectly this gave him political backing for the Common Market negotiations as well.

The French Government from this point on wanted to bring the Euratom talks to as rapid a conclusion as possible but to let the Common Market negotiations drag on as long as possible. The other countries' interest concentrated in the main on the Common Market. In this way an implied linkage arose between the two initiatives.

After agreeing with the various pressure groups – above all the farmers and the employers' association – the French Secrétaire d'Etat, Faure, put six conditions for France's entry to the Common Market to the heads of delegation on September 20:

1. The second of the three stages for the establishment of the Common Market should not begin before the Council of Ministers had unanimously concluded that the targets of the first stage had been fully attained.
2. The harmonisation of social costs should be achieved by the end of the transitional period, so that total labour costs would be the same in all the member states.
3. The French Government wished to reserve the right to maintain its system of export subsidies and import duties. This was to be dismantled as soon as France had a positive balance of payments again.
4. A state that had run into balance of payments difficulties should be allowed to reintroduce

protective measures.

5. The question of the inclusion in the Common Market of overseas colonial territories must be treated separately. The Government wished to submit more detailed proposals on this, and it thus underlined the demand it had already voiced at the Venice Conference.

6. Finally, exceptions to the implementation of the Treaty were to be made for France. In view of the crisis in Algeria, which could only be solved by additional French military spending and a drain on the country's resources, the Government was uncertain whether it would be able to introduce the economic changes needed for the customs union.

These demands, which were largely unacceptable to the other five negotiating partners, put the talks in considerable difficulty. Above all the harmonisation of social costs before the opening of the Common Market, as intended by the French delegation, led to bitter opposition from the representatives of Germany and the Benelux countries. From an economic standpoint the French demand was utterly unjustifiable. As a result of the French Government's inflexible attitude on this matter the negotiations quickly entered a cul-de-sac. When the six foreign ministers, meeting in Paris on October 20 and 21, 1956, were unable after protracted discussion to reach agreement on the opposing points of view regarding social harmonisation, the conference had to be broken off without achieving any result. For the time being the fate of the negotiations remained uncertain.

However, the tense international situation in the Near East and the Franco-German negotiations on the Saar, now approaching their conclusion, meant that neither Bonn nor Paris considered it advisable to heighten the confrontation in the Brussels negotiations. Both governments made an effort to resolve the crisis relatively quickly. During Chancellor Adenauer's short visit to Paris on November 6, 1956 - just at the moment when the French Government was being subjected to strong international pressure at the height of the Suez crisis - the decisive compromises were hammered out. (16)

The failure of the Franco-British Suez adventure once again made France's limited role as a great power between the two super-powers abundantly clear to the Mollet government. In a quest for closer co-operation with its European partners it gave up its hesitant attitude to the Common Market in the period that followed. Thus the essential breakthrough in the negotiations was achieved.

A further significant step towards the signing of the Treaty of Rome was the debate on the Common Market in the French National Assembly in January 1957. (17) Should France join the others in Europe or in future risk being isolated in the field of foreign policy? And with its economic security in mind, what must France do to bind the Federal Republic of Germany to the West? These were the leading questions in the debate. Considering its weak economy caused by its financial commitments overseas and in Algeria, as well as the defeat for its foreign policy in the Near East, France really had no alternative but to join the Community. If it wanted to play a determining part in the East-West conflict again it had to decide in favour of co-operation on an equal footing with its neighbours. As Mollet put it, only a consolidation of the West European states between the superpowers of the USA and the Soviet Union would enable France to avoid isolation. Further, the mutual economic dependence created by the Common Market offered France a degree of security in the face of the expanding German economy.

In spite of the fall of the French Government in May 1957 and the disappointment among Dutch parliamentarians at the lack of supranationality in the Economic Community's structure, the Treaty of Rome received the required majorities in all the parliaments of the six member countries without too much difficulty. It was again in the French National Assembly that the most significant decision was taken. The vote in favour in July 1957 signalled the breakthrough in the ratification debates. The close liaison between Government and Parliament during the Brussels negotiations ultimately had a decisive influence on the acceptance of the Treaty. The votes in July 1956 and at the beginning of 1957 were regarded as the relevant parliamentary decisions in favour of France's entry to the Community. Franco-German interaction during the process of ratification, when Monnet exerted considerable pressure both on the French Government and the German Social Democrats, served as a mutual guarantee in Bonn and Paris that the Treaty would be signed and a second EDC débacle avoided.

THE RATIONALE OF THE EEC TREATY

In Venice the six governments had recognised the thinking behind the Spaak Report as a basis for the treaty negotiations, but this had not cleared up the differences in interpretation and the conflicts of interest in individual specialised fields. Each government was intent on getting those arrangements written into the treaty that were advantageous to itself but on blocking less favourable solutions or toning these down by making them the subject of special regulations. When stipulating the important principles of the Common Market — e.g. the establishment of the common external tariff, the inclusion of agriculture, the rules of competition and the structuring of the institutions — it was the intention of the authors of the Spaak Report that the overall concept should not be watered down by a series of protective clauses and exceptions. It was feared that reservations and objections from the governments might cause the substance of the Spaak Report to fall apart and key areas of integration to be weakened.

It was Spaak's concern that such trends should be prevented and that political unification be achieved. The compromises arrived at were in large measure the result of his powers of persuasion and his negotiating skill. But leading negotiators, like von der Groeben, Franco Bobba, Theodor Hijzen and Johannes Linthorst Homan, also aimed at 'communautaire' solutions, only permitting exception clauses when technical constraints demanded them or the resistance of governments was insuperable. Apart from the settlement of the question of agriculture, the general provisions about economic policy, the inclusion of French, Belgian and Dutch overseas territories (deliberately not mentioned in the Spaak Report) and some rules of procedure, they largely succeeded in the course of the negotiations in incorporating the original aims of the Spaak Report in the Treaty.

The political concept of economic integration underlying the EEC Treaty was developed independently from the Coal and Steel Community Treaty. The contents of the EEC Treaty were influenced basically by three different economic concepts:

1. The <u>liberal, free trade concept</u> that aimed at freeing markets from protectionism and opening them up;
2. The German <u>market economy concept</u> that

envisaged an internal market in which the economic course of events would be determined by free competition.

3. The <u>French version of the market economy concept</u>, according to which the Common Market was to have a strong element of planning with the possibility for the national governments to intervene.

On the one hand the German protagonists of a neo-liberal national economy had to recognise that the rules of free trade would not suffice on their own. On the other hand the French line of thought could not prevail, because leading members of the French delegation realised that, with an increasing tendency to the liberalisation of foreign trade, the greater mobility of capital and labour, and a greater differentiation between demand and supply, planning could easily run the risk of no longer keeping in step with the realities of the economic situation. Also, as some of the French negotiators were prepared to let their domestic economy be subjected to keener international competition in the industrial sector – a line pursued actively by the Germans – in order to increase the efficiency of the French economy, the pure market economy school was able to win the day, particularly in matters of competition.

Excluded from this were, above all, the special rules for agricultural policy. Bearing in mind the decades of national interventionist policy in agricultural trade practised by all the member states, it is not surprising that in fact all the governments – and the French Government in particular – were only prepared to agree to a transfer of power to the Community if certain conditions were fulfilled and guarantees granted. It was in the interest of all concerned to select the right instruments for inclusion in the Treaty without for the time being specifying the content and aims of a common agricultural policy more clearly.

The situation was similar for some other areas like regional policy, energy policy and industrial policy. In general it became apparent that the more sensitive an area was for the national states, the more difficult it was to agree common policies.

This was particularly the case as far as economic and monetary policy issues were concerned. The arrangement whereby powers in such matters were left to the member states emerged virtually of its own accord. France was not prepared to grant powers of control to the Community in these policy areas, and in the Federal Republic of Germany there was a fear of a too highly planned system that would stand in the way of the principles of market economy. In this way significant areas of policy in the field of economic integration remained in the hands of the member states. The mere obligation to co-ordinate economic policies turned out in the end to be the most that could in effect be achieved in the course of the negotiations.

An important decision, that initially seemed to have little to do with the process of integration, concerned the agreements about relationships with the colonial territories - something the French Government had insisted on. The agreement was only made - following considerable financial promises by Adenauer at the conference of heads of government on February 19-20, 1957, in Paris - to meet France's demands for help over her colonial obligations and irrevocably to secure France's accession.

The nature of the institutions to be created and the description of the principles that were to guide them were determined by political compromise and by functional decisions needed to put the Treaty into practice. The dual system of Council and Commission arose on the one hand because the sovereign member states wanted to retain the ultimate powers of decision and legislation and on the other hand because of the necessity for an independent organ, representing the will of the Community, to ensure the application of the Treaty provisions at the supranational level. To this end an institutional system was set up with the aim of doing justice to both the intergovernmental and the supranational concepts.

It may be considered regrettable that the governments skilfully avoided being bound by a single concept in the EEC Treaty. However, in view of their particular national interests and of the circumstances of their domestic and foreign policies the Six would not have accepted any other solution. The institutional framework of the EEC Treaty therefore contains intergovernmental and supranational elements that possess both a static and a dynamic side to them. They are static inasmuch as substantial progress towards integration is hardly possible - in some cases even impossible - without the political will of the member states; just one example of this is economic and monetary policy. They are dynamic inasmuch as the member states are free to integrate further in the direction of a federation or some other form of grouping of states at any time.

THE ROLE OF THE UNITED KINGDOM

The unsuccessful attempt of the Six to include the British in the process of integration after the Conference of Messina (18), was at one and the same time a handicap and a relief for the course of the negotiations.

It was only with reluctance that the British Government had found its way to send a 'representative' to Brussels in July 1955. The leader of the delegation, Russell Bretherton, in announcing that Her Majesty's Government wished to take an active part in the deliberations, was only paying lip service to the idea, because it neither accepted the Messina resolution as a basis for negotiation nor was it interested in shaping the contents of the resolution after its own fashion. (19) The more the talks concentrated during the month of September on the creation of a customs union, the more the opinion surfaced in British Government circles that there should be a withdrawal from Brussels in order not to become even more entangled in the plans of the Six for further integration.

The rupture came at the beginning of November 1955 in the first session of the expert group. Spaak challenged the British delegate to express the clear support of his government to participation in the customs union. As Bretherton was unable to give an answer owing to the ambivalent attitude in London, Spaak made it absolutely clear that in future only those heads of delegation should take part in the discussions who were prepared to accept the proposal for a customs union.

After this withdrawal the British Government was faced, in the event of a market of the Six becoming a reality, with the alternative of being economically isolated from the rest of Western Europe or having to make sacrifices in the field of foreign trade in order to come to some arrangement with the Six. The far-reaching economic changes for the relationships of the West European states among each other, heralded by the Brussels negotiations, finally forced the British to modify their preferential trading system with the Commonwealth in favour of closer links with the Continent.

But in the meantime Britain, using the OEEC as a forum, introduced the proposal for a European Free Trade Area into the discussion in July 1956. (20) In London the Government wrongly believed an industrial free trade area that excluded agricultural produce would be politically and economically attractive in particular for France which did not find it easy to go along with the anti-protectionist philosophy of the Spaak Report.

On the French side, though, little understanding was shown for this British opportunism. The British were rightly criticised for putting forward the Free Trade Area plan simply as a reaction to the Common Market negotiations. Apart from that, the Fourth Republic's economic and monetary problems could not be solved within the context of a Free Trade Area.

The disparities to be expected from the participation of the OEEC countries were greater than those which the Treaty of Rome sought to settle. In addition, interests differed when it came to the inclusion of agriculture. Britain wanted to exclude the very aspect from the Free Trade Area that France was especially keen to see included. Besides, through the automatic opening up of a free trade area France would have lost just those guarantees for the transitional period that she had laboriously wrested from her partners in the Brussels negotiations. And the British plan did not promise an easing of the financial burdens brought on by France's colonial policy.

However, it was not least the British Government's vascillating posture that meant the plan for a free trade area was never a viable alternative to the idea of comprehensive integration. Britain gave the free trade area its full support only after the Suez adventure had failed and France had made her U-turn in Brussels. If the plan for a free trade area was ever considered by the British to be a genuine substitute for the Common Market, aimed at winning over France in particular but also her European partners, the project was condemned before it even started because it took no account at all of the interest of the Six in a customs union as the foundation for further political integration.

THE TREATIES OF ROME – AN ACCIDENT OF HISTORY?

The founding of the EEC and Euratom should not - as is generally the case - be traced back to the so-called 'relance européenne'. In reality a re-activation of the European idea never happened because after the failure of the EDC the efforts towards integration never came to a halt. It was rather more a matter of the Treaty of Rome coming about under uniquely favourable historical circumstances that were neither foreseeable nor consciously contrived. It was the external and internal political framework and the personalities involved as well as the method employed in the negotiations that proved to be the decisive factors.

External and Internal Environment

(a) Without the settlement of security and defence relationships between the Western European states and the USA (Treaties of Paris) the decisions taken at Messina would not have emerged and there would have been no possibility of making political progress towards closer economic integration.

(b) The deliberations on economic integration were made much easier by the premature withdrawal of the British delegation from the negotiating table in Brussels. The proposal put forward by the British for an industrial free trade area did not represent a genuine alternative for the Six, regardless of whether it was conceived as being an extension of the Common Market or a substitute for it.

(c) The change of government in France at the beginning of 1956 put a small group of European-minded officials into key positions in the government machine, which enabled them to manipulate a gradual change of course in French European policy in the direction of greater co-operation. They made sure that the Spaak Report was accepted and influenced the Cabinet in favour of commencing treaty negotiations.

(d) The decision on the creation of the Common Market depended in large measure on the vote in the French National Assembly. It was not the ratification debate but the two favourable votes during the negotiations that were the crucial parliamentary turning points for the acceptance of the EEC and Euratom Treaties.

(e) The course of events in the Suez Crisis finally tipped the balance for the French Government's decision in principle to join the Common Market. Defeat in the Near East, and the consequences of this for French influence in the world, pushed into the background the doubts which had previously been entertained about participation in the Common Market. In spite of this French diplomacy continued to display great skills in turning the country's weakness in the foreign policy and economic fields to advantage when it came to the tactics of negotiations: the negotiators deliberately let their hands be tied in the main areas of discussion by

ent and the pressure groups, thereby winning a
of concessions in Brussels.

he settlement of the Saar Question with the
cc   sion of the Saar Treaty improved Franco-German
relations, and this in particular helped to overcome
the crisis in the negotiations.
(g)   The Soviet intervention in Hungary brought home
the threat from the East for the West Europeans once
again and increased their feeling of solidarity. The
need for cohesion in Western Europe as an additional
element in the East-West conflict became that much
clearer.
(h)   The unqualified support by the USA, as the power
exercising   hegemony   in   the   West,   made   the
negotiations on the Common Market easier. It was in
Washington's interest to see a close association of
West European states, because it reckoned this would
strengthen   the   West   in   general.   The   American
Government was prepared to accept the disadvantages
for the United States economy and trade prospects
that the creation of the EEC caused. Confidence in
the economic strength of the country was such that
people were certain the domestic economy would be
able to compete with the economic potential of the
European Community.

The Actors
A small group of people was responsible for the birth
of the Treaty. Without the leadership of the Belgian
Foreign Minister the Treaty would never have been
signed.   His   negotiating   skill   and   political
dynamism, coupled with his determination to exert the
required pressure on individual delegations with the
aim of reaching a compromise, were just as important
an element as the close co-operation between a small
but   influential   group   of   officials   who   resisted
divergent tendencies within their own ranks and at
the conference table. These officials, who had a
sense of purpose and were convinced integrationists,
put the thinking behind the Treaty into words and
settled the details. The Treaty was given political
effect   by   the   foreign   ministers   and   heads   of
government.   The   step   forward   from   partial
integration in Europe towards total integration was
therefore a process that was guided by individual
figures and small national executive teams composed
of technocrats and politicians.

The Methods

(a)   At first no decision was taken on the method of integration to be followed. The various moves towards sectoral integration and comprehensive economic integration were so intertwined in the Messina Resolution on the basis of the Benelux Memorandum that both the German approach in favour of all-round integration for the Economic Community and the approach in favour of partial integration for the Atomic Community came to fruition.

(b)   In this way an implied linkage existed between the two projects from the very beginning of the negotiations. While France would not have agreed to the Economic Community without the creation of Euratom, the same applied the other way round for the Federal Republic of Germany and the remaining negotiating partners. If the two treaties had not materialised simultaneously or if they had been unhitched from one another, both projects would have automatically failed.

(c)   The material and institutional provisions of the EEC Treaty were a mirror image of the powers which it had been possible, with the agreement of their respective parliaments, to take from the national governments in the course of the negotiations and transfer directly or in stages to the Community institutions. The fact that, in spite of the unsuccessful attempt at supranational integration in 1954, agreement was reached on transferring sovereign powers to a supranational institution, can be traced back to the direction dictated by functional requirements and by the determination of supranationally inclined officials to strengthen the elements of federalism.

(d)   A series of favourable international circumstances, the weak economies of the West European countries and their interest in raising productivity and general prosperity, as well as the desire of the policy makers in each member state still to realise the idea of European unification, all ultimately contributed to the crucial driving force behind the progressive development from the partial integration of the Coal and Steel Community to the attempt at comprehensive economic integration in the EEC Treaty.

(e)   Not least of all, each member state realised that progress towards further integration and co-operation in a supranational organisation were important pre-conditions for their economic, political and social development; this too was a determining factor in the creation of the EEC.

CONCLUSIONS

With regard to the current discussion on further steps towards unification, and in the light of the knowledge gained during the early stages of the EEC Treaty, the following lessons can be drawn concerning the right approach to negotiations for integration:

1.   In the initial stages everything depends on the active involvement of a few leading political personalities whose intellectual and political attitude moves them to continue with the process of integration. They encourage interest in a new initiative by putting forward a plan and seeking the support of the governments concerned.

2.   This initiative is endorsed at an intergovernmental conference. Guidelines for the elaboration of a plan for integration are given to experts. The non-binding nature of the experts' studies makes it easier for the governments to agree to the opening of talks on further steps towards integration and prevents them from being tied to any unacceptable proposals the experts may make. It is useful to form a small group of experts under the chairmanship of a political personality especially if these experts are released from national obligations or instructions and thereby enjoy reasonable freedom of action. Their work should be essentially functional and be concerned with the examination of technical questions as well as practical political problems.

3.   The proposals contained in the report of the conference of experts do not, however, have any effect if the governments do not:

(a)   accept the principal proposals of substance in the report, i.e. there must be agreement on the basic aims to be pursued;

(b)   accept the report in its totality as a basic political document for future negotiations;

(c)   declare themselves ready to open official negotiations straightaway on the continuation of the process of integration.

The creation of a basis of negotiation in the form of a report is therefore of use for intergovernmental negotiations only if it takes the various implications and national interests into account and permits a pragmatic approach.

4.   The new steps towards integration are laid down in a treaty that is binding under international law. Conference diplomacy is the only possible method for the negotiations; the delegates act according to the instructions and guidelines of their governments.

5.   Integration can succeed only in those areas of

politics which in the long term can bring the existing problems of the national states more easily under control or completely solve them. It is not possible to dispense with the creation of institutions or properly organised co-operation in committees or other similar bodies. These ensure stability and durability for the common decisions and actions of the member states.

6.   Success in the negotiations depends above all on the support of leading personalities and a group of officials who identify with the aim of the negotiations and the main elements of the concept of integration as set out in the report.

7.   A crucial factor for the success of the negotiations is the presence of policy makers in the member states who are convinced of the need to negotiate further integration, support this, and are able to resist the opposition of government, bureaucracy, parliament or pressure groups.

8.   Under these circumstances a procedure agreed between the parliaments for the ratification of the treaty can have a stabilising effect, even if ratification depends on the parliaments of other community countries passing the treaty without reservation.

9.   A favourable constellation of historical circumstances is needed for the launching of a new initiative towards integration, as this will diminish opposition to the project at least to the extent that the implementation of the treaty will not be impeded.

10. Without the will to achieve integration on the part of all concerned, negotiations will be condemned to failure. In each Community country there must be a readiness to renounce sovereign national rights and transfer these to the Community. The destiny of integration depends ultimately on this.

Select Bibliography

Miriam Camps, <u>Britain and the European Community, 1955-63</u>. London, 1964

Michael Charlton, <u>The price of victory</u>. London, 1983

Wolfgang Harbrecht, <u>Die Europäische Gemeinschaft</u>. Stuttgart and New York, 1978

Karl Kaiser, <u>EWG und Freihandelszone. England und der Kontinent in der europäischen Integration</u>. Leiden, 1963

Hanns Jürgen Küsters, <u>Die Gründüng der Europäischen Wirtschaftsgemeinschaft</u>. Baden-Baden, 1982

Ernst van der Beugel, <u>From Marshall Aid to Atlantic</u>

Partnership. European Integration as a concern of American policy. Amsterdam, 1966
Hans von der Groeben, Aufbaujahre der Europäischen Gemeinschaft. Das Ringen um den Gemeinsamen Markt und die Politische Union (1958-1966). Baden-Baden, 1982. (Fr. ed. Combat pour l'Europe. La construction de la Communauté Européenne de 1958 à 1966. Brussels, 1985)
Peter Weilemann, Die Anfänge der Europäischen Atomgemeinschaft. Baden-Baden, 1982
F. Roy Willis, France, Germany and the new Europe, 1945-63. Stanford, 1965

Notes

1. Karl Kaiser, op.cit., p.2.
2. Hans R. Krämer, Die Europäische Gemeinschaft, Stuttgart, Berlin, Cologne and Mainz 1974, p.12.
3. Walter Lipgens, 'Europäaische Integration', in Richard Löwenthal and Hans-Peter Schwarz (eds.) Die Zweite Republik. 25 Jahre Bundesrepublik Deutschland – eine Bilanz, Stuttgart-Degerloch 1974, p.536.
4. Jean Monnet, Erinnerungen eines Europäers, Munich and Vienna 1978 p.506 ff.
5. Peter Weilemann, op.cit., p.17 ff.
6. On the discussions in the Dutch Government, see Adrian F. Manning, 'Die Niederlande und Europa von 1945 bis zum Beginn der fünfziger Jahre', in Vierteljahrshefte für Zeitgeschichte, 29, 1981, p.17ff.
7. Jan Willem Beyen, Het Spel en de Knikkers, Rotterdam 1968, p.234 ff.; Jean Charles Snoy et d'Oppuers, 'Un témoin raconte: Du plan Schuman aux traités de Rome', in 30 jours d'Europe, No. 285, 1982, p.22 ff.
8. On the controversies within the Federal German Government, see H.J. Küsters, Die Gründung der Europäischen Wirtschaftsgemeinschaft, op.cit. p.79 ff. and 112 ff.
9. Herbert Tint, French Foreign Policy since the Second World War, London 1972, p. 106 ff.; Walter Lipgens, 'Die latente Staatskrise der Vierten Französischen Republik', in Wilhelm Cornides (ed.) Die Internationale Politik 1956/57, Munich 1961, p.263. ff.
10. This document stemmed in the main from a memorandum of the Benelux States, dated May 20, 1955, and from a memorandum of the Federal German Government that was presented at the Conference; cf. the synopsis of the text in Howard Bliss: The

Political Development of the European Community. A Documentary Collection, Waltham (Mass.), Toronto and London 1970, p.34 ff.

11. Paul Henri Spaak, Erinnerungen eines Europäers, Hamburg 1969, p.297 ff.

12. Report of the Heads of Delegation to the Foreign Ministers, Brussels 21 April 1956, published by the Secretariat of the Intergovernmental Committee created by the Messina Conference.

13. Text to be found in Konrad Adenauer, Erinnerungen 1955-1959, Stuttgart 1967, p.253 ff.; cf. also Hanns Jürgen Küsters, 'Adenauers Europapolitik in der Gründungsphase der EWG', in Vierteljahrshefte für Zeitgeschichte, 31 (1983), p.659ff.

14. On the political changes see Pierre Guillen, 'Frankreich und der europäische Wiederaufschwung. Vom Scheitern der EVG zur Ratifizierung der Verträge von Rom', in Vierteljahreshefte für Zeitgeschichte, 28 (1980), p.1 ff.

15. L'année politique 1956, published by André Siegfried, Edouard Bonnefous and Jean-Baptiste Duroselle, Paris 1957, p.70 ff.

16. The compromises were formulated by Karl Carstens (at that time head of department in the Ministry of Foreign Affairs) for the Federal German Government and by Robert Marjolin for the French Government. See Karl Carstens 'Das Eingreifen Adenauers in die Europaverhandlungen im November 1956', in Dieter Blumenwitz, Klaus Gotto, Hans Maier, Konrad Repgen and Hans-Peter Schwarz (eds.) Konrad Adenauer und seine Zeit. Politik und Persönlichkeit des ersten Bundeskanzlers. Beiträge von Weg- und Zeitgenossen, Stuttgart 1976, p.591 ff.

17. On the course of the debate cf. Gerhard Kiersch, Parlament und Parlamentarier in der Aussenpolitik der IV. Republik. Wirtschafts-und Sozialwissenschaftliche Dissertation, vol. 1, Berlin 1971 p.290 ff.; Gabriele Latte, Die französische Europapolitik im Spiegel der Parlamentsdebatten, Berlin 1979, p.106 ff.; Pierre Guillen in Vierteljahrshefte für Zeitgeschichte, 28 (1980), p.9.

18. On British policy towards Europe in the 1950s see Camps, op.cit., passim; Charlton, op.cit., chs. 4-7; and Donald C Watt 'Grossbritannien und Europa 1951-1959. Die Jahre konservativer Regierung', in Vierteljahrshefte für Zeitgeschichte, 28 (1980), p.389 ff.

19. Harold Macmillan, Riding the storm 1956-59. London, 1971, p.69.

20. On the origins of the Free Trade Area negotiations see Camps, op.cit., p.9 ff; Hans Joachim Heiser, <u>British policy with regard to the unification efforts on the European continent</u>, Leyden, 1959, p.102 ff; Karl Kaiser, op.cit., p.96 ff; H.J. Küsters, op.cit., p.205 ff; Hans von der Groeben, op.cit., p.61 ff.

Chapter Five

IN SEARCH OF POLITICAL UNION: THE FOUCHET PLAN NEGOTIATIONS (1960-62)

Pierre Gerbet

General de Gaulle's proposal for a 'Union of States' among the six countries of the European Communities constituted, between 1960 and 1962, an important episode in the building of Europe. The Fouchet Plan, which put it into concrete terms, was the subject of long and difficult negotiations, but did not succeed, due to the deep differences of view which emerged between the Six over the aims as well as the methods of organising Europe: a 'European Europe' or an 'Atlantic Europe', a 'Europe of States' or a 'Community Europe', a Europe of the Six or a Europe enlarged to take in Great Britain?

THE INITIATIVE

The International and Community Environment
The international situation between 1958 and '61 was marked by growing tension in Europe following Soviet threats to Berlin and lack of certainty in American policy. On 27 November 1958 Kruschev issued an ultimatum on Berlin calling into question the rights and presence of the Western powers and demanding that negotiations be opened to change the city's status. The Western nations were unanimous in defending their rights against any pressure, but divided on whether it was opportune to open negotiations with the Soviet Union.

General de Gaulle was opposed to any negotiation under threat and to any change in the status of Berlin. This was also the position adopted by Chancellor Adenauer, who was very concerned about the more conciliatory stance of the British and Americans. Prime Minister Macmillan was keen to play intermediary betwen East and West and influenced President Eisenhower, who was more inclined to appeasement, above all since the retirement of his Secretary of State Foster Dulles in early 1959. A four-power Conference on Germany in the Spring produced no result, but Kruschev's trip to the United States in September caused considerable disquiet in Western Europe, above all in Federal Germany. There was an impression that American leadership was weakening. The US had fallen behind the Soviet Union in the space race, its balance of payments was in deficit and there were many uncertainties surrounding the end of the Eisenhower presidency and the early days of that of John Kennedy.

In Western Europe, on the other hand, the success of the EEC was becoming more assured. The first step in the freeing of trade had been taken on 1 January 1959, and on 12 May 1960 the decision was taken to speed up the application of the Treaty of Rome (by 1 July 1962 customs duties among the Six had been reduced by half and trade in industrial products between Community states was to double in the space of four years). In parallel, the foundations of a common agricultural policy were agreed after difficult negotiations and the first regulations adopted on 14 January 1962.

The EEC also began to play a role on the international stage. The establishment of a common external tariff confirmed the unity of the Community and led it to negotiate with a single voice in GATT for tariff reductions with the other industrialised countries. Britain, which had not originally wished to join the Six, set up the European Free Trade Association to counterbalance them, but then applied to join the EEC in July 1961. The Community was becoming an important actor on the international economic stage whilst being non-existent in the foreign policy and defence fields, since the Six co-operated only within the broader framework of the Atlantic Alliance. A striking contrast existed between an Economic Community on the road towards integration and the absence of any diplomatic and military Community.

The void left by the failure of the European Defence Community Treaty and the plan for a Political Community had not been filled, and the Western European Union (consisting of the Six plus Great Britain) had only a very limited role. The relaunching which took place at Messina had been cautiously limited to the economic sphere. Whereas the ECSC Treaty explicitly laid down a federal aim, the Rome Treaties went no further than affirming the wish to establish 'an ever closer union' between the

European peoples, without specifying the form it would take. It was indeed pointless to awaken opposition between federalists and the proponents of intergovernmental co-operation.

But the authors of the Treaties were gambling on the impact which the establishment of the customs union must inevitably have on the foreign policy of the member states and on the fact that the setting up of the Economic Community would give a strong stimulus to political co-operation or even integration. The functionalist theoreticians foresaw a well-nigh automatic 'spill-over effect' of Community action from the economic into the political sphere. The federalists did not believe this and urged the election of a constituent assembly. Jean Monnet, for his part held that there should be no headlong rush forward. He had no faith in any automatic evolution and held that 'political Europe will be created by men, when the moment comes, based on realities'. (1) First, it was necessary to make economic union a fact of life and to develop concrete links, then to move the Communities forward and strengthen their institutions. The Action Committee for the United States of Europe, created by Monnet, recommended in November 1959 the creation of a single commission for the three Communities, which would thus gain in prestige and authority. The Parliamentary Assembly, for its part adopted, on 17 May 1960, a proposal for its own election by universal suffrage and was to take on the name European Parliament on 30 March 1962. The EEC Commission was already confirming its propulsive role and believed itself to be a political force. But while some envisaged transposing the Community model, with Commission and Council, into new political fields and foreign policy, others wanted to give priority to 'consolidating economic integration and to extend only with caution and as the need arose, the powers and influence of the Community'. (2) Very soon, however the problem was put in a different context by General de Gaulle's initiative.

General de Gaulle's ideas on Europe
De Gaulle's accession to power on 1 June 1958 had been decisive for the implementation of the EEC treaty. The economic and financial reforms of December 1958 had enabled France to move towards freeing its trade. De Gaulle had safeguarded the embryonic customs union by opposing the British proposal for a wider free trade area. He had demanded

that a truly common agricultural policy be set up. He had done this firstly in the interests of the French economy and also because economic integration seemed to him to be the appropriate instrument for creating lasting solidarity between European countries. Yet he wished to go further and to set up a political Europe in conformity with his own views: a Europe of States, a European Europe.

De Gaulle had from the outset been critical of the Community method. He deemed it indispensable for the building of Europe to begin with politics and not economics and technical matters, which ought to be subordinated to the political sphere and not delegated to technocratic supranational institutions. It was, he believed, the task of sovereign States, using the method of intergovernmental cooperation, to take decisions of a political nature regarding the process of economic integration. He had already shown his hostility to the ECSC and Euratom; he was concerned at the growing authority of the EC Commission and opposed to the direct election of the Parliamentary Assembly. So the existing Communities must be 'capped' with an interstate political organisation which would neutralise their supranational potential, and in which individual national sovereignties would be preserved by the unanimity rule.

The co-operation method seemed to him all the more indispensable in that it would be applied in fields not covered by the Community Treaties: foreign policy and defence, which are at the very heart of the sovereignty of States. Indeed, de Gaulle believed that Europe, in order to exist, ought to make its personality clear, define its place in international relations, have its own foreign policy and even defence. He wanted to build a 'European Europe', less bound to the United States, a Europe which would be better able, within the framework of the Atlantic Alliance, to defend its own interests and which might even be capable of playing the role of a third force between East and West. As early as September 1958 de Gaulle had called for the creation of a three-nation directorate (the United States, Great Britain, and France) for the political and military management of the Atlantic Alliance. Having gained no satisfaction there, he now intended to draw his European Community partners along in the wake of French foreign policy in order to lend that policy more weight on the international stage. Among the Six France, with the support of Federal Germany, would provide the drive, since she alone possessed the attributes of a major power (in the UN Security Council, in Berlin and over the status of Germany; and as a member of the nuclear club since the first French nuclear explosion in February 1960). De Gaulle had already decided to set up a French nuclear force; had refused to stock American nuclear arms in France, was beginning the withdrawal of part of the France's fleet from NATO; and was thinking in terms of a European initiative to reform that body.

The Position of France's Partners. The attitudes of France's partners were quite different from those of General de Gaulle and remained much closer to those of Europe's 'founding fathers'. Certainly, none of the five governments was calling for a move towards federation, yet none wanted to give up the structures of the Communities. Most recognised the usefulness of setting up a system of political co-operation in order to increase their solidarity and facilitate the application of common policies, but on condition that the Community's institutions and the prospects for moving towards integration should be preserved, even in the political sphere. This was all the more so since Italy and the Benelux countries, fearing Franco-German hegemony, were greatly attached to an institutional system which offered them guarantees. With regard to foreign policy and defence, most of France's partners were interested, but worried by the aim of a 'European Europe' which would run the risk of drifting apart from the United States, whereas they all gave absolute priority to the Atlantic Alliance and to American protection within the framework of NATO. They feared that de Gaulle's policy might end up by weakening that organisation without France being able to protect them adequately herself. All in all the Five were happy enough with the status quo: development of economic integration within the Community framework through gradual extensions, and maintenance of foreign policy and defence within the NATO framework in close liaison with the United States. Nuances were, however, apparent in the position of each country.

Federal Germany: The government of the Federal Republic seemed closest to General de Gaulle's thinking, by virtue of Chancellor Adenauer's stance. This, however, was not shared by a segment of his political majority, nor even of his cabinet. Adenauer was attached to the Communities, which he had helped to found, whereas Erhard and the business community found them too 'dirigiste'. From his first meeting with de Gaulle, he was reassured by the latter's desire to bring the Common Market into being and to pursue Franco-German rapprochement. Unlike his foreign minister, von Brentano, he was not over-concerned at General de Gaulle's hostility towards supranationalism, all the more so since he believed that the EEC Commission ought to act with greater circumspection (3). As far as a system of European co-operation was concerned, Adenauer was favourable, judging that it would strengthen Federal Germany's international position, strengthen Germany's ties with Europe and make Europe less dependent upon the United States. In relation to defence, Adenauer held American protection to be vital, but being concerned at British and American uncertainty in face of Soviet pressure, he wished that France and Germany were better able to get their point of view across within the framework of NATO. Overall, and despite the reservations of some German politicians, Adenauer, wedded above all to the idea of Franco-German rapprochement, was to support General de Gaulle's initiative to the hilt.

Italy: Successive Italian governments, all of them Christian Democrat-led, remained very attached to the European idea and to the supranational Communities. Yet attachment to principles was accompanied by pragmatism in practice. Political co-operation was looked on with favour to the extent that it would tighten the bonds between European countries and allow Italy to play a role which would offset its economic weaknesses at that time within the Community. It would be Italy's way of showing itself more as a major nation within the Six, along with France and Federal Germany. Yet account had to be taken of public opinion, which was very 'European' in nature and suspicious of General de Gaulle; and care had to be taken to protect the Community institutions so as to prevent political co-operation from compromising integration. This is why Italy was to play a mediatory role between extreme positions and seek agreement by not accepting all General de Gaulle's ideas and by refusing to move away from the Benelux countries to form a triple directorate with France and Germany.

Benelux: The three Benelux countries were very

content with the economic and institutional aspects of the European Communities, yet had no common position regarding political co-operation. Luxembourg was the most favourable to French thinking, yet it wished to protect the Community system. Its role was necessarily rather minor and its position in relation to its large neighbour forced it to adopt a rather conciliatory attitude. Belgium's position was more complex. Paul-Henri Spaak, who had played a key role in the negotiation of the Rome Treaties, was convinced about the political purpose of building Europe. Yet he was very much an Atlanticist too and had been appointed Secretary General of NATO in May 1957. He was to return to the Belgian Ministry of Foreign Affairs in Spring 1961 and to prove quite favourable to the French viewpoint before adopting a hostile attitude which momentarily converged with the Dutch view. Unlike France's other partners, the Netherlands were hostile from the outset to General de Gaulle's plans (4). There was a strong 'European' and even federalist current in Netherlands public opinion, but the Hague government was particularly devoted to defending Dutch special interests and to the application of a clearly defined foreign policy. The Foreign Minister, Joseph Luns, played a crucial role in this regard. The Netherlands were happy with the European Communities, in particular the Common Market overall, which had been urged by J.W. Beyen as early as 1953, and with the common agricultural policy which Sicco Mansholt had largely contributed to setting up. Yet because of the country's structure (with external trade accounting for half of the country's GNP) they were seeking the widest possible market, and that provided by the Six seemed too narrow for them. They wanted to be open to the other countries of OEEC, in particular to Britain. They were greatly disappointed at the failure of the British proposal for a wider free trade area and desired an enlargement of the Communities. They were keen on the mechanisms of the Communities which guaranteed a certain degree of protection to the smaller countries, but were not disposed to go any further than functional institutions in the economic field. The Dutch government did not want a federal structure which might have been such as to prevent Community enlargement. But nor did it want intergovernmental co-operation which might have limited its freedom of action and weakened Community institutions, and which, within the framework of the Six, would have resulted in French hegemony, supported by Federal Germany. For the Dutch government political co-operation was acceptable only with Britain's participation as a factor of balance between the European countries and as an element of Atlantic orthodoxy. For the Netherlands, nothing was to be done outside the NATO framework. The United States were an effective protector and distant enough not to be troublesome, whereas a Europe of Six developing, at French instigation, a foreign and defence policy would risk weakening the Alliance without offering any credible guarantee to the smaller countries. Joseph Luns was, then, to oppose de Gaulle's ideas from beginning to end.

The French Proposals

By 1958 de Gaulle had begun, along with Chancellor Adenauer and Italy's President Fanfani, to talk about the idea of political co-operation, and this was quite well received. In March 1958 de Gaulle, on the occasion of a visit of Italian leaders to Paris and prior to the opening of the four-power Conference on Germany, wanted to have a common French-German-Italian stance on Berlin: 'too audacious a suggestion to be accepted' according to Couve de Murville, France's Foreign Minister (5). During his official visit to Italy in June, de Gaulle proposed the organisation of periodic meetings between Foreign Ministers, which would be prepared by a small common secretariat. The Italians agreed at once on condition that the meetings should not be limited to the three countries but extended to include the Benelux nations.

The Germans were then sounded out and von Brentano agreed without hesitation. But the difficulties began to emerge at a November meeting of the Six. Joseph Luns, supported by his Belgian colleague Pierre Wigny, came out against political consultations without Great Britain and outside the Atlantic framework. They would agree only if regular consultations took place in parallel within the WEU and NATO. They asked that the EEC Commission be invited to these meetings, but France declined, accepting only that it (and the Euratom Commission) might be consulted when the problems under discussion concerned the Communities. For their part, the smaller countries opposed the creation of a permanent secretariat because they had no wish to see political co-operation, to which they paid only lip service, being institutionalised and separated from the Community. The French proposals were steadily whittled down, yet this nevertheless marked the start of political co-operation among the Six. The quarterly meetings of Foreign Ministers were to deal both with the political follow-up to Community activity and also with other international problems. The first were held in January and May 1960.

De Gaulle very quickly decided to go one step further. In his press conference of 31 May, he announced his intention 'of building Western Europe into a political, economic, cultural and human grouping organised for action and self-defence ... through organised co-operation between States, with the expectation of perhaps one day growing into an imposing confederation.' De Gaulle was thus making a solemn declaration of his wish to build Europe and to have it play a role in international relations, yet he was also making clear his choice of a method different from that established within the Community framework. He was at pains thereafter to inform the governments of the Five, beginning with Chancellor Adenauer. Objections were raised by his partners regarding NATO, the future of the Communities, and Britain's absence. General de Gaulle took no account of this and decided to face public opinion directly with his proposal at his press conference of 5 September 1960. He compared nation states ('the only realities upon which one can build, the only entities invested with the right to order matters and the authority to act') with 'vaguely extra-national bodies having some technical value, but which do not and cannot have any authority and thus any political authority'. Decisions he argued, could only be taken by states working in co-operation:

> Making sure that there is regular co-operation within Western Europe is what France believes to be at once desirable, possible and practical, in political, economic, cultural and defence matters. This implies a regular, organised system of concertation between responsible governments and also work by specialist bodies in each of the common fields working under government control; it would include periodic discussions in an Assembly made up of delegates from the national Parliaments and it ought, in my view, also to include as soon as possible a formal European referendum in order to lend this new beginning for Europe a sense of belonging and the popular involvement so vital to it.

II THE NEGOTIATIONS

General Features

General de Gaulle's press conference impressed public opinion, but also created anxiety about the future of NATO, and of the Communities themselves. The proposed organisation would, moreover, be a concert of sovereign states with no independent body to represent the general interest or capable of defending the smaller nations, and it would not be really democratic in nature since its Assembly would be nominated and have only a consultative role. As far as a referendum was concerned, this was forbidden by the Federal German constitution and would have caused constitutional and political problems in the other countries. All in all, de Gaulle's proposal appeared to constitute a total change in the objectives and methods of European unity.

Nevertheless, it had to be accepted that it was a major political initiative which could not be brushed aside. Monnet saw its positive side, believing that one had to take advantage of the presence in government of two great men, de Gaulle and Adenauer, to push Europe forward. He was willing to accept that a confederal political structure might exist alongside the integrated structures of the Communities, but only on condition that these were safeguarded and remained able to develop towards a federal-style body. He defended this view in the Action Committee and made approaches along the same lines to Chancellor Adenauer and Joseph Luns. This was also the view taken by the majority of the 'European' elite. Political co-operation could be useful, but only on condition that the existing Communities should be preserved along with their potentiality for development in a supranational sense. Similarly, political co-operation might enable the Six to establish themselves more firmly in the field of international relations, but only on condition that it was within the Atlantic Framework and not aiming to set up a 'third force'. Thus, it was necessary to negotiate in order to secure these guarantees. This was what France's five partners had in mind.

Chancellor Adenauer was the most determined, despite some reservations expressed by his entourage and by some German politicians: since he was pragmatically-minded, he was willing to start down the road of strengthening Franco-German co-operation and moving Europe forward. The Italian and Luxembourg governments adopted a positive approach and showed a readiness to talk. In Belgium, Paul-Henri Spaak, who was to become Foreign Minister once more in Spring 1961, was very favourable to regular foreign policy co-operation whilst nevertheless wishing to make it more supranational in structure. Yet the Netherlands government proved from the outset very sceptical and reticent because of Britain's absence.

The negotiations were essentially intergovernmental and never took place within the Community framework, which would not have been permitted by de Gaulle. (6) The Commissions were neither invited nor consulted. The European Parliament was neither consulted nor informed; it was on its own initiative that it discussed the plan and drew up suggestions, some of which were taken up by several governments. There was no Committee, chaired by an independent political figure, to look after the common interest and able to arbitrate, between individual national interests, as the Spaak Committee had done in the preparation of the Treaties of Rome. The Intergovernmental Committee on Political Union was chaired by diplomats, firstly by the Frenchman Christian Fouchet, then by the Italian Attilio Cattani, who were to seek to reconcile opposing ideas but were not in a position to make final decisions. Classic diplomatic procedures were used: summits between heads of State and government, meetings of Foreign Ministers, prepared by detailed negotiations between civil servants in the Intergovernmental Committee. But bilateral diplomacy constantly got at cross purposes with the multilateral meetings. De Gaulle used bilateral diplomacy to the maximum to exploit the particular relations of France with each of her partners.

The Five also used the same method because they did not have identical positions and they could not form a bloc - above all due to Dutch hostility. De Gaulle threw his whole weight into the scales and increased the number of bilateral meetings preceding six-nation meetings in order to secure support. He was able to use his influence and tactical skill to reach compromises with each of his partners except the Dutch who found themselves even more isolated than France. Quite naturally, de Gaulle used the more favourably inclined to put pressure on the more reticent and Chancellor Adenauer did much the same, whereas the Italians sought to play a mediatory role, fearing too close a Franco-German rapprochement. Consultations were above all frequent between the 'Big Three' who were the most inclined to go ahead and who had evolved similar points of view. This worried and annoyed the smaller states, who were afraid of being presented with a <u>fait accompli</u>. They reacted by hardening their position. This led to a gradual deterioration of the atmosphere among the Six, in which personal sensitivities as well as divergent stances also played a part, together with suspicion of ulterior motives and doubts about real intentions. If General de Gaulle sought to reassure them, he was suspected of wanting to destroy NATO and the Communities and to dominate Europe by the Paris-Bonn axis. If France's partners cast themselves in the role of defenders of the Community system, de Gaulle suspected them of using this as a pretext and of really making the maintenance of NATO and the avoidance of annoyance to Great Britain their top priority, since Britain was indeed becoming concerned.

Successive Stages

Following bilateral contacts with each of France's partners, de Gaulle called a meeting in Paris of the six Heads of State and Government on 10 February 1961. On the day before, he met Adenauer and reassured him about France's loyalty to the Atlantic Alliance and the Treaties of Paris and Rome. At the meeting, the German Chancellor and Italy's Prime Minister Fanfani were in agreement that the political vacuum in Europe should be filled with something which was feasible, that is with co-operation. The Belgian and Luxembourg Prime Ministers, Eyskens and Werner, were of the same view, provided that neither the Communities nor NATO were damaged. But the Dutch Foreign Minister Joseph Luns refused to agree to regular summit meetings or institutionalised political co-operation. He had been shocked by the prior agreement between de Gaulle and Adenauer; was fearful lest consultations on defence questions damage NATO; and above all felt that the key question of Britain's involvement remained unsettled. He insisted, also, on his country's attachment to integration, which was somewhat in contradiction with the desire to see the British take part.

In order to avoid an outright failure, Italy proposed that a Commission be set up with the task of drawing up specific proposals for a later meeting. 'European political co-operation had an inauspicious beginning. It took just over another year for it to reach its final failure', Maurice Couve de Murville, France's Foreign Minister, was later to observe. (7) In the preparatory committee, which met in Paris under Fouchet, efforts were made to bring views closer together. Five delegations agreed to regular meetings betwen Heads of State and Government with a view to discussing and, if possible, harmonising the foreign policy of the Member States. The Community Treaties were to· be respected even if the Heads of State and Government might take decisions when the Council of Ministers was unable to agree. The representatives of the Community institutions were to be invited to the meetings of the Six when the matters discussed involved the Community's fields of responsibility. The European Parliament would also be kept informed.

But the Dutch remained firmly opposed. At the Foreign Ministers' meeting of 5 May, Luns expressed the view that the proposed intergovernmental system would cast doubt on the political structure of the Communities and that diplomatic questions of global importance should not be dealt with, since they fell within the scope of NATO. He also called for Britain's participation in political consultations. Still there was stalemate, yet prospects altered with Paul-Henri Spaak's return to the Belgian Ministry of Foreign Affairs. He proved very favourable to de Gaulle's ideas and accepted the principle of regular political consultations with no limit on subjects for discussion, including defence, along with a political secretariat which could be based in Paris. Henceforth, it became difficult for the Dutch government to persist, in isolation, with a totally negative attitude. Luns at length agreed to the calling of a new summit meeting following efforts at conciliation by the Italians.

The Bad Godesberg Conference on 18 July, chaired by Adenauer, went off well. Efforts were made on various sides. France abandoned the idea of a referendum, which had been turned down by her partners, and agreed to the reference in the declaration to the Atlantic Alliance and the Communities, whose work would go forward and to which other states might be admitted. The Netherlands seemed to accept the principle of regular summit meetings without demanding Britain's presence. The final declaration stated the resolve of the Six 'to give substance to the wish for political union already implicit in the Treaties establishing the European Communities', to develop their co-operation to this end by regular meetings of Heads of State and Government in order to confer on foreign policy and to reach common positions. The co-operation of the Six would not be confined to the political field and would extend to education, culture and research.

The Bad Godesberg declaration aroused many hopes. The press and public opinion saw it as the birth of a political Europe. A major step forward seemed to have been taken in the construction of Europe. Yet this was only a declaration of intent: no concrete decision had been taken as to the methods of co-operation. A treaty had still to be drawn up. The Fouchet Committee was given the task of putting forward concrete proposals. It set to work again. France took the initiative by presenting a draft treaty on 19 October. This aimed at establishing a 'Union of States' which would adopt a common foreign and defence policy and develop scientific and cultural co-operation. The economic field was not mentioned, which implied that the Union of States would not interfere with the Communities' institutions. In the defence area, mention was made of 'co-operation with the other free nations'. The Union's institutions were to be purely intergovernmental: a Council of Heads of State and Government meeting quarterly and taking decisions by unanimous vote (with the possibility for a state to abstain and not be bound by the decision), a Council of Foreign Ministers meeting in the intervening periods, a Political Committee, based in Paris, to prepare the Council's work and composed of national officials, and a Parliamentary Assembly (that of the Communities) with consultative powers but the right to draw up recommendations. The Union would be open to new Community countries following a unanimous vote. One clause proposed that after three years the Treaty would be revised to strengthen the union by moving towards a unified foreign policy and decentralising the European Communities within the Union itself. The 'Fouchet Plan' took up the ideas of the Bad Godesberg declaration and took into account the observations made by France's partners. Yet differences of view persisted and were to be aggravated by changes in the international situation.

The International Context

East-West relations had worsened still more with the building of the Berlin Wall on 13 August 1961. Whilst making clear the Western powers' will to maintain freedom of access to Berlin, President Kennedy proved inclined to negotiate with Kruschev, who stood by his threat to conclude a separate peace with East Germany if Berlin's status were not changed. Macmillan adopted the same stance. Adenauer was opposed to any concessions, but was obliged to take Anglo-American pressure into account. He was all the more appreciative of de Gaulle's position, therefore, hostile as he was to any negotiation under duress. This led to a strengthening of Franco-German relations and a greater will on Adenauer's part to achieve political union in the interests of greater cohesion among the Six in the face of Soviet pressure. On the other hand, this situation brought about a change in direction by Spaak, who was also in favour of negotiation and who was alarmed at seeing Paris take a different stance from Washington. He clashed with Couve de Murville over this in the Atlantic Council. In these circumstances, European Union in foreign policy and defence no longer seemed to him desirable but, on the contrary, dangerous if that Union were to find itself drawn along by the bigger powers away from American policy and towards the weakening of NATO, unless supranationality were to be introduced into it or the British brought in. Henceforth, Belgium was to join the Netherlands in their hostile attitude to the French proposals.

American policy towards Europe was another element of discord. Kennedy's 'Grand Design' was emerging in outline with the November 1961 plan for a commercial association between Europe and the United States (worked out in detail in the Trade Expansion Act of January 1962) which might develop into an Atlantic free-trade area between America and a European Community enlarged to include Great Britain and other countries. This prospect naturally interested France's partners but de Gaulle saw in the proposed 'partnership' the method by which the United States might assure its leadership and submerge the European Community within an Atlantic Community. This danger seemed all the more plausible as President Kennedy, who was putting into action the new nuclear strategy of 'flexible response', wished to control his allies' nuclear forces and had been suggesting, since May 1961, the establishment of a multilateral nuclear force within the NATO framework. De Gaulle was thus all the more eager to get a European Union based on his own ideas, even more so since the American President was anxious about Gaullist policies and was urging Britain to join the Six.

In fact, the Macmillan government announced its application in July 1961, and negotiations opened in Brussels in the autumn. The plans for Political Union were not without influence on the British decision.

As early as 1958, London had been concerned at such a possibility (8), and still more so in 1960, in face of the French proposals, which Britain had sought to slow down via diplomatic contacts with the other Five. Yet the intergovernmental co-operation urged by de Gaulle was in line with British ideas and the Conservative government approved the Bad Godesberg declaration. At that time it did not ask to take part in the negotiations on Political Union but simply wished to be kept informed. The prospect of Britain's imminent entry into the Community could only encourage the Netherlands and Belgium to slow down the negotiations on Political Union and de Gaulle, on the contrary, to speed them up.

Failure

Belgium now joined the Netherlands in arguing that since the Six were negotiating with the British on membership of the Community, they ought to bring them in also into the negotiations on Political Union. But this was not accepted by the others, and the six Foreign Ministers decided on 15 December 1961 to proceed to draw up a treaty for a Union, while recognising that countries entering the Community would also be admitted to it, and continuing to keep the British informed of their work. Within the Fouchet Committee, the Germans, Italians and Luxembourg delegations accepted the French plan as a basis for discussion but, together with the Belgians, asked for a series of amendments. The most important of these related to the link between the proposed Union and NATO; the autonomy of the Community; and the introduction of certain 'Community' elements into the Union's institutions - an independent Secretary General, a wider role for the Assembly, and a more precise revision clause providing for future development towards single entity. The French made concessions on these points in December. (9)

Agreement then seemed possible, apart from Belgo-Dutch fillibustering. At the same time the EEC took an important step forward on 4 January 1962 with the adoption of the principles of the common agricultural policy and the unanimous decision of the Six to move to the second stage of the transitional period laid down in the Treaty of Rome.

It was at this time that General de Gaulle, eager to reach a conclusion and fearing that the concessions made by French diplomats might ruin his plan, decided to put his partners on the spot by hardening his position. On 18 January a new text was communicated to the Preparatory Committee by its chairman, Christian Fouchet (hence the name Fouchet Plan II). It had been scrutinised and corrected by de Gaulle himself who now cancelled the concessions previously made. It was now proposed that the scope of the Union should be extended to the economic field but without any guarantee of respect for the existing treaties. With regard to defence, all reference, even indirect, to the Atlantic Alliance was expunged. As for the institutions of the Union, there was no question now of an independent secretariat: a committee composed of national diplomats was again proposed. The powers of the Assembly were to remain consultative and there was no further mention of direct elections. Finally, the revision clause no longer embodied the aim of rationalising co-operation between states and spoke merely of the future possibility of developing Political Union towards a Community system.

Why this eleventh-hour toughness on de Gaulle's part? Was it a tactical move in order to obtain further concessions from his partners? Was it a declaration of the principles which seemed to him vital, and which were in danger of being watered down in the compromise which was emerging? Whatever the explanation, it surprised even the French diplomats who had worked for an agreement in good faith. Couve de Murville later expressed the view: 'That was of course the risk, and thus the disadvantage, of such an initiative. Without fundamentally altering anything of what France was willing to accept, the initiative awoke mistrust and seemed to justify that mistrust.' (10) France's partners were amazed and indignant: they saw themselves brought back to the original starting point.

As the French delegation had no latitude to allow the text to be amended, the Five decided for the first time to form a bloc and put forward a counter-proposal.

This they tabled on 25 January 1962. Their text is of particular interest in the context of this study because it introduced the expression 'European Union' in its first article to describe the 'union of States and of European peoples' which was to be created. The same expression was also used on repeated occasions elsewhere in the text. (11) In using this phrase its authors appear to have been seeking to find an expression to distance themselves from the Gaullist projects, both of which had proposed that 'the Union' should consist of 'a union of States', even though the first title of each of the two Fouchet drafts was headed 'Union of the European peoples'. (12) It was out of such political and linguistic nuances that the expression 'European Union' emerged at this time - though not with any great fanfare or success. It was only ten years later, when the old files were dusted and re-read, that it was to be exhumed and consecrated by the leaders of the enlarged Community. (See next chapter).

It was not easy for the Five to agree. The German, Italian and Luxembourg delegations agreed with the principle of Political Union provided that NATO obligations and the autonomy of the Communities were respected and a Community character given to the institutions of the Union, and reinforced when the treaty was revised. But the Five did not agree on the changes to be made. The Dutch maintained their strong reservations about the principle of Political Union and demanded that defence policy be developed 'within the NATO framework' (the other delegations wanted a policy 'aimed at strengthening NATO').

De Gaulle, perhaps aware that his brutal tactics had upset his partners, now showed greater flexibility. He went to see Adenauer on 15 February and Fanfani on 4 April. He reassured them by showing himself open to inserting references in the draft treaty to the Atlantic Alliance and the autonomy of the Communities. But he refused to offer any undertakings regarding its later revision. The German government agreed to this but the Italian did not. The Foreign Ministers' conference of 20 March made some progress, despite the tense atmosphere. The Five dropped their demands on numerous institutional points, in particular on the creation of an independent secretary general. Attilio Cattani, who had become chairman of the Intergovernmental Committee, drafted new proposals based on compromises between France, Germany and Italy on the relationship with NATO and safeguarding the existing Communities.

The basic problem, however, remained the precondition of British participation, on which the Netherlands and Belgium continued to insist, all the more so since Edward Heath, the British Minister responsible for entry negotiations, while approving the intergovernmental nature of the plan for Political Union, declared that any European defence policy must be directly tied to the Atlantic Alliance. He also asked that Britain be allowed to take part in the negotiations. This unexpected demand could not fail to strengthen the resistance of Dutch and Belgians who were also irked that an agreement should have been sought between the 'Big Three'. At the ministerial meeting in Paris on 27 April, Luns and Spaak, whlist recording their disagreement with the draft texts which appeared to provide a basis for compromise between the other delegations on NATO and the safeguarding of the Communities, refused to go on with the negotiations until it was known whether the British would be joining the EEC. Faced with this disagreement, the ministers broke up, giving no new mandate to the Cattani Committee and fixing no date for another meeting.

III THE BALANCE SHEET

The Final Efforts
The serious nature of the failure struck public opinion forcibly and political leaders sought to justify themselves. Spaak explained that if a supranational Europe could not be achieved, a Europe of states with Great Britain would be preferable to one without her. General de Gaulle, in a caustic press conference on 15 May, launched a strong attack on the proponents of a supranational Europe, accusing them of playing into the hands of the United States. He also came out against Atlantic integration, thereby justifying the misgivings of his partners.

However, the idea of Political Union was not abandoned. The Italians tried to win over the Belgians. In July, de Gaulle and Adenauer asked Fanfani to take the initiative in setting up a new summit conference. But the Italians were cautious and felt that preparations must be made. Spaak himself, who had become sceptical about the prospect of British membership of the Communities, declared he was ready to accept a Union of Six on the condition that it included a political Commission independent of the governments. But this was unacceptable to de Gaulle. He and Adenauer then began to move in the direction of close bilateral co-operation and sought to involve Italy in order to set up a kind of directorate of the 'big powers' capable of carrying the 'smaller' ones along with them. Couve de Murville went to Rome with this objective on 12 October. He proposed that the same agreements be concluded with Italy as with Germany (13). But Fanfani did not agree. He had no desire to break with Belgium and the Netherlands by dividing the European Communities in this fashion; nor did he favour a three-country Political Union in which Italy would necessarily play

a secondary role and which would have distanced her
from the United States and Great Britain. In the end
the plan for Political Union was reduced to the
Franco-German Treaty of 22 January 1963, the other
partners having successively dropped out.

The signing of this bilateral treaty between the
two largest countries was deeply resented by the
other partners. They saw in it the confirmation of
their fears of a Franco-German bloc which could
impose its will on the other Community members. To
offset this danger, they attempted to re-open talks
on Political Union. They were all the more keen to do
this since the British question was no longer
relevant, at any rate in the short term, because of
the veto on British entry imposed by de Gaulle on 14
January 1963. Once the stir created by this had
calmed down, several proposals were put forward in
1964. Spaak, who was concerned at the deterioration
in Community spirit, suggested at the WEU the
creation of an independent Committee to discuss with
governments and to try to find a basis for a Treaty
of European Union. Erhard, who had succeeded Adenauer
as German Chancellor in October 1963, made a rather
similar proposal in November: he also suggested that
in the meantime the Six should consult each other on
foreign, defence and cultural questions before
taking decisions. The Italian government, for its
part, proposed on 28 November regular intergovernmental meetings to be prepared by a committee of
national officials but with a Secretary General who
would be an independent figure with the right of
initiative. The Dutch government, however, remained
hostile to union among the Six and insisted on the
need to work with Britain in WEU. The Belgian, German
and Italian proposals were not taken up by the French
whose foreign policy moved further and further away
from that of the other governments. Agreement on
fundamentals no longer seemed possible. This was
Couve de Murville's answer to Fanfani when the latter
proposed calling another summit in March 1965.
Subsequently, the 1965-66 constitutional crisis was
to aggravate still further the disagreements between
France and the Five over the issue of
supranationality. The French withdrawal from the
military organisation of the Atlantic Alliance in
March 1965 then made it impossible to envisage any
common foreign and defence policy among the Six. As
long as de Gaulle remained in power, Political Union
remained out of the question.

The Causes of Failure

Political Union was, then, probably not achievable because of the fundamentally opposed ideas of the member states regarding Europe's structure, direction, and dimensions. De Gaulle's plan was very coherent: 'A Europe of the states' with no supranationality in politics or economics; 'a European Europe' with its own foreign policy and defence. The Dutch position was diametrically opposed: economic integration but no political Union without Britain, the guarantor of an Atlantic Europe. Both sides were convinced that the European interest coincided with their national interests. The positions were irreconcilable and rigidly defended. Between the two protagonists, attitudes were less clear-cut: the usefulness of Political Union to fill a vacuum and to contribute to the construction of Europe was recognised; Union was not rejected in principle but it was thought that immediate national interests called for guarantees about its objectives in order not to weaken the Atlantic Alliance and NATO, which were the only effective defence, and for guarantees on the institutional level, since a degree of supranationality was held to be a protection for the smaller countries. At different times and with different personalities the proportions in this mixture varied: Adenauer gave priority to Franco-German understanding; Italy's leaders wished to achieve union, but wanted to play their role of a medium-sized power and refused to side with the 'big' countries against the 'small'. Spaak was undecided between the need for supranationality and the participation of the British. Luxembourg had, in its own interests, to remain closer to France than to the other Benelux countries.

If the basic disagreements played a more important role than the actual details of the negotiations, these latter also contributed to failure. The absence of a Community framework made itself felt. The negotiations were conducted according to the norms of classic diplomacy, with its deals, manoeuvres, and attempts at intimidation. Above all, the negotiations focussed on the structures of the future Union and not upon its precise objectives: after the very broad Bad Godesberg agreement, the governments set the Fouchet Commission to work on the institutions instead of first tackling the question of aims. A common foreign and defence policy, certainly, but which policy? Since differences of view existed, they preferred not to go into the subject but to begin by setting up a framework in which they might be gradually reduced. But this was to leave the door open to questions about motives, particularly those of de Gaulle, whose foreign policy worried some of his partners and who had no wish to find themselves dragged along behind him. Conversely, de Gaulle suspected them of wishing to do nothing outside the Atlantic framework and of behaving like satellites of the Americans.

Could Political Union have succeeded at the price of a little more flexibility on the part of the protagonists? Certainly, de Gaulle proved far too rigid in defending his principles. He wanted at one and the same time to create an intergovernmental union and to eliminate the supranational nature of the existing Communities. This was too much. Had he made concessions towards supranationality, or at least respected it, he might have rallied his partners to him and isolated the Netherlands, which would have been deprived of any excuse and risked appearing anti-European. Wishing to make a British-style Europe without the British was a hard position to defend. Yet, above all, de Gaulle clung to his ideas, which would brook no compromise. Were France's partners to accept what de Gaulle offered them while taking no account of their misgivings? Adenauer and the Italian leaders thought they would be able to use Political Union to bridle de Gaulle and avoid crises, or at least resolve them in a way favourable to Europe. Attilio Cattani believe that if an embryonic Political Union had come into existence, things would have gone very differently afterwards (14). This is doubtful, since de Gaulle on the contrary conceived of Political Union as an instrument for drawing his partners along in the wake of French policy, which he believed to be the only right one for Europe. Would de Gaulle have submitted for prior discussion by a Council of the Six his decision to say no to Great Britain in 1963, his recognition of China in 1964, his decision to withdraw from Atlantic military integration in 1966, his second veto against Great Britain in 1967? What unified foreign and defence policy would have been possible, given such divergencies? Had Political Union existed, could it have been anything more than an arena for confrontation, or at best an empty framework?

The Consequences

The failure of the project for a Union of States meant that there was no political co-operation in the Communities throughout the whole of the 60s. There

were no more summits (apart from a very formal one in
Rome in 1967) and the periodic meetings of Foreign
Ministers begun in 1960 were no longer held after the
first veto against British entry. New possibilities
of political co-operation emerged only after de
Gaulle's departure. But the affair of the Fouchet
Plan had left its mark, and useful lessons were
learnt for the future.

At the Hague Summit (December 1969) the
necessity of political co-operation was recognised.
This was becoming possible because the principle of
Britain's entry had been accepted and defence issues
set to one side. But there was no longer any question
of institutions distinct from those of the
Communities. President Pompidou's suggestion of a
political secretariat seemed like a revival of the
Fouchet Plan and was abandoned. It was therefore a
question only of developing co-operation in the field
of foreign policy. It was no longer a question of
'capping' the Communities, which were in any case
weakened by the 1966 Luxembourg compromise on
unanimous voting. Political co-operation did not
develop outside the Communities and in opposition to
them, but in liaison with them.

With President Giscard d'Estaing, political co-
operation was intensified with the transformation of
irregular Summit meetings into a European Council
bringing together Heads of State and Government three
times a year to deal with foreign policy and
Community affairs. This development of intergovernmental co-operation was accepted only because it was
very pragmatic; because it involved the participation of the Commission; because, in return, France
gave up its opposition to direct elections; and -
above all - because differences over foreign policy
between France and her partners had been reduced, and
Britain was now a member of the Community.

Select Bibliography

Robert Bloes, Le 'Plan Fouchet' et le problème de
l'Europe politique. College d'Europe, Bruges, 1970.
Susanne J. Bodenheimer, Political Union, a microcosm
of European politics, 1960-66. Leyden, 1967.
Alessandro Silj, Europe's Political Puzzle, a study
of the Fouchet negotiations and the 1963 veto.
Cambridge (Mass.), 1967.

General Works

Miriam Camps, Britain and the European Community

1955-63, London, 1964.
Hans von der Groeben, Combat pour l'Europe, Brussels, 1984.

Memoirs
Konrad Adenauer, Mémoires. vol 3 (1956-63), Paris 1969.
Charles de Gaulle, Mémoires d'espoir. vol 1 Le renouveau 1958-62. Paris, 1970.
Maurice Couve de Murville, Une politique etrangère 1958-69, Paris, 1971.
Paul-Henri Spaak, Combats inachevés, 2 vols, Paris, 1969.

Documents
The relevant diplomatic archives are not yet open. But the main texts have been published by the European Parliament (Political Committee) in Le dossier de l'Union Politique. Recueil de documents avec preface d'Emilio Battista, Luxembourg 1964. See also the more recent Selection of texts concerning institutional matters of the Community from 1950 to 1982. Committee on Institutional Affairs, Luxembourg (undated).
General de Gaulle's statements and other documents are to be found in Edmond Jouve, Le general de Gaulle et la construction de l'Europe, 1940-66. 2 vols, Paris, 1967.

Notes
        1.   Jean   Monnet,   Mémoires,   Paris,   1976. pp.505-6.
        2.   Von der Groeben, op.cit., pp.98-99.
        3.   Idem, p.101.
        4.   See   especially   Bodenheimer,   op.cit., ch.VI.
        5.   Couve de Murville, op.cit., p.356.
        6.   See Bodenheimer, ch.IV.
        7.   Couve de Murville, op.cit., p.362.
        8.   Idem, p.44.
        9.   See Bloes, op.cit., pp.254-6.
        10.   Couve de Murville, op.cit., p.370.
        11.   Text   reproduced   in   Selection   of   texts concerning   institutional   matters   of   the   Community from 1950 to 1982. European Parliament, Luxembourg, 1982, pp.122-6.
        12.   For a comparison with the Fouchet drafts, ibid. pp.112-121.

13.   Couve de Murville, op.cit., p.377.
14.   Attilio Cattani, 'Essai de coopération politique entre les Six, 1960-62 et échec des négociations pour un statut politique' in <u>Chronique de Politique étrangère</u>, vol II, no 4, Brussels, July 1967.

Chapter Six

NEW AMBITIONS: FROM THE HAGUE TO PARIS SUMMITS (1969-72)

Christian Franck

On 1 July 1968, eighteen months ahead of schedule, the E.E.C. completed its liberalisation of trade in industrial goods. This customs dismantling, together with the application of the common external tariff, meant that the customs union had been achieved. This success, which the Federal Republic of Germany had pressed for, did not however mean that the Community would henceforth sail on under clear skies. Certainly, it had successfully carried through a programme of negative integration, which consisted in removing the tariff barriers. Would it then be able to go on to undertake a phase of positive integration which would create an organic solidarity in the fields of economic and monetary policy? The completion of the customs union in the middle of 1968 was not sufficient guarantee of this. In fact, several problems exposed the Community to difficulties which would not be easily overcome. The entry of Great Britain, the first disturbances within the International Monetary System, and the financial arrangements for the common agricultural policy, a question closely linked to the issue of increased budgetary powers for the European Parliament: all these represented obstacles looming in the path towards the building of Europe. Obstacles which, at the end of the sixties, seriously darkened the horizon.

Nevertheless, in 1969, a large gap in the clouds came into view. Following de Gaulle's resignation in April, the Hague Summit in December untangled the main knot which had been hampering the community's progress: President Pompidou won the final financial arrangements for the common agricultural policy. This opened the door for the entry of Great Britain. At the same time the step by step creation of an Economic and Monetary Union was contemplated and the

Foreign Ministers were instructed to table proposals concerning political unification (amounting in fact to cooperation in the field of foreign policy), by 1 July 1970. If the final declaration of the Summit, announcing that 'the Community has today arrived at a turning point in its history' (1), was to be believed, then the triptych of completion, further development and enlargement which sums up the meeting at The Hague did indeed mark the resumption of progress.

The forward march was to lead to the Paris Summit of October 1972, where the creation of a European Union was proposed for 31 December 1979, and the completion of the Economic and Monetary Union for 31 December 1980. This was the Summit of Euro-optimism. Working to ambitious deadlines, the Community was to fix itself a series of objectives in the fields of monetary policy, science and technology, and environment and social policy. In the short term, the main external economic policy dossiers were concerned with relations with the Eastern countries, the developing countries, and the G.A.T.T. multilateral trade negotiations. Improvement of the Community's decision procedures and the progress of Political Cooperation were also on the agenda. Before the end of the decade, all the relationships between Member States were to be converted into a European Union (2).

The movement between the Summits of The Hague and Paris had been created by a dynamic force working within the Community. A will to go forward succeeded the tensions and blockages which had arrested the Community's development during the discussions surrounding the Fouchet plan, and when France had left its 'empty chair' betwen June 1965 and January 1966. The British question was resolved. The so-called 'theological' disputes over the institutions were toned down. The term 'European Union' adopted by the Paris Summit foresaw no predetermined style of institutional architecture: it was put forward as the outcome of a procedure, and not as an institutional formula.

THE DRIVING FORCE OF A NEW DYNAMIC

It was the debate over enlargement which gave rise to a new driving force. The renewed applications for membership made by Britain, Ireland, and Denmark reached the Presidency of the Council in Brussels on 11 May 1967. Norway's application followed in July.

London's application reflected the reorientation of British policy towards the continent. Various factors were working in that direction: the evolution of trading patterns showed a decline in trade with the Commonwealth; on the strategic level, a relative aloofness towards the United States had come about (Britain had decided against asking the USA for Poseidon missiles to replace its Polaris). Participation in European political cooperation would enable Britain to retain its place in major international debates, especially with regard to East-West relations.

On the side of the Six, tension had arisen between France's opposition to enlargement, reaffirmed by General de Gaulle on 27 December 1967 (3), and the backing given by the other Five to Britain's application. The Hague Summit found the beginnings of a solution to this tension. As long as dissension existed to divide its members, the Community's development was blocked. But France's change of attitude during the summer of 1969 set the Community in motion again. On 22 July in Brussels, the French Foreign Minister, Maurice Schumann, revealed to his colleagues the link which France was prepared to make between the completion and strengthening of the Community on the one hand, and its enlargement on the other. Whence the triptych: 'completion, further development, enlargement' which the French Minister put forward for discussion at the following Summit in The Hague in December 1969.

How can we explain the change in Paris's attitude towards British membership? Several reasons can be put forward, which have to do with the prevailing international situation, the Community context, and domestic policy. Stanley Hoffman has shown that after the Soviet invasion of Czechoslovakia, de Gaulle initiated a rapprochement with the United States. In February 1969, he received President Nixon in Paris. He restored France's strategic doctrine to a western perspective (4). The politico-strategic reasons underlying the first veto against enlargement were therefore less evident at the end of the 1960s.

On the Community level, two elements were to play on the French attitude. The first had to do with the emergence of West Germany's economic and monetary power. André Fontaine wrote that Georges Pompidou, having become President of the French Republic, 'mistrusted the Germans. He considered their weight within the Community to be excessive, and judged it necessary to counterbalance it as much as possible'

(5). British entry into the Community would ensure this counterbalance. Reasoning in classical 'balance of power' terms, Paris re-evaluated British membership: it would no longer act as a Trojan horse for America, but rather as a counterweight to West Germany. More important still, and without doubt the decisive factor, would be the link between enlargement and completion. France demanded that the Community be endowed with definitive financial arrangements, based on a system of own resources and guaranteeing the financing of the common agricultural policy. The provisional regime inaugurated in 1966 and financed by national contribution was due to expire at the end of December, 1969. Paris was seeking to win the agreement of its partners on this question. It was France's acquiescence to negotiations with London which incited the other member states to settle in return the Community's definitive financial arrangements, which would ensure the proper working of the agricultural policy. During a televised interview, on 24 June 1971, President Pompidou admitted the connection between completion and enlargement:

> ... I could see that our partners did not want to go further, that there was very little hope, especially, of the common agricultural market's being renewed and, so to speak, definitively installed. That is why, at the Hague Conference, I confronted them with a clear choice. And I secured, on the one hand, that definitive arrangements should be made for the agricultural market, in exchange for the opening of negotiations with Great Britain, on the other. (6)

As candidate for the 1969 presidential elections standing against the centrist and pro-European Alain Poher, Georges Pompidou had won over to his side Giscard d'Estaing's Independent Republicans and Jacques Duhamel's Christian Democrats, who were in favour of a revival of the Community, and not opposed to enlargement. The Chaban-Delmas Government formed from the presidential majority included four ministers who were members of Jean Monnet's Action Committee for a United States of Europe, which was in favour of British membership. (7) The stage of domestic French politics was ready for a scene change. During the presidential campaign, Pompidou had declared that

133

'it would be dramatic to leave England outside Europe'. (8) The prevailing state of international affairs, the Community context and France's domestic policy made it possible at the end of 1969 to contemplate her entry.

Completion, further development and enlargement: the triptych proposed by France was submitted for discussion at the Hague Summit on 1 and 2 December. Point 5 of the final Communiqué sealed the agreement concerning completion: in order to ensure 'the definitive financial arrangement for the common agricultural policy', national contributions would be progressively replaced by the Community's own resources, with the object of achieving in due course the 'integral financing of the Community's budgets'.

As for further development, also referred to as reinforcement, this would involve the 'creation of an Economic and Monetary Union' (point 8 of the Communiqué). Enlargement was dealt with in point 13: there was 'agreement on the principle of the enlargement of the Community' and on the opening of negotiations with the applicant States. A last point, number 15, also mentioned 'the matter of political unification'.

At The Hague, the Community deadlock was overcome. How was the triptych put into practice? Negotiations on completion followed immediately in the wake of the Summit. A marathon session lasting from 19 to 22 December settled the system of the Community's own resources: these would be obtained by payment to the Community of the agricultural levies, customs duties and a fraction not exceeding 1% of the receipts from value added tax. The financing of the Community by its own resources would become fully operational in 1975. After Italy had insisted on the common agricultural policy's being extended to include wine and tobacco, the Council's Decision of 21 April 1970 on the financing of the Community by its own resources confirmed the December agreement.

This Decision was complemented by the Treaty of Luxembourg, signed on 22 April, concerning the European Parliament's budgetary role. It amended articles 78 of the E.C.S.C. Treaty, 203 of the E.E.C. Treaty and 117 of the Euratom Treaty, so as to reinforce the Parliament's participation in the budgetary procedure. The distinction made between compulsory and non-compulsory expenditure dates from this Treaty. (9) The control of the national parliaments over the national contributions was being replaced by the European Parliament's control over a budget financed by the Community's own resources.

This increase in its budgetary powers was, however, kept separate from the question of the election of the members of Parliament by universal suffrage. Despite strong insistence by the Netherlands (10), the latter issue was neither linked to the Treaty of 22 April, nor even included in the timetable resulting from the Paris Summit of October 1972. On this matter, France found itself isolated, since all of its partners were in favour of direct election. It was at the Paris Summit of December 1974 that the French government finally accepted to treat jointly the issues of instituting the European Council and direct election to the Parliament.

Whilst completion was brought to a rapid conclusion after the Hague Summit, reinforcement and enlargement were tackled simultaneously in the course of 1970. The enlargement negotiations opened in Luxembourg on 30 June. The ad hoc group for Economic and Monetary Union, set up in March and presided over by Mr Pierre Werner, submitted its report in October.

ENLARGEMENT: CONDITIONS OF ENTRY

After February 1970, the Six defined their position with regard to enlargement. Since the Hague Summit, it was no longer a question of yes or no to British entry. The issue was now the conditions of membership: the candidates would have to accept the provisions of the Treaty, and the decisions which had been taken in accordance with these, which went to make up the 'acquis communautaire' - the patrimony of derived Community legislation. The Community also laid down the modes of negotiation. (11)

When negotiations opened on 30 June 1970 in Luxembourg, Britain and the three other applicants accepted the rules laid down by the Treaty, and all subsequent derived legislation. They did not call for a revision of the rules, but for a system of progressive adaptation, during a transitional period of five years. The agreement on the general doctrine of membership was merely a preliminary condition. Next, it was necessary to broach individual problems which raised prickly issues. The main difficulties were the level of the British contribution during the transitional period, the application of Community preference in the agricultural sector, which would hit above all the import of dairy produce from New Zealand and cane sugar, the fate of the Sterling

balances held throughout the world, and the
Community's fisheries policy.

The negotiations remained bogged down until
April 1971 (12). The main obstacle was Britain's
financial contributions. London argued that these
would be several times greater than the sum of
Community expenditure in and on Britain. The notions
of 'net contributor' and 'fair return' made their
first appearance in the language of Community
diplomacy. Britain's agricultural sector made up
less than 5% of its active population. It was obvious
that Community expenditure, more than 80% of which
went to finance the common agricultural policy, would
be of little benefit to Britain. So London wanted to
place a maximum limit on the contribution which it
would have to make to the Community's own resources
at the end of the transitional period, and proposed
until that time to pay a progressive contribution
which fell well short of its partners' expectations.
In December 1970, the British negotiator, Geoffrey
Rippon suggested that his country pay a contribution
of about 3% of the Community budget in the first year
of membership, while France held the view that the
British should immediately agree to pay 20% ....

This controversy made it clear that Britain was
no party to the Franco-German compromise agreed upon
at the outset of the common market: German industry
wanted a large market for its products; France wanted
a common agricultural policy. Bonn accepted that the
financing of agricultural expenditure should
compensate the 'trade effect' of the customs union.
Although it would also be a 'net contributor', West
Germany had accepted the system of 'own resources'.
Britain's ideas were different; the 'trade effect' of
the common market had nothing to do with the
financing of the Community's budget. It was 'unfair'
that Britain should have to pay much more than it
would receive in payments.

Geoffrey Rippon's offer of 3% for 1973 was
perhaps an extreme position typical of the early
stages of negotiations. It nevertheless found a
counterpart, in March 1971, in the French demand that
London should annually repatriate a fixed percentage
of the Sterling balances held abroad. In Paris's
view, these balances represented a huge floating debt
which, in the event of a rise in speculative
pressure, could weaken the Pound and prevent future
monetary union. France's partners found this demand
excessive, and London replied that the problem fell
within the competence of the IMF. These extreme
positions on the British contributions and the

regulation of the Sterling balances had blocked the negotiations. A meeting in Paris on 20 and 21 May 1971 between Pompidou and Heath cleared the ground for the central compromise: Britain would bow to the budgetary rule of the Community's own resources, and France would tone down its demands for the rehabilitation of the Sterling balances (13). At the close of this meeting Britain's readiness to accept the 'acquis communautaire', and France's 'yes' to enlargement were both clarified and confirmed.

Shortly before the Paris encounter, the sixth ministerial negotiation meeting had been held in Brussels on 11 and 13 May. That meeting initiated the reconciliation of views which would crystallize several days later. By tracing the rough lines of solutions to various problems, the meeting came to be considered as a 'breakthrough'. (14) The Six extended the transitional period by six months for agricultural produce, thereby acceding to a demand which the British had been making from the outset of the negotiations. As for the cane sugar which London imported at a price which was higher than that on the world market, it was decided that this problem should be dealt with within the context of the renewal of the Yaoundé Conventions. The sixth ministerial meeting had finally made it possible to contemplate more realistic rough estimates for the annual contributions of the future Member States. In short, after the Brussels and Paris meetings in May, not only was the deadlock raised, but the negotiations had also made considerable progress. Only the problems concerning New Zealand dairy produce and the fisheries remained to be solved.

The final round of negotiations took place in Luxembourg, on 20 June 1971. The British budget quota for the transitional period was fixed: it would progress from 8.64% in 1973 to 18.92% in 1977. The New Zealand dairy produce imported into Great Britain (15) would be subjected to special regulations, to be gradually phased out by the end of the transitional period. Agreement on the problem of fisheries policy was not reached until 15 January 1972. The Norwegians in particular wanted to protect their extremely well stocked waters. (16) In Articles 100 and 101 of the Treaty of Accession certain fishing limitations were conceded to the applicant States within the 6 mile and 12 mile zones of their territorial waters. On 22 January 1972, this Treaty was signed at the Egmont Palace in Brussels. Despite its parliament's approval, the referendum organised in Norway in September delivered a majority verdict (54%) of 'no'.

The new Community would be one of nine members only.

TOWARDS ECONOMIC AND MONETARY UNION

At the same time as it was negotiating enlargement, the Community embarked on the road towards Economic and Monetary Union, the 'Royal Route' to unification, a term coined by President Pompidou (17). Whilst the former action had been dominated by the Franco-British confrontation, it was differences between France and West Germany which crystallized the positions concerning the second. Moreover, the two divisions crossed paths in May 1971. On 10 May, West Germany, followed by the Netherlands, decided to let its currency float. In the view of President Pompidou, who was preparing to receive Edward Heath, the flotation of the Deutschmark overrode the regulation of the Sterling balances, and helped push through the compromise with London. (18)

Economic and Monetary Union was in keeping with the extension of the customs union. According to the theory of integration, a 'spill over' effect would cause the one to follow the other. (19) In terms of integration logic, monetary stability and the harmonisation of economic policies would simultaneously consolidate and reinforce the advantages of the Common Market. The harbingers of the international monetary system's derailment were to lend these theoretical considerations the force of urgency and practical necessity.

In Washington in March 1968, following a strong increase in the private demand for gold, the Gold Pool was suppressed and the convertibility of the Dollar into gold was reserved for the Central Banks alone. This was the prelude to the total inconvertibility decreed on 15 August 1971, and the devaluations and ultimate flotation of the American currency which were to follow. This monetary instability left the Common Market open to the adverse effects of unilateral measures. 1969 brought proof of this danger. In November 1968, General de Gaulle refused to resort to devaluation in order to expunge the inflationary effects of the Grenelle agreements which had put an end to the social disturbances of May 1968. On 8 August 1969, however, President Pompidou ordered an 11.1% devaluation of the Franc. Several months later, in October, it was the turn of the Mark, under pressure from speculation diverted away from the Dollar, to be revalued by 9.3%.

These unilateral monetary adjustments had a double impact on the Community. Firstly, they forced the introduction of the 'compensatory amounts' intended to maintain agricultural price unicity; secondly, they showed how low the coordination of monetary policies stood on the governments' list of priorities. 'Whatever illusions still remained as to the existence of a de facto monetary union were dispelled as a result of these changes of parity, and the lack of coordination which characterized them' (20).

The lessons of August and October 1969 were brought to The Hague. On the initiative of Chancellor Brandt, Economic and Monetary Union became a major issue. Agreement on the overall objective was, however, coupled with an important strategic division between 'Monetarists' and 'Economists'. The former, namely France, Belgium and Luxembourg, were of the opinion that monetary cooperation would bring the coordination of economic policies in its wake. The latter, namely West Germany, the Netherlands and to a lesser degree Italy, believed that monetary union could only be the result of harmonisation of economic policies (21).

An 'ad hoc' group, set up in March 1970 by the Council of Ministers, was instructed to devise the elements of Economic and Monetary Union. Presided over by Pierre Werner, the Prime Minister and Minister of Finance of Luxembourg, the group submitted its report in October of the same year. The report advocated a parallelism of the monetary and economic approaches. Besides the harmonisation of economic, fiscal and budgetary policies, it proposed centralised decision-making in the field of monetary policy. The Werner Report included an important section concerning the institutions: a decision-making centre for monetary policy, a Community system of central banks, and supervision by the European Parliament. The plan would also proceed by stages, the first of which, lasting for three years, would set the process in motion. On the monetary plane, the first phase would provide for the limitation of fluctuations between the Community's currencies through interventions carried out in those currencies.

In February 1971, the Council examined the Werner report. On 22 March, it adopted a Resolution concerning the phased execution of Economic and Monetary Union. (22) This Resolution diluted the institutional proposals contained in the Report considerably, since these had aroused a very negative reaction from the French. Without specifying the conditions necessary to complete the first stage and go on to the second in January 1974, the Council nevertheless took three decisions which confirmed certain proposals contained in the Report, namely to increase coordination of short term economic policies, to strengthen cooperation between the central banks, and to establish a mechanism for medium-term financial aid.

The flotation of the Mark and the Guilder at the beginning of May called into question monetary stability within the Community. It was necessary to superimpose a specifically European device on the common rules of Bretton Woods, which had been undermined by the Dollar crisis. This device was intended to maintain a certain degree of cohesion within the Common Market. After the fluctuation margins for all currencies vis-à-vis the dollar were widened to 2.25% on either side of the new par value, following the agreement signed on 18 December 1971 at the Smithsonian Institute, the members of the Community decided to narrow the maximum fluctuation margins between their own currencies to 2.25% (23).

An agreement betwen the central banks of the Member States, signed at the Banks for International Settlements in Basle on 10 April 1974, arranged the 'snake in the tunnel': the width of the snake (the 2.25% fluctuation band between the currencies of the Community) was twice as narrow as that of the tunnel (4.5% fluctuation vis-à-vis the Dollar). But the Community's cohesion was soon to be shaken. In June, Britain, Ireland and Denmark left the snake. The Paris Summit in October nonetheless maintained the principle of narrow fluctuation margins. It assigned to a European Monetary Cooperation Fund, which would be set up on 3 April 1973, the task, amongst others, of 'concertation between the central banks over the required narrowing of fluctuation margins between their currencies' (24).

Although the Community managed to carry the enlargement through to a successful conclusion, between the Summits of Paris and The Hague, the development of Economic and Monetary Union which followed the Werner Report was immediately confronted by monetary instability and a wave of inflation. Instead of the monetary and economic crisis accelerating the movement towards integration, it created pressures of such magnitude that the member states could do no more than maintain a minimum of concertation and cohesion. Rather than speeding up progression to the second phase of

Economic and Monetary Union, the crisis slowed it
down, and finally rendered it quite untimely. The
'Royal Route' turned out to be narrow and tortuous.
However, the ride was to be much less bumpy for
another scheme undertaken at The Hague, namely
Political Cooperation.

BEGINNINGS OF POLITICAL COOPERATION

At The Hague, the prospect of enlargement revived the
quest for political union. The December Summit
reaffirmed 'the political objectives which give the
Community its meaning and purport' and assigned to it
the task of 'promoting the relaxation of
international tension and the 'rapprochement' among
all peoples, and first and foremost among those of
the entire European continent'. (25) In the context
of forthcoming multilateral East-West negotiations
and a crisis in the Near East, revived by the 1967
war, concern for the Community's role on the
international stage returned to the forefront. This
concern was shared in London, where the initiation of
European Political Cooperation was taken as one of
the grounds for its application for membership. And
so a link was forged between enlargement and
political union.
     At the Summit of The Hague, the Ministers of
Foreign Affairs had been instructed to 'study the
best way of achieving progress in the matter of
political unification, within the context of
enlargement' (26). In what directions could this
progress go? Would it be a matter of institutional
construction, as had been provided for by the draft
Statute of the European Political Community of 1952-
4? France, soon to be followed by Britain, would
reject this idea. Would it be a move in the direction
of common defence? The differences between the
independent attitude of the French and the Atlantic
leanings of their partners, and the neutrality of
Ireland - an applicant for membership - made any stps
in this direction impossible. Should political
unification be linked to 'the reconciliation,
coordination and unification of the member states'
policies' in the fields of education, science and
culture, as proposed by Article 2 of the 2nd Fouchet
Plan (January 1962)? As soon as attention came to
focus on a Community science and technology policy,
and on the question of own resources for the EEC
budget, it seemed preferable to link the new policies
to the Community's institutional nucleus, in the

context of 'further development' evoked at The Hague. Consequently, it was increased political cooperation which was finally accepted as the step forward towards political unification. 'It appeared to the Ministers that it was in the field of concertation of foreign policies that the first concrete efforts should be made to show the world that Europe has a political vocation' (27).

The implementation of cooperation in the field of foreign policy was linked to the prospect of enlargement. This is explained both by the interest declared by the British Government in Europe's role in the world, and by the attempts made amongst the Six to break out of the stalemate in which they had been caught since the failure of the Fouchet Plan (1962). On the British side, Foreign Minister George Brown had made clear the political motivations of the application for membership, during a meeting of the WEU on 4 July 1967 in The Hague. 'We believe that Europe can finally become a Community expressing its point of view and exerting an influence on international affairs, not only in the commercial and economic field, but also in the fields of politics and defence' (28). This insistence on the international role of the European Community showed one of the underlying motives for Britain's desire to join (at least for those leaders who took the European option): having lost her status as a world power and her colonial empire, Great Britain would find in an enlarged Europe the dimensions and resources which make active participation in international affairs possible. Statements by Duncan Sandys and Roy Jenkins illustrate the British expectations. According to the former: 'If we can make European unity an accepted force not only for European but for world progress, then we shall indeed be fulfilling a new leadership role'. The latter announced that '... Britain will make the European Community itself much stronger and more of a force in its own right among the great world states' (29).

Corresponding to the British interest in the international role of the European Community were the efforts of the Six to rise above the failure of the Fouchet Plan of January 1962. These attempts were made within the framework of the Council of Ministers of the West European Union, which acted as a forum for debate between the Six and Great Britain. In October 1968, the Belgian Foreign Minister, Pierre Harmel, proposed the institution of cooperation between the seven countries in the fields of foreign policy coordination, defence and security,

technology and currencies. This amounted to
installing a formula for inter-governmental
cooperation similar to that of the Fouchet Plan,
within the framework of the WEU. The Belgian proposal
was a departure from Benelux's traditional
integrationist doctrine. But such pragmatism made
British participation a necessary precondition of
any resumption of dialogue on Political Cooperation.
    In order to áchieve this 'reconciliation,
coordination and harmonisation in the field of
foreign policy', Minister Harmel advocated
'consultation ... gradually becoming obligatory,
insofar as the States consent to this, on a list of
subjects to be decreed annually' (30). The Belgian
proposal was well received, by all except France.
Paris correctly saw in the transfer of cooperation
into the sphere of the WEU an attempt to bypass the
French veto against enlargement (31). The Belgian
initiative was soon to be followed, in February 1969,
by an Italian initiative, also concerned with
obligatory consultation on matters of foreign policy
(32).
    When, with the coming of President Pompidou,
French attitude towards British membership changed,
the elements which, in 1968-1969 were working in
favour of Political Cooperation, could find concrete
form in the Davignon Report. The prospect of
enlargement lent the European Community a more
broadly representative European dimension: it should
enable it to express itself upon international
political issues. Thus the Davignon Report set up the
consultation procedure which would be reinforced by
the Reports of Copenhagen (1973) and London (1981)
before being legally codified in the Single European
Act of 1986. Consultation was to involve meetings of
the Ministers, a Political Committee (made up of the
Political Directors of the Foreign Ministries) and
working groups specialised by regions or according to
specific problems. The first ministerial meeting was
held in Munich in November 1970, and the first joint
declaration (concerning the Middle East) was made in
May 1971. In the meantime, the question of a
permanent political secretariat for activities in
the field of political cooperation had been raised by
Bonn and Paris. President Pompidou proposed that this
Secretariat be based in Paris. The Benelux countries
were opposed to this as it would be too far removed
from the Community Institutions, and thus in danger
of permanently cementing the distinction between
Political Cooperation and Community activities. The
creation of another institutional pole could well

reduce the Community's role. As a consequence, the project for a secretariat was abandoned.

TOWARDS EUROPEAN UNION

In spite of this and other difficulties, substantial progress had been made by the autumn of 1972 with the triptych of measures outlined at The Hague. It was against this background that the leaders of the enlarged Community met in Paris in October to chart its future course. An ambitious programme was mapped out, accompanied by a series of deadlines. At the heart of this programme was a reaffirmation of 'the determination of the member states of the enlarged Community irreversibly to achieve economic and monetary union'. The necessary decisions including the setting up of a European Monetary Cooperation Fund were to be taken in the course of 1973 so as to allow the transition to its second stage by January 1 1974 and the achievement of EMU not later than December 31 1980. In addition a Regional Development Fund was to be established by the end of 1973, and a series of action programmes agreed: for environment-al policy by 31 July 1973, and for social policy and science and technology by 1 January 1974. At the same time a common commercial policy towards the countries of eastern Europe was to be implemented by 1 January 1973; a policy for the next round of GATT talks by 1 July 1973; and a policy towards developing countries by the end of that year. A commitment was also made to 'take practical steps to improve the decision-making procedures in the Council and the cohesion of Community action' by mid 1973. And, finally, the member states affirmed their intention 'to transform the whole complex of their relations into a European Union before the end of the present decade'. (33)

How exactly this last decision came to be taken is a story which remains to be told. The expression 'European Union' was not new: as we have seen (Chapter 1) the term 'union' had been used frequently in the immediate post-war years to indicate a generic objective, as well as having been incorporated in the title of several specific organisations. More recently, at the beginning of 1962, the expression 'European Union' had been used by the Five in the Draft Treaty they presented as a counter to the second Fouchet project. (See Chapter 5). It was there defined as a 'Union of States and of European peoples' (34). It was conceived as being initially separate from and parallel to the Communities, being concerned essentially with foreign and defence policy matters, while also providing a vehicle for intergovernmental cooperation in such other policy areas as educational, scientific and cultural fields. However, the draft also provided (Art. 16) for a general review at the time fixed for the move from the second to the third stage of the EEC's transitional period. One of the aims of this review would be 'to establish the conditions under which, at the end of the transition period of the Common Market, the European Union and the European Communities will be incorporated in an organic institutional framework, without prejudice to the machinery provided for in the Treaties of Paris and Rome'. At the same time procedures were to be established for the gradual introduction of the majority principle in decisions of the Council of the Union (which were initially to require unanimity).

Both the phrase and the concept of an organic over-arching framework surfaced again at the Paris Summit. But this time 'European Union' was used as the name for the latter, rather than just cooperation taking place alongside the Community. The initiative in proposing 'European Union' in this sense as a new objective appears to have been taken by the Belgian Prime Minister, Gaston Eyskens, at a meeting with his Benelux colleagues in advance of the Summit. Fortified by their support, the Belgian delegation then proposed at the meeting itself the creation of a 'complete European entity' as a framework for the actions decided on for the rest of the decade. (35) Another source suggests that the concept of European Union was also suggested to Pompidou by a member of his entourage, Eduoard Balladur. To Michel Jobert, then Secretary General of the Elysee, who asked him: 'But what does it mean?' Balladur replied: 'Nothing ... But then, that's the beauty of it'. (36)

It is no doubt this imprecision which helped greatly in gaining acceptance for this new commitment. The concept of European Union was vague enough to suit a wide variety of different approaches to the future of the Community - including the confederal model supported by Pompidou himself. (37) But at the same time European Union also symbolised the way ahead. It expressed a teleology which was intended to mobilise political will and energies. It reflected a driving force which the period 1969-72 appeared to have fired with new life. Having agreed on it as an objective, the leaders of the enlarged Community asked the institutions to draw up a report on the subject before the end of 1975 for submission at another summit conference. A new objective had been set - but what it meant and how it was to be achieved were problems deliberately set aside for later consideration.

Select Bibliography

Max Jansen and Johan K De Vree, The ordeal of unity, Bilthoven 1985. (Ch. 10 'Moving again')
Uwe Kitzinger, Diplomacy and persuasion, London 1973
Loukas Tsoukalis, The politics and economics of European monetary integration. London, 1977

Notes

1. Final Declaration of the Conference of Heads of State and Government of 1 and 2 December 1969 at The Hague, EC Bulletin, 1/1970.
2. See point 16 of the Declaration of the Paris Summit, 19 and 20 October 1972, EC Bulletin 10/1972.
3. For an analysis of General de Gaulle's two vetoes, see Uwe Kitzinger, op.cit., p.37-40. The January 1963 veto was based above all on political considerations concerning relations with the United States; the main motives underlying the November 1967 veto were of an economic nature.
4. Stanley Hoffman Essais sur la France, Paris, 1974, p.348-354.
5. A. Fontaine, Un seul lit pour deux rêves, (One bed for two dreams), Paris, 1982, p.158.
6. L'Année Politique, Fondation Nationale des Science politiques, Paris, 1971, p.417.
7. See Pierre Gerbet, La construction de l'Europe, Paris 1983, p.349.
8. Quoted by A. Fontaine, op.cit., p.157. It would be wrong to conclude from this declaration that President Pompidou was pronouncing himself clearly in favour of British membership. Until May 1971, there would be continuing uncertainty as to his personal convictions and his definitive option.
9. In the first budget financed by the Community's own resources, in 1975, compulsory expenditure accounted for 85.1% of the total, and non-compulsory expenditure for the remaining 14.9%. By 1980 this had risen to 20%.
10. At the Paris Summit in October 1972, the Dutch Prime Minister Biesheuvel had pleaded for direct election by universal suffrage: 'If we want to involve all Europeans in European politics ... we cannot dispense with general European elections to a

European Parliament', quoted by <u>Le Monde</u>, 20 October 1972.
11. On the negotiation procedures, see Uwe Kitzinger, op.cit., pp.77-89.
12. Ibid, Chapter III. ('The Negotiations Dig In').
13. See Yann de l'Ecotais, <u>L'Europe sabotée</u>, Rossel édition, 1976, p.63.
14. See U. Kitzinger, op.cit., p.127.
15. These imports accounted for about 85% of New Zealand's cheese and butter exports.
16. See Michael Shackleton, 'Fishing for a Policy? The Common Fisheries: a Policy of the Community', in <u>Policy Making in the European Community</u>, ed. by H. Wallace, W. Wallace, Carole Webb; London, 1977, p.349-371.
17. Quoted by Jean Lecerf, <u>La Communauté en Péril</u>, Paris, 1975, p.267.
18. 'This display of Bonn's readiness to go its own way in monetary matters ... doubtless strengthened President Pompidou in his resolve to let Great Britain join the Six', Yann de l'Ecotais, op.cit., p.69.
19. See Leon H. Lindberg, <u>The Political Dynamics of European Economic Integration</u>, Stanford, 1963, p.10: 'In its most general formulation, spill over refers to a situation in which the original goal can be assured only by taking further action ...'.
20. J. van Yperseele, J.-Cl. Keoune, <u>Le système monétaire européen</u>, Brussels, 1985, p.40.
21. See Loukas Tsoukalis, op.cit., p.85-93.
22. EC <u>Bulletin</u>, no. 5/1971, p.47.
23. Council Resolution of 21 March 1972, EC <u>Bulletin</u> no. 4/1972, p.41-44.
24. See EC <u>Bulletin</u>, no. 10/1972, p.17.
25. Point 4 of the final Communiqué of the Conference of the Heads of State and Government, The Hague, 1-2 December 1969.
26. <u>Idem</u>, Point 6.
27. 'Report of the Ministers of Foreign Affairs of the Member States on the Problems of Political Unification', (Davignon Report) 27 October 1970, Part I, point 10. EC <u>Bulletin</u>, 11/1970. Besides cooperation in the field of foreign policy, Political Cooperation was later extended to two other areas: the fight against terrorism (from 1975 onwards), and a European Judicial area (from 1977 onwards). See Philippe de Schoutheete <u>La Coopération politique européenne</u>, Brussels, 1980, ch. 6.
28. Quoted by Pierre Gerbert, in <u>La construction de l'Europe</u>, Paris, 1985, p.336.

29.   Quoted in Roy Pryce, <u>The politics of the</u> <u>European Community</u>, London, 1973, p.125.
30.   Belgian proposals concerning cooperation within the WEU, 21 October 1969, text quoted by Jean-Claude Masclet, in <u>L'Europe politique</u>, Paris, 1975, p.82.
31.   See Pierre Gerbet, <u>La construction de</u> <u>l'Europe</u>, op.cit., p.343-344.
32.   Following which France suspended its participation in the meetings of the WEU.
33.   Point 16 of the final Declaration of 20 October 1972. EC <u>Bulletin</u> 10/1972.
34.   Art 1. The text of the Draft Treaty is reproduced in <u>Selection of texts concerning</u> <u>institutional matters of the Community from 1950 to</u> <u>1982</u>. European Parliament, Luxembourg, 1982.
35.   See <u>Le Monde</u>, 21 October 1972.
36.   Michel Jobert, <u>L'autre regard</u>. Paris, 1976 p.164.
37.   'Building Europe is possible and necessary ... this can only mean building on what already exists, a confederation of States determined to harmonise their policies and integrate their economies ...' Press conference of 21 January 1971, quoted in <u>L'Année politique</u> 1971, p.246.

Chapter Seven

THE TINDEMANS REPORT (1975-76)

Jacques Vandamme

Although no definition of the concept of European Union can be found in the October 1972 Summit declaration, it is possible to extract some explanation from the general context of the European revival which began at The Hague in December 1969.

One of the major decisions taken at The Hague was to go beyond the customs union by creating an Economic and Monetary Union. On the agenda for the Paris Summit were the accompanying industrial, regional and social policies, and there was also talk of a project for social union. (1)

So the idea of 'European Union' covers a whole set of different policy areas and commitments, as opposed to the partial approach developed as a consequence of following the logic of functional integration. This idea was expressed by Chancellor Willy Brandt in a statement to the European Parliament on 13 November 1973:

> The Federal Republic has made European Union its homeland. The classical nation State belongs to yesterday. European Union will not be the outcome of a supranational revolution, nor of an uprooting of frontier posts, but of an acceleration of the fragmentary, functional efforts to achieve Economic and Monetary Union, Social Union and Political Union.

The first component of the concept of European Union was, then, the idea that progress must be global and no longer fragmentary. This is one of its essential features. The second component was the idea that all progress must imply a qualitative transformation of the whole. This new element was the contribution made to the concept of European Union by the Tindemans Report.

THE CIRCUMSTANCES AND CONTEXT OF THE TINDEMANS MISSION

The Paris Summit of December 1974 stood at a turning point in the history of the Community. In France, Giscard d'Estaing had just been elected President of the Republic, whilst in West Germany Chancellor Schmidt had succeeded Willy Brandt. This was the occasion for a new attempt at revival after the failure of Economic and Monetary Union. The revival programme decided upon in Paris contained three main elements:

- the decision to proceed to direct elections to the European Parliament;
- the institutionalisation of the Summits by the creation of the European Council, which would meet three times a year;
- the decision to entrust Leo Tindemans, the Belgian Prime Minister, with the task of drawing up a report on the concept and the shape of European Union.

These three decisions enable us to perceive the significance of this mission. On the one hand, the democratic nature of the Community was to be reinforced by the direct election of the Parliament. On the other hand, in the face of the Community's governmental inadequacies, a kind of super-Executive was created to resolve conflicts and determine the major orientations of Community action. It remained to put these reforms in a wider context, thereby giving the newly created whole that coherence and dynamism which it so desperately needed.

The communiqué of the Paris conference specified that Tindemans was to draw up a report after consulting the European institutions, the governments and economic and social groups within the Community.

Why did this mission fall to Leo Tindemans?

During the summer of 1974, a series of bilateral ministerial contacts had revealed a desire for a revival in the Community, and more especially in its political aspects. It was the ambition of the French Presidency of the Council (July-December 1974), the first under Mr Giscard d'Estaing, to convert this will for revival into practical steps forward.

In October 1974, in a speech delivered at the University of Leuven, Tindemans proposed that the Heads of State, who were due to meet in December, should agree to entrust to a group of three Wise Men, presided over by a Prime Minister in office, the task of preparing, in the space of a year, a proposal defining the content of European Union.

This proposition was discussed in the capitals in November. At· the beginning of December, Harold Wilson, to whom Tindemans had presented his proposal, suggested that the mission be entrusted to one man, after the fashion of the mission entrusted during the war to Lord Beveridge, who was to draw up a programme to reform the Social Security system: Wilson had been his assistant.

The British Prime Minister was all the more in favour of this proposal as it put off the moment of decision: he had to get the 'renegotiation' package which had been promised to his electors accepted before the following June. Before that deadline, the British government could not pass judgement on any important question concerning the future of the Community. Wilson succeeded in convincing his colleagues, and in particular Giscard d'Estaing, who was to play a decisive role in the formulation of the final proposition. As far as the latter was concerned, the idea of giving this exploratory mission about European Union to the prime minister of a small and friendly country could in no way harm the European ambitions which he fostered for his seven-year term in office. Giscard doubtless attached more importance to other and more immediate decisions to be taken at the first meeting of the European Council which he was to chair: namely the insertion of this Council into the Community's machinery, and the direct election of the European Parliament.

CARRYING OUT THE MISSION

The text of the Communiqué of the Conference specified the mandate given to Tindemans:

> They (the Heads of Government) consider that the time has come for the Nine to agree as soon as possible on an overall concept of European Union. Consequently, in accordance with the requests made by the Paris meeting of Heads of Government in October 1972, they confirm the importance which they attach to the reports to be made by the Community institutions. They request the European Assembly, the Commission and the Court of Justice to bring the submission of their reports forward to before the end of June 1975. They agreed to invite Mr. Tindemans,

Prime Minister of the Kingdom of Belgium, to
submit a comprehensive report to the Heads of
Government before the end of 1975, on the basis
of the reports received from the institutions
and of consultations which he is to have with
the Governments and with a wide range of public
opinion in the Community. (2)

Scope and Method

The scope of the mission was determined by this
Communiqué. A report was to be made based not only on
the reports requested from the other Institutions but
also on consultations with the Governments, and with
bodies representative of public opinion.

It was, then, a very personal mission: what was
expected was an opinion, and proposals, from one man.
He should draw his inspiration from other reports,
and chiefly those of the Parliament, the Commission,
the Court of Justice and the Economic and Social
Committee. These were the 'privileged' interlocutors. But the governments were also to be prime
interlocutors. They would not be called upon to
negotiate, but merely to express their points of
view. This was, in some respects, the 'diplomatic'
side of the mission.

But it also had a 'popular' or democratic aspect
through consultation with the representative bodies
of public opinion. This was without doubt the
mission's most original aspect. Never before had such
a mission been asked to consult the populace on the
future of Europe. Nor had so many opinions and
documents, and such a diversity of positions,
concerning this same future ever before been
collected together.

And the promise was well and truly kept, even if
traditional diplomatic circles were far from pleased
with this novelty. If proof of this is needed, it can
be found by perusing a list of the thousand
individuals and groups consulted (3).

How was the mission carried out from a technical
point of view?

Tindemans' first step was to formulate the
problem carefully. After consulting a group of
professors specialising in European affairs, he had a
questionnaire drawn up, which would later be given to
all participants, and especially to the representatives of public opinion (4). This document defined the
questions to be elucidated concerning as much the
content of European Union as the role of the
institutions and the implementation procedures. It

covered virtually all of the central questions which are still topical today.

The discussions held with the representatives of public opinion were built up around this questionnaire. They took place for the most part in the capitals of the member states of the Community, at the same time as the exchanges of views with the governments and political parties.

The latter exchanges also broadly followed the same lines. Tindemans and his colleagues stayed for two or three days in each capital. An intensive use of the time available made it possible to organise meetings, on the premises of the Belgian Embassy, with the political leaders of the different parties, and representatives of employers' and workers' organisations, of the financial world, farmers, small firms and traders, women's associations and youth movements. Documents and written notes were passed on to the Prime Minister. Between these meetings, Tindemans would go to the offices of the Prime Minister of the country he was visiting, there to hold conversations with the chief members of the Government.

What arose from these consultations and from the opinions expressed in the reports of the Institutions?

Opinions expressed by the Institutions

We shall limit ourselves to the suggestions made by the Commission and the European Parliament. (5)

The Commission. The Commission believed that only by transforming the Community into a European Union could the aspirations of its citizens for security and change be satisfied. This Union had to be based on Community principles, namely the endowment of powers on common institutions which could ensure, better than the states, Europe's continued well-being and influence in the world. But only those tasks which the states individually could no longer carry out effectively were to be entrusted to the Union. Its spheres of competence would be determined in an Act of Constitution. All other areas were reserved for the states.

The Union would have as its principal objective Economic and Monetary Union. This could be achieved on the one hand through coordination of the economic policies of the states, and reinforcement of the Community's exchange rate system, and on the other hand through the development of a new monetary instrument issued by the Union's Monetary Authority. Initially this would only be used in transactions between Central Banks. Its management should be entrusted to the European Monetary Cooperation Fund, as forerunner of a future Central Monetary Authority under the political control of the Community institutions.

The Union would have to be endowed with a considerably larger budget allowing flexible measures to be taken in response to the needs of the Union as a whole. The size of this budget should not be linked to an increase of public spending in the Member States. Quite the contrary, it should enable economies to be made in the national budgets, thanks to a more rational utilisation of resources.

As regards the improvement of economic structures and the elimination of economic disequilibria, direct intervention by the Union was necessary in order to solve problems arising directly at Community level. The Union would have to be able to finance actions by using Community means and methods (regional and environmental policies).

In the social field, the Union would encourage the progressive introduction of systems ensuring minimum social welfare − a fact which must not prevent the member states from setting themselves more ambitious objectives. In certain areas, such as the protection of migrant workers, the Union should have a common policy endowed with its own finances.

The need for coherence between internal and external action meant that the Union would have to have a foreign policy of its own. Some areas would remain within the competence of the Member States. In others concerted action would be necessary. But for some areas, deriving from internal Community competences, the Union had to have external competence of its own. And it was not possible to speak of a European Union without bringing up the problem of defence. Greater integration in this field would depend on the progress made regarding foreign policy and the strengthening of solidarity.

A list of human rights should be incorporated in the Act creating the Union, so as to assert the democratic nature of the Union.

On institutional issues, the Commission opted firmly for a single structure covering all the activities of the Union, rather than separate structures for different policy areas. It also expressed a preference for a qualitative leap forward rather than step-by-step change. Discussing the type

of changes to be sought, it stated that 'European
Union means nothing if it does not involve the
development of a European governmental executive'.
It then discussed three institutional models. It
rejected the first in which executive power would be
exercised by a body consisting of national ministers;
stated a preference for a second model in which the
functions of government would be exercised by a body
independent of national governments, but accepted
that for a limited transitional period a third model
might be needed, in which a body representing
national governments would be given a role in
decision-making alongside this supranational body.
In all three models a bicameral parliamentary system
was envisaged.

The Parliament
The European Parliament's Resolution of 10 July 1975
suggested an evolutionary process towards European
Union. The resolution was divided into two parts, the
first of which indicated the broad outline of what
this Union should be, whilst the second concerned the
preparatory phase, and proposed immediate measures
intended to improve the existing situation and to set
the process in motion.

The Resolution dealt with the objectives of the
Union, which should be conceived of as a 'pluralist
and democratic Community'. Like the Commission, it
thought that its tasks should be limited to those
'which the Member States could no longer effectively
carry out alone'. Among these the Resolution cited
foreign policy (including security policy), and
social, regional, economic, monetary, budgetary,
energy and research policies. This list was by no
means exhaustive.

The Resolution also described the institutional
structure upon which the Union should be founded.
The central pillar should be 'a single decision-
making centre, which would be in the nature of a real
European Government, independent of the national
governments, and responsible to the Parliament of the
Union'. As for the Member States, they would remain
in control of all those fields not lying within the
competence of the Community; furthermore, they would
participate in the decision-making process of the
Union. This should involve a bicameral system, made
up of a Parliament elected by universal suffrage and
representing the European peoples, and another body
representing the Member States. This institutional
structure should in all events assume a truly unitary

character. It was not so much a question of
relinquishing sovereignty, as of exercising in
common those powers which the Member States could no
longer exercise in isolation with the desired degree
of effectiveness.

Opinions Expressed by Organisations representing Public Opinion

It is most striking to note that an overwhelming
current of opinion in Europe was in favour of
substantial reinforcement of the powers and fields of
competence of the European institutions.

This current was expressed, in the first place,
through the three main European political groupings:
the Federation of Socialist Parties, the European
Popular Party and the Federation of Liberal and
Democratic Parties, whose leaders all expressed
their members' deep desire for further integration.
On the political level, the only misgivings were
those expressed by the French Communist Party (and
the French Communist trade union, the CGT), the right
wing Gaullists (such as Michel Debré) and certain
Danish parties. In Great Britain, the Labour Party,
then in power, was far from negative, especially
after the June 1975 referendum. The same was true of
the Danish socialists.

Many 'transnational' groupings also made known
their organisations' points of view concerning the
future of the European Union and the structure of its
institutions. (6) It is striking that all of them
were in agreement about one essential point: European
Union needed efficient institutions with political
authority, democratic legitimacy, real powers and
effective means of ensuring that the Union could act
efficiently both internally and externally, and of
making its activities both transparent and
comprehensible.

Without having actually adopted an official
position regarding the European Union, the European
trade union confederation (ETUC) believed that at the
present stage of development, concertation with the
trade union organisations was of the utmost
importance: less for the trade union organisations
than for the building of Europe itself. Indeed, if
the Community institutions failed to find a way of
quickly arousing greater interest of the workers in
the objectives of European construction, then the
organisation was convinced that there was a danger of
apathy, and even of an anti-European attitude growing
up in trade union circles.

The Tindemans Report (1975-76)

The importance of the European Parliament's
election by universal suffrage and of an increase in
its powers in the legislative field were by no means
underestimated in these circles. But there was a
continuing belief that the real function of the
European Parliament lay more in the reinforcement of
its power to control the policies which were carried
out.

As for the Council of Ministers, discussion
centred more on improving its functioning, and, above
all on guaranteeing that all its decisions were
subsequently translated into action.

In these same circles, there were some who
believed that the essential institutional reforms
should be focussed on the Commission. First and
foremost, the Commission should initiate proposals.
The execution of the policies decided on should be
left to specialised agencies. The creation of such
agencies would at the same time enable the Commission
to resume its original functions, as a body which
proposed policies. In this respect, it was considered
that the members of the Commission should be placed
on a level where they could discuss as equals with
the national politicians.

The farmers' organisations as a whole did not
give priority to the creation of new institutions.
They did however think it necessary to move towards
the creation of a real European executive body,
capable of effective government in those fields where
responsibility was to be progressively handed over to
the European institutions. The European Parliament,
elected by universal suffrage, should have both
legislative powers and powers of control. The
structure of a European Union should be based on the
principles of subsidiarity and decentralisation. The
Council, which currently has both legislative and
executive functions, should be progressively
replaced, on the one hand by a body with extensive
legislative powers - namely the European Parliament -
and, on the other hand, by an executive body - namely
the Commission.

The Union of Industries of the European
Community (UNICE) came out in favour of further
progress in the field of European political
construction, with a view to creating a European
Union founded on a democratic distribution of power,
and a constitutional guarantee of rights. According
to UNICE, the main interest of industry lay in a more
efficient decision-making process (an acceleration
without loss of quality) and in the most extensive
possible participation, ensured by close

consultation, for industry in this process. The crux of the qualitative leap forward which they considered essential to the realisation of European Union, should consist of two measures: the creation of a real European executive, capable of 'governing' effectively in those areas and fields of competence which would be transferred, increasingly progress- ively, to the European institutions; and direct election by universal suffrage to the European Assembly, which would be given power both to legislate and to control.

So it can be seen that the economic and social organisations active at a European level attached great importance to the establishment of a reinforced institutional structure for the European Union.

THE CONTENT OF THE REPORT

Leo Tindemans' mission was not an easy one. In drawing up his report, three possibilities were open to him. He hesitated for a long time before making his choice.

The first possibility was to make a report relying on the majority tendency which had emerged from the 'popular consultation', and which was in favour of substantially strengthening the European construction, with regards both to the powers and the working of the institutions. Such a report would have identified the new challenges facing the Community, and the solutions with which to deal with them, in the short and medium term. It would have been a kind of 'message' to the European people, looking further afield than the immediate prospects.

The second possible solution would have been to make a report like the Spaak Report which had followed the Messina Conference in 1955, in other words, a document whose general lines, after approval by the Heads of Government, would have provided the basis for future negotiations to draw up a Treaty of European Union.

The third solution was to submit a rather more 'diplomatic' report taking into consideration the short term constraints, but capable of extracting from the governments an agreement on a set of general guidelines. On the basis of this agreement, legally binding texts could gradually be elaborated, putting the accepted guidelines into practice in such areas as Political Cooperation, Economic and Monetary Union, social and cultural policy, etc. The totality of these texts would finally constitute the European

Union.

In the end, Tindemans opted for the third solution. He justified this in the letter which accompanied his submission of the report to the Heads of Government:

> This is the reason why I deliberately refused to draw up a report claiming to be, at least in part, the Constitution for the future European Union. Nor did I wish to describe what Europe ideally should be, while remaining personally convinced that Europe will only fulfil its destiny if it espouses federalism.
>
> The crisis in Europe is so serious that we must, in the immediate future, save what has already been achieved and, working on this basis, take drastic measures to make a significant leap forward.
>
> I had to make a difficult choice. My proposals do not directly concern the final phase of European development. They state the objectives and the methods whereby Europe can be invested with a new vitality and current obstacles can be overcome.
>
> My choice is based on the belief that at the present time any other approach would be either unworthy of our faith in Europe, or else, because of its utopian nature in the present circumstances, would lose all credibility with the parties in power. Consequently, it represents a realistic yet feasible approach. (7)

Taking the report as a whole, it would appear that European Union, according to Tindemans, was a new phase in European integration, entered upon through a decision of the Heads of Government to take measures in different areas (domestic and foreign policy, mobilization of public opinion, institutions) amounting, as a whole, to qualitative progress capable of leading, at a later stage, to a new Treaty confirming this progress in legally binding texts, and providing for the necessary adjustments to the institutional mechanisms.

The idea of globality, to which we referred earlier, quoting Chancellor Brandt, recurs here. But a new element appeared in the Tindemans Report, namely the quality of progress. Accordingly, it would not be possible to state that European Union existed on the basis of, say, differentiated progress made in the monetary field (progress which was actually made in 1979, with the foundation of the European Monetary System). Nor could this be said if the Council were functioning correctly in the way indicated by Tindemans, and by so many others, before and since. What was necessary was a complete package of measures which, when taken together, amounted to qualitative progress.

The measures which Tindemans proposed should constitute such a package were set out in the five chapters of his report which was submitted at the beginning of January 1976.

Need for Common Vision

The first expanded upon the need for a common vision of Europe built around the concept of European Union, the components of which were listed as being:

1.   to present a united front to the outside world;
2.   to recognise and accept the economic interdependence of our States and to organise a certain number of common policies, especially in the economic and monetary fields;
3.   to express this solidarity effectively through regional and social policies;
4.   to develop a European awareness at the individual level.
5.   to enhance the authority of the institutions so as to increase the effectiveness and legitimacy of their actions.

Europe in the World

The second chapter dealt with Europe in the world, and enlarged on the mechanisms of a common attitude in certain areas of foreign policy.

As far as procedure was concerned, Tindemans suggested a single decision-making centre, in other words, an end to the distinction between Community affairs and Political Cooperation. This central authority would be the Council of Ministers.

Besides this, the report proposed that the political undertaking of the Member States, which underpinned Political Cooperation, should be transformed into a legal obligation, in the form of a protocol restating paragraph 11 of the 1973 Copenhagen Report. (8)

As for the substance of Cooperation, the report proposed four areas to which this commitment to obligatory consultation should be applied, with a view to establishing a common, or majority position:

the new world economic order; relations between
Europe and the United States; security; and crises
occurring within Europe's immediate geographical
surroundings.

Economic and Social Policies

In the third chapter, dedicated to European economic
and social policies, the idea of differentiated
progress in economic and financial fields was
proposed. The crux of the matter, said the Report,
was that it was impossible to submit a credible
programme of action if it was deemed absolutely
necessary that in every case all stages should be
reached by all the states at the same time. The
objective divergence of their economic and financial
situations was such that, if this requirement were
insisted upon, progress would become impossible, and
Europe would continue to crumble away. It must be
possible to allow that:

- within the Community framework of an overall
  concept of European Union accepted by the Nine,
- and on the basis of an action programme drawn up
  in a field decided upon by the common
  institutions, whose principles have been
  accepted by all,

(1) those States which were able to progress had a
    duty to forge ahead
(2) those States which had reasons for not
    progressing which the Council, on a proposal
    from the Commission, acknowledged as valid,
    would not do so,

- but would at the same time receive from the
  other States any aid and assistance that could
  be given them to enable them to catch up with
  the others,
- and would still take part, within the joint
  institutions, in assessing the results obtained
  in the field in question.

What was being considered here was not a Europe
'à la carte': the participants would be bound by the
agreement of all as to the final objective to be
attained; it would only be the timescales for
achievement which would vary.

A Citizen's Europe
The report underlined that the Community was not just a form of cooperation between states, but was also a bringing-together of peoples. To strengthen this aspect, the report recommended that action be taken to protect citizens' rights (fundamental rights, consumer rights, protection of the environment); and to create external signs of solidarity, with regard in particular to the movement of persons, transport and communications, payment of medical expenses and mutual recognition of diplomas. It is also in this chapter that we find the proposal to create a European Foundation to promote initiatives intended to improve better understanding between peoples.

Strengthening the Institutions
The fifth chapter was dedicated to the institutions. As regards the Parliament, the Report advocated that it should be given the possibility, gradually becoming a right, as the Union progressed, to initiate legislation.

As for the European Council, its task should be: (a) to determine coherent general policy guidelines, based on a comprehensive vision of the problems, such being the indispensible precondition for any attempt to produce a common policy; and (b) to provide the necessary impetus for European construction and to search for that political agreement which would allow dynamic progress to be maintained, in spite of difficulties.

For the Council of Ministers, the Report recommended enhanced coherence (better coordination of the specialised Councils), recourse to majority voting, and a strengthening of continuity, by extending the term of Presidency to a whole year.

Lastly, in order to give the Commission increased authority and cohesion, Tindemans proposed the following amendments to the Treaties:

(a) The President of the Commission should be appointed by the European Council.
(b) The President when appointed should have to appear before the Parliament, to make a statement and have his appointment confirmed by vote.
(c) The President of the Commission would then appoint his colleagues, in consultation with the Council, and bearing in mind the number of Commissioners allocated to each country.

Finally, the report recommended various measures to delegate executive power, particularly by the Council of Ministers.

The chapter concluded by saying:

> In the last resort, the institutional framework will reflect the spirit behind it. It is the political consensus of our states described in the first chapter of this report which must give new life to the common institutions. The belief that the Union is vital and necessary will enable us to overcome conflicts of interest and differences of opinion. The resolve to achieve Union will bring us to give the necessary powers to the common institutions. Without this political kiss of life the institutions of the Union will always lack substance and force.

THE FOLLOW-UP TO THE REPORT

In general terms, the report was received as a positive contribution to the development of European cooperation. It certainly fell far short of the expectations of militant Europeans, but such people were aware that the general climate was scarcely favourable for the attainment of great ideals.

In this context, the congress organised in Brussels by the European Movement in February 1976 proved to be an interesting test. In a declaration, carried by a very large majority, the Congress took note of the progamme proposed by Tindemans with approval. (9) It called for a two phase realization of European Union: the first phase running from 1976 until the direct election of the Parliament in 1978, and the second phase beginning after the elections, and involving the revision of the Treaties. The Congress asked that the Council adopt the proposals of the report during the first phase. It nevertheless added that the principle of a two-speed Europe should be rejected. For the second phase, the Congress called for modifications to the Treaties which would result in a strengthening of the powers of the Commission and the Parliament going well beyond the recommendations contained in the Tindemans report.

During this gathering, various political leaders also made known their points of view. Former Chancellor Willy Brandt pleaded above all for the direct election to the European Parliament, which should be seen as 'a permanent constituent assembly for Europe. We should ensure that it obtains more than just a right to initiate legislation. Leo Tindemans has shown in his realistic and laudable report that our path is lined with concrete stages to help us on our way'. (10). Regarding differentiated integration, he stated that: 'realistic differentat- ions, if they exist in a spirit of solidarity, can facilitate further progress.'

The French Socialists were less positive. Their leader, Francois Mitterrand said that regrettably, and despite its positive aspects, the Report was guilty of a sort of 'other-worldliness' which neglected to examine certain economic and political realities. (11) Other French socialists spoke of 'the total absence of a global political project for European Union'.

For the Italian Christian Democrats, Giulio Andreotti considered the Report a good synthesis between the ideal and the practical. According to him, however, study of the institutions should be taken much further. Helmut Kohl, at that time President of the CDU was of the opinion that there was no alternative to the 'step by step' method. He judged the Tindemans proposals to be realistic, constructive and immediately applicable.

The most criticised part of the Report was without doubt the one in which Tindemans advocated differentiated progress in the economic and monetary fields. This proposition, erroneously christened 'two-speed Europe', is also the one which will give rise to the most heated discussions in the future. (12)

Governmental Negotiations

Throughout 1976, under the presidency first of Luxembourg, then of the Netherlands, the Tindemans Report was discussed in the Council of Ministers, and in working parties.

As a conclusion to his Report, Tindemans had asked that the political consensus as to the goals and characteristics of the Union be defined. But the drawback of this procedure, for a report of this nature, was evident: it was to become embroiled in the Council's habitual discussions without anyone assuming the responsibility for reaching a conclusion. The element of impetus was lacking. Moreover, it was far from evident that a Liberal Luxembourg Prime Minister, followed by a Socialist Dutch Prime Minister, would be prepared during their presidency to get their feet wet, just to pave the way for a victory for their Christian Democratic

Belgian colleague.

The main points of the controversy were as follows:

(1) The definition of common action, and therefore majority voting in certain relevant areas of political cooperation. France and Britain were against this.

(2) The new forms of economic and monetary cooperation: many delegations considered these propositions unrealistic because of the considerable divergence in results achieved by the economic policies of the different member states;

(3) the proposed increase in the powers of the European Parliament;

(4) the nomination procedure for the President of the Commission.

At no time, however, was the possibility considered of real negotiations on the conclusions to be drawn from the Report. Moreover, within the 'normal' institutions such as the Council, a large number of current matters headed the list of priorities for the attention of the Ministers. That year, 1976, persistent economic and financial difficulties and diverging national policies darkened the political horizon.

Consequently, it is hardly surprising that the final conclusion of the discussions of the November 1976 European Council in The Hague were restricted to extremely vague considerations concerning the Report's 'great interest' and the necessity of arriving, in due course, at a 'comprehensive and coherent common political approach'.

In the end, the only practical outcome was to invite the Council and the Commission to produce an annual report on the results obtained and any progress which could be achieved in the short term in the various sectors of European Union, without ever actually defining either its content or the implementation procedures, unless, of course, it was to consider that the progressive development of the Community was, in itself, European Union. But that was, in any case, not the conception of the Tindemans Report.

GENERAL CONCLUSIONS

It is possible to take stock of the Tindemans phase

in the process towards achieving European Union from various angles.

The first is that of political effectiveness. In this respect, the Report did not live up to the expectations of its author, since it did not create an initial political consensus indispensible to any subsequent action.

There are several reasons for this. The first has to do with the political and economic climate prevailing in Europe in 1976, at the moment when the Report came under discussion. This climate was not favourable to grand political projects, because economic crisis was plunging the member states into ever greater difficulties. Without having found a common solution in this area, which was after all within the competence of the existing Communities, it was hardly credible to discuss more advanced integration programmes.

A second reason can be found in the conditions under which the Tindemans mission itself was carried out, and in the personality of the former Prime Minister. Leo Tindemans was alone in accomplishing his mission: he was not, as was the case at the time of the negotiations for the Spaak Report, surrounded by a group of representatives of the Heads of Government, who would have ensured permanent contact with their 'chiefs' throughout the elaboration of the Report, thereby endorsing the Report's conclusions, at the moment of its presentation.

Also, Leo Tindemans has a conciliatory nature: he likes to seek the compromise which will reconcile the points of view of his interlocutors. In an interview given to a Belgian newspaper shortly after completion of his mission, he said:

> If I had had a little more time, I could have convinced those countries who are now still hesitating. For example, in my view there is a great transformation taking place in Great Britain. If I had been able to gain three to six months, I am sure that I would really have been able to formulate propositions in the name of the Nine. (13)

Leo Tindemans would certainly have hoped to be able to attain his objective of presenting a project for acceptable compromise. But he did not have the time.

In the end, the Report went beyond any political compromise which might have been possible at that time, but, on the other hand, it fell short of being a grand mobilising design. As one Dutch commentator puts it: 'It did not, as many had hoped, lay down a ready-formulated concept, to be carried out in stages, which the governments would have subscribed to, as had happened in the past with the Spaak-Beyen Report, which culminated in the EEC Treaty. The Dutch Government had also hoped for something of that sort.' (14)

The third reason for the Report's lack of impact is the fact that, from 1976 onwards, the European debate was directed towards the question of direct election to the European Parliament, which had to be the object first of an inter-governmental agreement, and then of a ratification procedure in each Member State.

In such an uncertain climate, it appeared unduly risky to add to the problems of this dossier the further difficulties involved in yet another ambitious project. (15)

The Tindemans Report should, however, also be evaluated using criteria other than simply those of short term political effectiveness. Firstly, it should be noted that, after the Report, the concept of European Union assumed a more definitive form. As we saw at the beginning of this chapter, the Report's main merit is that it added that qualitative element to the concept of European Union. It was not yet certain that progress towards this should also be based on new legally-binding texts, but from then on, alongside the idea of globality which had already been established before the Report, the qualitative element was to be inescapable.

Finally, the Report's chief contribution was not only to re-state and reaffirm the long-term aims which had been formulated in 1972, but to give much more precise content to the concept of European Union and also to the steps which needed to be taken to advance towards it. The failure to reach agreement on the minimum programme proposed by Tindemans showed, however, the differences of opinion that existed among the members of the enlarged Community with regard both to the aims and substance of further integration. (16) Until these have been resolved no real progress towards European Union will be possible: it is to the credit of the Tindemans Report that it made this quite plain.

Annex A
Questionnaire on European Union
I.   **Preliminary Questions**

1.   What does Europe stand for? What are its <u>raisons</u>
       <u>d'etre</u> and its specificity in 1975?
2.   What experience can be gained from the first
       twenty years of European construction?

II.   **Content of European Union**

1.   As regards the field of application of the
       Treaties, do you envisage a development of the
       policies which have been provided for, and an
       improvement in the actions and procedures
       currently in use? If so, in what way?
2.   In certain areas not explicitly provided for in
       the text of the Treaties, common action has been
       undertaken by the Member States. Should the
       scope and content of the policies in question be
       further clarified? Should more binding
       commitments be envisaged in the application of
       the common actions which have been decided upon?
3.   More particularly, would you like to say what
       Economic and Monetary Union implies? What are
       the conditions for its attainment?
4.   Beyond Economic and Monetary Union, what does
       European Union entail?
5.   Would it be useful to provide - in the
       relatively short term - for the insertion of
       certain areas into the framework and procedures
       of the Community? If so, which ones?
6.   In certain areas, it is possible to envisage a
       division of powers between the States and the
       Institutions of the Community: what should
       these areas be? how should the division of
       powers be envisaged in practical terms?
7.   Regarding the extension of the decisions taken
       by the Heads of State and Government in their
       meeting in Paris on 7 December 1974, what
       initiatives could be taken to concretize the
       European reality in individual everyday life?

III.   **The Institutions**

A.   **Generalities**
1.   Should the objectives of European Union be
       attained through the existing institutions, or
       must parallel institutions be created? If so,

which?
2.	Is it possible to conceive of a single
	institutional structure, having recourse to
	different procedures - Community and intergov-
	ernmental - depending on the matters in
	question?

B.	**The European Council** (meeting of the Heads of
	Government in the Council of Ministers and in
	the context of Political Cooperation)

	What role can be played by the European Council?
	What missions should eventually be entrusted to
	it: coordination, impetus, arbitration ...?

C.	**The Parliamentary Assembly**
	Starting from the principle of election to the
	Assembly by direct universal suffrage,

1.	What kind of power should be acknowledged for
	it? Participation in the normative power of the
	Council? If so, following which modes? Control
	over the activities of the Commission? The right
	to initiate legislation? Intervention in the
	investiture of the Commission?
2.	In which areas could it exercise its powers?
3.	Structure of the Assembly and election methods.
	(See the general document drawn up following the
	debates in the European Parliament on January
	14th 1975, concerning the adoption of a draft
	Convention instituting the election of the
	members of the European Parliament by direct
	universal suffrage.)

D.	**The Council**
1.	Should adjustments be made to the execution of
	the legislative function?
2.	Should provision be made for delegation by the
	Council to the Commission of wider powers in the
	management of the common policies?

E.	**The Commission**
1.	Should its powers be strengthened? How? In which
	areas?
2.	What sort of procedure should be envisaged for
	the nomination of the members of the Commission?
3.	What should be the composition of the

Commission?

F.   **The Court of Justice**
     Do you have any observations regarding the
     fields of competence and powers of the Court of
     Justice?

G.   **The Economic and Social Committee**
     How can the representation of economic and
     social interests within the Community be
     improved?

IV. **Method**
1.   Should the exact content of the Union be fixed
     at the point of departure, or should the
     institutions of the Community be instructed to
     define the content, taking as their starting
     point a general concept to be agreed upon
     beforehand?
2.   Should progress be made in stages, following a
     schedule of fixed deadlines?
3.   What should be the legal foundations upon which
     European Union should be built? Certain clauses
     of the present Treaties? Additional clauses?
     New treaties?

V.   **Conclusion**
     In your view, what positive actions should be
     taken by the existing structures (political
     parties, trade union and employers' organisat-
     ions, other professional organisations) in
     order to achieve the indicated objectives?

Annex B
Conclusions of the European Council of November 30,
1976
1.   The European Council examined the report on
European Union submitted to it by Mr Tindemans at its
request. It heard an account given by the Chairman of
the work carried out, and approved the general lines
of the comments by the Ministers for Foreign Affairs
on the various Chapters of the Report.
2.   The European Council indicated its very great
interest in the analyses and proposals put forward by
Mr Tindemans. It shared the views expressed by the
Belgian Prime Minister on the need to build European

Union by strengthening the practical solidarity of the nine Member States and their peoples, both internally and in their relations with the outside world, and gradually to provide the Union with the instruments and institutions necessary for its operation. It considered that European Union should make itself felt effectively in the daily life of individuals by assisting in the protection of their rights and the improvement of the circumstances of their life.

3.   On this occasion the European Council had a wide-ranging discussion of the principles which must underlie the construction of European Union over the coming years. European Union will be built progressively by consolidating and developing what has been achieved within the Community, with the existing Treaties forming a basis for new policies. The achievement of Economic and Monetary Union is basic to the consolidation of Community solidarity and the establishment of European Union. Priority importance must be given to combating inflation and unemployment and to drawing up common energy and research policies and a genuine regional and social policy for the Community.

4.   The construction of Europe must also make the best use of possibilities for cooperation between the nine Governments in those areas where the Member States are prepared to exercise their sovereignty in a progressively convergent manner. This form of cooperation in the field of foreign policy must lead to the search for a common external policy.

5.   In the light of future developments as defined by the report on European Union, the Heads of Government, with the intention of establishing a comprehensive and coherent common political approach, reaffirm their desire to increase the authority and efficiency of the Community institutions, as well as the support of the peoples for them, and confirm the role of the European Council as a driving force.

6.   On the basis of the conclusions reached by the Ministers for Foreign Affairs, the European Council invites them, and the Commission, in the sectors for which it is competent, to report to it once a year on the results obtained and the progress which can be achieved in the short term in the various sectors of the Union, thus translating into reality the common conception of European Union.

Select Bibliography
Primary sources:
European Union. Report by Mr Leo Tindemans to the European Council. EC Bulletin, Supplement 1/1976.
Report on European Union. Commission of the European Communities, EC Bulletin, Supplement 5/1975.
Resolutions of the European Parliament on European Union (Bertrand Reports) 17 October 1974 and 10 July 1975. EC Bulletin, Supplement 9/1975.
Report of the Court of Justice on European Union. 22 July 1975. EC Bulletin, Supplement 9/1975.
Opinion of the Economic and Social Committee on the European Union. 16-17 July 1975. EC Bulletin, Supplement 9/1975.

Secondary works:
Heinrich Schneider and Wolfgang Wessels (ed.). Auf dem Weg zur Europäischen Union? Bonn 1977.

Notes
1.   Speech delivered by Chancellor Brandt to the European Parliament, November 13 1973.
2.   Extract from the Communiqué of the Conference of the Heads of Government of 7-8 December 1974. EC Bulletin, 12/1974.
3.   This list appears in the Annex to the edition of the Tindemans Report published by the 'Texts and Documents' series of the Belgian Foreign Ministry.
4.   For text see Annex A.
5.   For sources of the complete texts, and the reports of the other institutions, see Select Bibliography.
6.   For more details on this subject, see the exposé given by Jacques Vandamme at the 27th Round Table on European Problems, at Bonn, 2 and 3 April 1976.
7.   The complete text of the letter from Tindemans to the Heads of Government is given in EC Bulletin, Supplement 1/1976.
8.   The text of the relevant paragraph of the Copenhagen Report is as follows: 'Governments will consult each other on all important foreign policy questions and will work out priorities, observing the following criteria:
-       the purpose of the consultation is to seek common policies on practical problems;
-       the subjects dealt with must concern European interests whether in Europe itself or elsewhere where the adoption of a common position is

necessary or desirable.
On these questions each State undertakes as a general rule not to take up final positions without prior consultation with its partners within the political cooperation machinery.' EC <u>Bulletin</u>, 9/1973.

9.   European Movement. Congress of Europe 5-6-7 February 1976, Brussels. Declaration. Duplicated note.

10.   Duplicated note of a statement made by Willy Brandt, President of the SPD, at the opening of the plenary session of the Congress of the European Movement of February 6 1976, in Brussels.

11.   Agence Europe 7 February 1976.

12.   See especially our commentary in <u>Integration</u>, Bonn, No. 3/78.

13.   <u>La Libre Belgique</u>. 7 October 1975.

14.   L. Metzemaackers. Het Tindemans rapport: Samenvatting en karakteristiek. In <u>Nieuw Europa</u> 1 1976.

15.   H. Schneider, 'Anlauf ohne Sprang?' in H. Schneider and W. Wessels, <u>op.cit</u>.

16.   See also Jacques Vandamme, 'L'Union européenne et le Rapport Tindemans', in <u>Studia Diplomatica</u>. vol. XXXIV. 1981 No. 1-4.

Chapter Eight

THE GENSCHER–COLOMBO PLAN AND THE 'SOLEMN DECLARATION ON EUROPEAN UNION' (1981–83)

Gianni Bonvicini

The Genscher-Colombo plan to relaunch the integration process and quicken the pace toward European Union was conceived at the beginning of 1981 and had unique characteristics with respect to similar initiatives. (1)

First of all, the initiative was taken outside any institutional framework. In fact, it was announced by the German Foreign Minister, Hans-Dietrich Genscher, on January 6, 1981 at an FDP Party Congress in Stuttgart (coincidentally, the initiative came to an end more than two years later in the same city).

Secondly, Genscher did not have a precise mandate from his government or from a European institution, as was the case on other occasions (e.g. the Tindemans Report or the Three Wise Men's report). His was the expression of the personal views of a minister who had always looked toward Europe with conviction and interest.

Thirdly, the initiative, to which the Italian Foreign Minister, Emilio Colombo, soon lent his name, was not the only one of its kind. On the contrary, a number of plans concerning the future of the Community were in the air.

The agreement between Genscher and Colombo matured after the European Commission drew up a report in response to a mandate given it on 30 May 1980 to make proposals for the reform of the Community budget. The origin of the report dates back to the contentious procedure taken by the Thatcher government against the Community budget. But the Commission's response was not limited to financial proposals, it also touched on the field of institutional reform.

Another plan was presented at the beginning of 1981 by the British Foreign Secretary, Lord

Carrington, within the framework of European Political Cooperation. With a very pragmatic approach, Carrington suggested that certain aspects of the EPC be strengthened, in particular, the role of the president and the ability to respond quickly and decisively to international crises (crisis management).

Lastly, pressure directed in the European Parliament at that time to deal directly with Community reform by drafting a new Treaty. The pressure exerted by Altiero Spinelli and the Crocodile Group finally won out over the caution and scepticism of other European parliamentarians. (See Chapter 9).

The reasons for these various attempts to relaunch the process of integration was mainly based on the clear perception of 'a state of necessity' to answer internal and external challenges to Europe. Among the many questions the members of the Community had to face were: its enlargement to include Spain and Portugal (Greece had just entered in January 1981); the need to increase monetary co-operation to match the growing power of the dollar; the struggle against inflation and the diverging economic trends inside the Community; the worsening of European-American relations on issues related to Detente; and Middle East problems.

Once again the Community found itself in the position of needing to counterbalance its enlargement with a deepening of its policies and decision-making mechanisms. Not having done so during the first enlargement in 1973, there was a shared feeling of urgency to exploit the last chance left to restore a certain 'communitarian' character to the process of integration and a greater efficiency to the decisional apparatus.

The moment was one of great activism in which almost all aspects of European integration were examined, from strictly Community matters to European political cooperation, to more ambitious attempts at a total revision of the terms and manner in which European integration was evolving. As we shall see, this context was to have a profound effect on the outcome of the Genscher-Colombo plan, limiting the scope of its proposals and the possibilities of constructing those broad political alliances necessary for its success.

ORIGINS AND CONCEPT

In his January 6, 1981 speech at Stuttgart Genscher gave some explanation of the reasons that had persuaded him to undertake such an initiative, and its basic objectives. But in order better to understand his motives and aims, there is also evidence from one of his close collaborators, Von Niels Hansen (2). Hansen points out that for a number of years no progress had been made towards closer integration and underlines how the last important steps taken were the direct elections of the European Parliament, decided upon in 1975 and the creation of the European Monetary System (EMS) in 1978-9. In the meantime, two important plans for reform, the Tindemans Report of 1975, and that of the Three Wise Men of 1979 had come to naught. What was more alarming was the fact that both projects were sponsored and backed by EC government heads but failed nevertheless.

In his speech, Genscher put the emphasis on Europe's pressing political, rather than economic, needs. This also was to have an important effect on the form of the plan. The German minister reasoned in terms of international politics and the deterioration of the climate between the superpowers, even if he was aware of the fact that the EC's internal policies had to be changed and strengthened to stand up to the impact of enlargement.

Genscher then indicated the fundamental objectives of European Union: development of a common European foreign policy; extension of the scope of economic cooperation provided by the Treaties of Paris and Rome; agreement on security policy, closer cooperation in the cultural sector, and legal harmonization.

Continuing his interpretation of Genscher's speech, Hansen discusses the method to be followed, which included the taking up of a number of points from previous plans such as the Fouchet plan of 1961/62 and some of Tindeman's ideas. He adds that the initiative was not intended to result in immediate European Union, but rather in an as yet undefined intermediate stage, adding another stone to the construction.

Probably domestic political reasons convinced Genscher to take the lead in a struggle for Europe, such as the need to reaffirm his leadership over his party and a certain tendency to distance himself from Chancellor Schmidt's declining interest in Europe. And, in fact, as the subsequent history of this plan showed, some of the major obstacles to the maintenance of the high profile of the original version were found inside the same German government (hostile, for example, to accepting any further budgetary engagement or economic constraint).

After having announced his proposal, the German minister went to Rome on January 21, where he repeated it, seeking the political support of the Italian government. This was readily assured him by Emilio Colombo, the Italian Foreign Minister, in a speech given January 28 at Florence to delegates of the Assembly the Conseil des Communes d'Europe, in which he expressed his willingness to make this attempt at progressing more rapidly toward European Union. This was the first step in a long story linking the two ministers' names.

ITALO—GERMAN TALKS AND THE LAUNCHING OF THE PROPOSAL

Naturally, the Italo-German alliance was not immediately achieved. There were problems of understanding concerning the strategy to be adopted that created difficulties in the work of the group of foreign ministry officials headed by their respective political chiefs, Bruno Bottai and Franz Pfeffer.

There were two main problems. The first concerned the final form of the plan. The Germans were in favour of the adoption of a juridical instrument (a Treaty) binding all parties to respect the agreement, while the Italians preferred a more flexible arrangement that would not call for national ratification, jeopardizing the success of the initiative. Successive events swayed opinion toward the latter solution: a Solemn Declaration (3).

The element of the greatest disagreement, however, was the content of the plan. The Italians outlined their position almost immediately, suggesting a considerable increase in the part dedicated to internal Community progress and the development of common economic policies. The basic idea was that if the Community was not effective internally, it would also be weaker and less credible externally.

This was also the Commission's thesis in its response to the 'May 30 Mandate' which underlined the dramatic need thoroughly to re-examine and reform common policies — and in particular the common agricultural policy — in order to avoid destroying the meagre results obtained up to that time. Italian reasoning was flawless, but it touched upon a matter which was unpopular with the German government and for which Genscher had no backing. Increasing the Community budget (because that was the obvious consequence of the Italian proposal) was a subject which was fast becoming taboo in Germany. Chancellor Schmidt had already repeated numerous times that the Germans were tired of being net payers to the Community. Furthermore, Genscher objected that the British would never agree to such a proposal and that the Germans were not willing to deprive themselves of British support.

On the other hand, there were two very precise reasons for the thorough examination called for by the Italians. The first was that Italy was not sure of the economic impact enlargement of the Community would have and did not want to lose the relatively advantageous position the Community still offered her. The second was that the Italian government was particularly sensitive to European and federalist movements which were still pushing for internal Community progress towards a single European currency and new common policies.

The conflict continued until autumn with a succession of proposals and counterproposals from both sides. In two consecutive meetings of ministers, on September 11 and 12, and October 3 in Rome, the problem was momentarily shelved, with priority going to the announcement of and acceptance by their European partners of, the bilateral initiative. The Italians settled for an abridged version of their proposals with the intent to continue talks at a later date.

On November 12, the two ministers sent a copy of the joint plan to their colleagues and to the presidents of the Commission and the European Parliament. The understanding was that both ministers write an accompanying letter, so that divergent motivations and perceptions would come to the fore. In fact, in Colombo's letter, his concern about development of Community economic policy was emphasised in its opening paragraph. (4)

The Italian-German plan was given only a lukewarm welcome. The Council of Ministers and European Parliament had no original remarks. The European Council in London on November 26 dedicated very little time to it, inviting foreign ministers to present another report. Denmark objected to the word 'appreciation' appearing in the description of how the plan had been received and proposed merely to refer to its 'reception'.

EXAMINATION OF THE PLAN BY THE TEN

On January 4, 1982, the EC Council of Foreign Ministers decided to set up an ad hoc group composed of high foreign ministry officials to start talks about the plan. These ended a year and a half later, in June 1983, with the European Council's Solemn Declaration on European Union in Stuttgart.

For the first six months the group was chaired by the Belgian ambassador Philippe de Schoutheete, since his country was also exercising the presidency of the Community at that time. He was succeeded by the Dane Gunnar Riberholdt in the second half of 1982 and the German Franz Pfeffer at the beginning of 1983. Other countries were generally represented by their respective Directors for Political Affairs, aided by lower level stand-ins. Although the method followed - that of forming an ad hoc group composed of diplomats - was not new to the Community, there were two original elements.

The first was that, at the urging of the Italian and German ministers, the European Parliament was kept closely associated with its work. This was done by means of a number of meetings with the assembly in Strasbourg keeping it informed of all progress. Of course, as a consequence, Parliament pressed for its opinions to be taken into consideration.

The second element was that Genscher and Colombo never relinquished their paternity of the plan to the Community. In other words, they followed closely the evolution of the plan and, by means of a special procedure, were always the ones to explain the progress and difficulties encountered within the various Community institutions. They flanked the president in office at all times and on several occasions, such as reports to the European Parliament, even replaced him.

Nevertheless, the three presidencies of the ad hoc group played different roles in implementing the task given by the Foreign Ministers. The Belgian presidency, for example, took up with great authority the lead in preparing the first draft of the revised version of the German-Italian proposal, which was presented already on 23 February 1982 at an EC Council meeting. In contrast, the Danish presidency of the second half of the year made a less enthusiastic contribution to the work of the group, presenting at the Copenhagen European Council of 3-4 December 1982 only a brief report on the various points of disagreement among the Ten. The real effort to bring the Genscher-Colombo initiative to a successful conclusion was made in the first semester of 1983, when Germany used its spell in the presidency to push forward the proposal.

In any case, the alliance between Genscher and Colombo was the decisive element in maintaining interest in the proposal. But while on the one hand this novel fact of German-Italian cooperation helped the initiative to come to a concrete conclusion (and not end up shelved, as had happened so often in the past), on the other hand it created problems of alliances with other countries.

Why, for example, was there so little enthusiasm for the Italo-German plan on the part of the French? At no stage in the talks did the French government display interest in the plan as a whole (though it had specific objections to some points). In fact, almost as if to counter it, on October 13, 1981, Paris presented a memorandum on means of overcoming the economic crisis and reasserting Europe's political existence, thereby demonstrating its propensity to deal with the European Social sphere - Mitterrand's banner of Europeanism - and, more generally, its disapproval of initiatives excluding it from a central role. In other words, initiatives originating outside of the traditional French-German scheme have slight probabilities of success and recent history has borne this out. (5)

Besides France's reluctance during the talks, two other countries - Denmark and Greece - turned out to be clearly against all proposals implying greater restraints on their sovereignty and national policies. The British position was less distinct. While in favour of greater cooperation in EPC (as they had proposed in the October 1981 London Report) and the inclusion of security problems as part of political cooperation, they were opposed to reforms of Community institutions as urged by those who wished to make them more supranational in character.

Britain's main reluctance regarded, naturally, the restoration of majority voting inside the Council in order to solve the negative effects on the decision-making process of the 1966 'Luxembourg compromise'. This attitude (and fear) was reinforced by the decision of the EC Ministers, on May 18, 1962 for the first time for many years, to take a majority vote in the Council on agricultural prices to overcome British opposition.

The most convinced supporters of the Genscher-Colombo proposals were the Benelux countries and Ireland, but they had reservations too. Both Ireland and the Netherlands (to a certain extent) were not particularly in favour of an extension of security competences (albeit limited to political and economic aspects) and the prospect of a Defence Ministers' Council.

INSTITUTIONAL ACTORS

We have already briefly mentioned the contacts the two ministers had with the European Parliament. It was no easy relationship. Generally, the European Parliament, or some parts of it, were convinced that the realism contained in the Genscher-Colombo plan would have a double negative effect: on the one hand, it would not help solve the Community's more serious problems and on the other, it would constitute an alibi for governments to neglect the European Parliament's own parallel institutional initiative: a Draft Treaty for European Union. (See Chapter 9).

Nevertheless, contacts between the two ministers and the Assembly at Strasbourg were frequent. When it was presented there on November 19, 1981, the climate was encouraging and a year later, when the Ad Hoc Group already had done a great deal of work, the parliamentary Report of the Belgian Christian Democrat Croux (discussed on October 14, 1982), expressed a rather positive judgement on the Genscher-Colombo plan. Emphasis was laid on the need to associate it closely with Parliament.

The Danish were the first to oppose this association in the Council of Ministers on November 23, 1982. Colombo suggested then that the next president, a German, could maintain at least informal contacts. But despite the new president's efforts, conflict broke out with Parliament during the course of 1983. On March 16 of that year, the president of Parliament, Dankert, suggested minor improvements to the plan to ensure it the support of the Assembly. But the second Croux report of April 12, 1983 set the tone of parliamentary demands: inclusion of the Genscher-Colombo Act in the European Parliament's initiative; implementation of resolutions calling for parliamentary power of initiative in the legislative sector; Parliament's participation in the conclusion of international treaties and an improvement of conciliation procedures. The conditions were tough, but besides their refusal of the power to ratify international treaties, the two ministers were in agreement with the rest of Parliament's requests. Meetings continued, but in the meantime, the Genscher-Colombo plan underwent a number of negative changes in the course of negotiations between the Ten. Just before Stuttgart, Parliament made one last attempt to have its proposals accepted, but by now the course was set and it certainly did not seem to be going the Assembly's way.

Other institutions were involved to a lesser degree. Besides the Council of Ministers which institutionally deals with these matters, other bodies kept a rather low profile. The European Council gave it little consideration; in the December 1982 session in Copenhagen, it merely listed the differences between the various member countries while in Brussels the following March, government heads listened to an informative report. Only at Stuttgart in June 1983 was the time finally ripe for its approval.

For its part, the Commission hardly ever dealt with the matter and the Committee of Permanent Representatives (COREPER) was entrusted with discussion of the strictly institutional aspects.

What was to play an important role in determining the outcome of the Genscher-Colombo initiative were bilateral and multilateral relations among the member states. Besides obvious and continuous contacts between Germany and Italy, the two ministers continued to press their colleagues indirectly, through trips to the various capitals, to convince them to keep the initiative alive and not excessively distort its original character.

The decisive element in the outcome of the plan was the fortunate coincidence of the German presidency during the final stages. Being directly involved in the entire development of the project, the president was able to take advantage of his six months in office to bring the matter to a conclusion in the form of a 'Solemn Declaration on European Union' formally agreed at the meeting of the European Council in Stuttgart on June 19, 1983.

FROM THE INITIAL PLAN TO THE FINAL VERSION

Naturally, in order to judge the validity of the Solemn Declaration, and more generally the entire matter, the premises from which the Genscher-Colombo initiative originated must be compared with the final text approved by the EC heads of government.

Institutional Reform

The basic principle behind the European Act is similar to that which inspired the Tindemans Report: to bring together the European unification process split into two components, that of the Community and that of political cooperation.

More specifically, the plan proposed:

(1) To give the European Council a strategic role and insert it in a permanent and definitive way in the common decision-making structure;

(2) To create a single Council of Ministers responsible both for EC and EPC matters;

(3) To create new specialised ministerial councils, including culture and defence.

(4) To improve the decision-making process with a return to majority voting in the Council and the adoption of a new procedure designed to reduce the use of the veto;

(5) To give a more important role to the European Parliament, by extending its authority and power of intervention (such as consultation about the nomination of the Commission president, an investiture debate on a new Commission's programme, consultation on international agreements, etc.);

(6) To strengthen the role of the Presidency and to create a small secretariat for European Political Cooperation.

Of all these important suggestions, very few survived the year and a half of exhaustive talks. Essentially, what were to be innovative institutional mechanisms were turned into verbal expressions of good intent.

As far as the European Council is concerned, the most innovative aspect concerned the recognition of the possibility of it taking direct decisions and setting guidelines. Substantially, it was to become an organ similar to the Council of Ministers but with a strategic role in setting development guidelines for the integration process. In the Stuttgart Declaration this innovation was not even taken into consideration. A phrase from the Communiqué of the Paris Summit of 1974 (which established the European Council) was repeated almost literally to the effect that 'when the European Council acts in matters within the scope of the European Communities, it does so in its capacity as Council within the meaning of the Treaties' (point 2.1.3.).

There was also strong opposition to the idea of

making the European decision-making process more unitary through the creation of a single Council of Ministers. The main objection was that a solution of the kind would have implied revision of existing Treaties (6) and would have modified the strictly intergovernmental nature of the EPC. If one takes into consideration the request to return to a majority vote in the Council and to give EPC decisions a more binding character, then the strong opposition to the proposal from the ad hoc group and the Council can be understood. So the Stuttgart Declaration made no mention of a single Council. It did recommend greater respect of the Treaties as far as voting was concerned, reaffirming that 'the application of the decision-making procedures laid down in the Treaties of Paris and Rome is of vital imprtance in order to improve the European Communities capacity to act. Within the Council every possible means of facilitating the decision-making process will be used, including, in cases where unanimity is required, the possibility of abstaining from voting' (point 2.2.2.).

The idea of creating new specialised councils (especially for Ministers of Defence) was completely discarded, and things were not much rosier for an organisational strengthening of EPC. On the one hand, the need for a more important role for the presidency was reaffirmed (but this problem was already dealt with and partially solved in the 1981 London Report), yet no position was taken concerning the creation of a small secretariat.

Equally disappointing was the part of the Stuttgart Declaration dealing with the role of the European Parliament. If one cuts away emphatic statements on the importance of the institution in Strasbourg, hardly anything is left. There was no mention of parliamentary power of investiture of the president of the Commission, nor of extension of the conciliation procedure provided for by the 1975 Treaty.

What actually was obtained in the institutional field was more along the line of confirmation and development of current institutional practice than real innovative change. Not even a total return to respect of the provisions of the Treaty of Rome and the overcoming of various compromises arrived at through the years, starting with that of Luxembourg in 1966 was achieved. What is worse, not even the rationalisation of existing structures which was one of the prime objectives of the Genscher-Colombo plan was achieved.

184

New Common Policies and Foreign Policy

We have already mentioned the differences which existed even within the German-Italian duo with regard to common economic policy. Italy's main aim was to reinforce and develop the Community economy. During talks in the ad hoc group, these differences were not ironed out and, on the contrary, the Germans found precious allies in the British. The opposition of these two countries and the substantial indifference of the others reflected on all aspects of the Italian proposal, from definition of a common industrial policy, a considerable increase in own resources and the establishment of the European Monetary Fund, to the reform of the common agricultural policy. Finding itself up against such compact opposition and to avoid weakening its alliance with its German partner, Italy in the end settled for vague promises in the sector of Mediterranean agricultural policy and generic statements for the rest.

The most innovative elements of the original Italo-German plan were the proposed transformation of political cooperation into a real common foreign policy and the extension of the sector's authority to security and cultural affairs. As far as the first issue is concerned, the Italo-German proposals were numerous and articulate and aimed at giving more substance to the purely declaratory statements of policy of the EPC. They proposed linking preliminary consultations of the Ten more closely to later common action; making reactions more timely; making the so-called 'acquis politique' more binding; improving links with the European Parliament; strengthening the presidency; creating a permanent small secretariat; and modifying the rules of consensus.

It soon became clear, however, that the main difficulty lay in including the expression 'foreign policy' in the text, which would have underlined the link between the declaratory phase and action. Both France and Denmark felt that the time was not yet ripe for a step of this kind. Objections on other points were no less numerous.

The same occurred for an extension of the scope of cooperation to security and culture. With regard to the former, all hypotheses of common action, co-ordination of respective national policies and creation of an ad hoc body to deal with them were immediately discarded. At best, Germany and Italy's allies agreed to reaffirm a phrase in the 1981 London Report stating that Europeans could discuss some political and economic aspect of security.

CONCLUSIONS

Conflict also arose between Genscher, Colombo and their partners about the revision clause of the Declaration. The two leaders had thought that after a five year period, the Declaration could be turned into a Treaty binding for all. The compromise solution reached at Stuttgart speaks of a re-examination of the text at the latest five years after, the approval of the Declaration and a consequent decision on whether or not to incorporate progress achieved in a Treaty on European Union, which is tantamount to starting all over again from scratch.

The successive changes in the form of the proposal, which was first called a Treaty, then an Act, and finally a Solemn Declaration, well illustrate the downgrading action led by some governments to empty the proposal of its political significance and binding character. At Stuttgart, the general atmosphere was still very gloomy and the unresolved issue of the British contribution to the Community budget continued to hang like a Sword of Damocles over the development of the process of integration. In addition, too many problems and dossiers were on the table of the heads of governments to permit them to devote enough attention to the Genscher-Colombo proposal. It must be remembered here that the paralysis had reached such a great intensity in the Community, that the Stuttgart Council desperately decided on a special procedure to link all the unresolved problems together in a package deal and set up a Special 'Jumbo' Council for the preparation of the next summit in Athens in December 1983 - which was another failure.

So Germany and Italy's great effort was cut down to a declaration with little innovative content which, above all, did little to indicate the road to be taken toward attainment of European Union. Genscher and Colombo's plan to 'Communitarize' existing forms of cooperation and study the competences of the Union more thoroughly came out of Stuttgart lacking the concrete means needed to start the process. The Declaration was not a credible instrument of progress toward European Union nor did its wording help to clarify the concept of European Union. It was just another attempt to move forward and will probably be remembered more as a missed opportunity than for the role it has played or will play in the future.

Select Bibliography
Ferdinando Lay (ed), L'iniziativa italo-tedesca per
il rilancio dell'Unione europea. Origini e sviluppi
della dichiarazione di Stoccarda. Padova, 1983.
Pauline Neville-Jones, 'The Genscher-Colombo proposals', Common Market Law Review, December 1983.
Joseph H.H. Weiler, 'The Genscher-Colombo Draft
European Act: the politics of indecision', Revue
d'Integration Européenne/Journal of European Integration, vol vi, Winter-Spring 1983.

Texts
Draft European Act (November 6 1981). EC Bulletin,
vol 14, 11/81 pp.87-91
Solemn Declaration on European Union (June 19 1983)
EC Bulletin vol 16, 6/83 pp.24-29

Notes
    1.   A great deal of the information on which
this chapter is based is drawn from the book edited
by Ferdinando Lay (see above). This is an
indispensable source containing not only a very rich
collection of information but also a political
interpretation of the initiative.
    2.   Von Niels Hansen, 'Plaidoyer für eine
Europäische Union', Europa Archiv no 5/1981, pp.141-
8
    3.   This interpretation is suggested by Lay,
op.cit., p.14
    4.   Ibid, p.17
    5.   See Gianni Bonvincini, 'European integra-
tion and the future of the Community', The
International Spectator No 1/85, p.22 and Wolfgang
Wessels, Alternative Strategies (op.cit.)
    6.   Lay, op.cit., p.40

Chapter Nine

THE EUROPEAN PARLIAMENT'S DRAFT TREATY ESTABLISHING THE EUROPEAN UNION (1979-84)

Otto Schmuck

An important new element in the search for European Union was introduced by the initiative taken by the European Parliament in drawing up its own proposals for a Draft Treaty to establish such a Union. This followed the first direct elections of its members in 1979, and pressure from a significant group of them that it should develop a role as a Constituent Assembly. The protagonists of this view, led by Altiero Spinelli, succeeded not only in drafting, but also in gaining the support of a very substantial majority of their colleagues for, a Draft Treaty which was approved on February 14 1984 by a vote of 237 to 31, with 43 abstentions. (1) Many regard this as one of the main achievements of the first directly-elected European Parliament. This chapter examines briefly the background to the initiative, the discussions which led up to the Draft Treaty, its substantive proposals, and their subsequent impact.

THE POINT OF DEPARTURE: THE FIRST DIRECT ELECTIONS, 1979

The holding of the first European elections in 1979 was a milestone of considerable importance in the development of the European Community and the European Parliament. Many observers saw in this a real opportunity for far-reaching changes in the Community's system in the direction of a European Union. It meant that in June 1979 there appeared on the Community stage for the first time an actor who could claim a direct mandate from the citizens of Europe, unlike the Council or Commission, for example, whose legitimation stemmed from national parliaments or governments. The election campaign had already showed clearly that a directly elected EP would not be satisfied with the secondary role it had been playing hitherto, and the prospect of the EP acquiring greater importance after the elections featured in innumerable election manifestos, pronouncements by politicans and newspaper reports. (2)

During the preparations for the elections opposition to a strengthened role for the Parliament also became apparent; the French Assemblée Nationale and the Danish Folketing obliged their governments to reject the idea of extending the EP's powers. The election campaign in France aimed specifically at adhering strictly to the Treaties of Rome and resisting any movement towards reforms. On February 15, 1979 President Giscard d'Estaing had stressed 'that the powers of the Assembly would not be changed as a result of the elections and that these powers must be exercised strictly within the terms of the Treaties'. It was therefore clear as early as 1979 that the calls for reform in individual member states would come up against outright opposition.

In the spring of 1979 a poll was conducted of 742 candidates for the EP (a representative cross-section), of whom 62% were later elected; 54% of those questioned were of the opinion that the EP should become the European constituent assembly.

Table 9.1: The EP should become the Constituent Assembly. Answers of candidates for the EP in Spring 1979 according to nationality. (3) (Figures show percentage of those questioned)

Country	For	Don't know	Against
Belgium	88	3	9
Denmark	11	16	74
Federal Republic of Germany	89	6	5
France	3	3	94
Ireland	20	10	70
Italy	93	3	4
Luxembourg	93	7	0
Netherlands	65	14	21
United Kingdom	29	11	60
EC total	54	7	39

This showed support above all from Belgian, German, Italian and Luxembourg candidates, while most of the Danish, French, Irish and British in the poll were against. Nevertheless a clear majority in favour of such a project was already emerging in the EP, and this was to prove a viable basis for working out the Draft Treaty in the subsequent discussions. The EP continued deliberately on the same track as its predecessor, the nominated Parliament of the years up to 1979. The latter had already voiced its demands for a reform of the Community on many previous occasions. These included the proposals of the Ad Hoc Assembly for a Draft Treaty for a Political Community (see Chapter 3); the EC Assembly's reactions to the first Fouchet Plan (see Chapter 5) when it demanded the introduction of direct elections, more budgetary powers, and responsibility for the ratification of international treaties (4); and its submission on European Union in 1975 when it demanded also co-decision in legislation. (5)

More recently, on May 19, 1978 the Political Committee had voted in favour of a comprehensive report by Lord Reay on future relations between the institutions. (6) However, on September 13, 1978 it was decided in plenary to send this report back to the Political Committee, because discussion of it just before the direct elections was considered inappropriate ('... It is for the future parliamentarians elected directly by the people to enter into discussion with the Council and Commission about how the relationship between them should be formed further'). (7) The nominated Parliament did not want to bind its successor with regard to the substance of European Union, because far-reaching initiatives in this domain were expected of the directly-elected EP.

These expectations were reflected in the manifestos of the three party groupings formed in advance of 1979.

- The Liberals and Democrats declared themselves in favour of a union of European citizens in which legislative and budgetary powers of decision were to be exercised jointly by the Council and the European Parliament. It was to be the EP's duty to draft an appropriate treaty and to press for a speedy ratification by the member states. (8)
- The European People's Party (Christian Democrats) called for a strengthening of the Community institutions by giving them more authority; making them more effective; better internal cohesion, and increased national and Community legitimation. New constitutional and

institutional initiatives were expected of the directly-elected parliament. (9)
- The statements of the <u>Socialist and Social Democrat parties</u> were less unequivocal. A common electoral platform demanding a legislative responsibility for the EP, although subject to the agreement of the Council, was rejected in particular by the British Labour Party and the Danish Social Democrats for inclining too much towards integration. (10) In the final, very brief, declaration by the party leaders of June 23, 1978 mention was simply made of the need for the EP to develop for the time being within the framework of the existing treaties; transfers of responsibility, both for the EP and for the European Community as a whole, were to come about only as a result of the clear agreement of national governments and parliaments. (11) The national manifestos of the Socialist and Social Democrat parties differed considerably from one another on this issue. (12)

Other political parties, like the British Conservatives, came out in favour of limiting the European Community mainly to economic tasks and of limited pragmatic improvements in the institutional field, (13) or, like the French Gaullists, they argued for a retention of the existing treaties, (14) or again, like the Danish Folkebevaegelsen mod EF (People's Movement against the EC), strove in principle for the withdrawal of their country from the European Community. (15)

After the June 1979 elections it became apparent that the pro-European forces in the EP had a clear majority. (16) Nevertheless it took a considerable time before work began on comprehensive proposals for reform. The reason for this lay in the many teething troubles with which the Parliament had to contend once it had been constituted. The Euro-MPs, many of whom had no parliamentary experience at all, had to adjust themselves to the daily routine of the EP with its three different locations and its six (seven, from 1981 onwards) official languages. It was only gradually that positions capable of commanding a majority in the EP emerged.

The diversity of attitudes among the members of the EP stemmed above all from the variety of their political and regional backgrounds, and this explains the comparatively long period of time between the first session of the EP in July 1979 and the setting up of the Institutional Committee in January 1982. To have tackled the subject of European Union prematurely would without doubt have led to greater opposition among the 'new boys' in the EP than was the case later on, as they first of all had to learn the hard way about the idiosyncracies of the Community system and the Council's reluctance to make concessions to the EP. (17)

PARLIAMENTARY DELIBERATIONS – THE SEARCH FOR VIABLE COMPROMISES

It was not until a year after the direct elections that the EP took up institutional questions in earnest. A dual strategy was then developed. One part of this consisted of a 'policy of small steps' aimed at better exploiting the existing powers of the EP vis-à-vis the other institutions. (18) But in parallel with this a start was made on a far-reaching plan for the establishment of European Union which, when put into operation, would mean a qualitative change in the status quo in the Community. Leading MEPs have described these two approaches as being complementary to one another. (19)

At the beginning of its work on European Union, however, party political rivalries emerged and there were differences of opinion on where the emphasis should be placed. As early as September 1979 a motion for a resolution on the further development of the legal foundations of the European Community was introduced by the European People's Party member, Jochen van Aerssen, although it bore no fruit. (20)

The initiative that was ultimately to be decisive was taken in July 1980 by Altiero Spinelli who, together with Felice Ippolito (another Italian MEP) and several other like-minded colleagues, founded the 'Crocodile Club', named after a restaurant in Strasbourg where the supporters of reform first met. (21) Since October 1980 the group has kept its parliamentary colleagues regularly informed of its aims and activities through the medium of the 'Crocodile Letters'. (22) A motion for a resolution was formulated, in which they emphasised that it was the duty of the EP to draw up proposals for institutional reforms. These proposals would have to be presented to the relevant constitutional bodies in the member states direct for ratification. An ad hoc working party was to be charged specially with the study of these questions. (23)

By 1981 170 MEPs from nearly all party groups

had given their signatures in support of the
Crocodile initiative. There were, however, distinct
reservations at the outset on the part of the EPP,
who themselves would have liked to be the originators
of the project. When it became clear that the motion
would succeed even without their support, they
decided to cooperate actively too. In the plenary
discussion on the motion in July 1981 the EPP pressed
successfully for the creation of an Institutional
Committee instead of the proposed ad hoc committee.
(24) On the day when the Institutional Committee was
constituted the EPP members produced a comprehensive
draft of a treaty providing for the establishment of
a European Union. (25) In this way a degree of
rivalry was introduced into the Committee: but this
had a positive effect.

Four basic trends regarding the aims of the
Crocodile initiative emerged in the Committee and
later on in plenary sessions:

- About half of the MEPs were in favour of working
  out a European constitution following fairly
  closely the lines of national federal models.
  Supporters of this idea were to be found among
  the Liberals, the European People's Party, some
  Socialists, the Italian Communists and some
  Independents.
- A substantial minority wanted pragmatic
  improvements to the existing Community
  structures. According to them the EP should
  concentrate on working out policy proposals and
  institutional agreements that could be applied
  within the framework of the Treaties, instead of
  re-hashing the institutional blueprints of the
  1950s. This point of view was shared by a
  majority of the Socialists, the British
  Conservatives, the French Gaullists and some
  others.
- Several independent MEPs favoured the idea of a
  'Europe of the Regions', which aimed at a far-
  reaching decentralisation of the decision-
  making process.
- A fourth (and weaker) group, consisting of the
  majority of the Danish MEPs, the French
  Communists and some others, were in principle
  against any reforms leading to a European Union.

In the work both in committee and in plenary
Altiero Spinelli played a leading role. The Committee
made him a 'co-ordinating rapporteur'. Working out
the plans for reform was too big a task for one MEP

193

alone; consequently six rapporteurs for separate aspects were appointed and Spinelli co-ordinated their work. This procedure also provided an opportunity to involve Members reflecting a variety of political and national trends in the process. This assured broad-based support while at the same time preventing individual groups from taking over the project. Spinelli, a convinced federalist who had made known his views about a united Europe on many past occasions, (26) did not push his own aims but gave pride of place to compromises formulated in such a way as could be accepted by as broad a majority as possible both in committee and plenary. However, not too much of the substance of a democratically structured and viable future model of the Community was to be sacrificed in the interest of positions that could be sure of attracting a majority.

An important characteristic of the procedure was the regular liaison between the Committee and plenary sessions in order to assure the latter's permanent support for the former. The Parliament had four full-scale plenary debates on the subject, and each time the substance of the proposals became more detailed. Table 9.2 shows that the Institutional Committee could always depend on a broad majority in plenary, even if the participation in such significant votes might have been greater.

In the Institutional Committee the influence of the German and Italian MEPs was considerable. Both the Chairman, (Mauro Ferri) and the Co-ordinating Rapporteur, (Altiero Spinelli) were Italian, while out of the six rapporteurs, two were German (Gero Pfenning and Hans-Joachim Seeler) and another Italian (Ortensio Zecchio). An analysis of the Committee members present at the adoption of the various reports confirms this observation. Each time about half the MEPs present were Germans and Italians (see Table 9.3).

Nevertheless the Draft Treaty is more than just a German-Italian agreement within the EP. As Co-ordinating Rapporteur, Spinelli proceeded in such a way as to include all the forces that wished to see reform and to avoid confrontations at the votes. This constant search for compromises explains why there are many imprecise formulations in the texts that were drawn up. Spinelli himself stressed that he could have imagined a more far-reaching and precise plan for reform, but then it would not have been possible to achieve the goal of a broad majority in plenary. In his opinion the support of at least some of the British Conservatives and the German Social

Table 9.2: Voting in the European Parliament at the Different Stages of the Elaboration of the European Union Treaty. (The percentage figures relate to the total of 434 members of the EP)

	For		Against		Abstentions		Total votes	
	No.	%	No.	%	No.	%	No.	%
Setting up of Institutional Committee EP Doc. 1-889/80 rev. (9.7.81)	159	(36.6)	24	(515)	12	(2.8)	195	(44.9)
Guidelines on Draft Treaty EP Doc. 1-305/82 (6.7.82)	259	(59.7)	36	(8.3)	23	(5.3)	318	(73.3)
Preliminary Draft Treaty EP Doc. 1-575/83 (14.9.83)	202	(46.5)	37	(8.5)	71	(16.4)	310	(71.4)
Draft Treaty EP Doc. 1-1200/83/A (14.2.84)	237	(54.6)	31	(7.1)	43	(9.9)	311	(71.7)

Table 9.3: The Majority Patterns in the Institutional Committee at the Final Votes on the Motions for Resolutions Submitted to the Plenary (plus, in brackets, the number of non-voting MEPs present)

	Total present	Italians	Germans	Voting results		
				For	Against	Abstentions
Guidelines (Doc. 1-305/82/A) 24.-26.5.82	33	12	6	31	–	2
Substance (Doc. 1-575/83/A) 5.7.83	35 (+10)	8 (+8)	6 (+1)	29	4	2
Preliminary Draft Treaty (Doc. 1-1200/83/A) 14.12.83	34 (+4)	12 (+2)	5 (+1)	31	3	0

Democrats was a pre-condition if the project was to succeed. The analysis of the vote in plenary on February 14, 1984, listing the MEPs by nationality and party affiliation, shows that it was possible to a large extent to achieve this aim (see Table 9.4).

THE CONTENTS OF THE DRAFT TREATY

The Draft Treaty takes the form of an international treaty requiring ratification by all the member states of the European Community. The text consists of a preamble and 87 articles. The EP decided in favour of drawing up an entirely new treaty: the alternative would have been to propose changes to the existing Treaties, but this would not have led to a coherent overall draft and in addition would have meant that the EP would have had no role to play once an Intergovernmental Conference had been summoned, other than giving its formal opinion to the proposed changes, as provided in article 236 of the EEC Treaty.

It was the EP's intention to maintain and develop the 'acquis communautaire' so as to avoid unnecessary institutional changes and the accusation of too federalist an approach. Its reform proposals had two major objectives:

- First, the inclusion among the tasks of the Union of political areas that were not within the scope of the Community but for which the latter could provide a suitable framework; and the inclusion within a single Community framework of areas where cooperation had already developed - such as EPC and the EMS;
- Secondly, measures to make the decision-making process more democratic and efficient.

The Scope of European Union

In the Draft Treaty both European Political Co-operation and the European Monetary System, are placed together under the same roof of European Union. At the same time new areas of activity, for which the European level seems more suitable as an operating framework, are envisaged, while avoiding an undesirable degree of centralisation. In order to achieve these aims the principle of subsidiarity is applied: this means (Article 12.2) that the union 'shall only act to carry out those tasks which may be undertaken more effectively in common than by the

Table 9.4: Analysis of vote on February 14 1984 in the European Parliament on the Draft Treaty, by nationality and party affiliation of MEPs (27)

Political group Country		SOC (125)	EPP (117)	ED (63)	COM (45)	L (33)	DEP (22)	CDI (11)	NA (10)	Total
Belgium	+	6	10	–	–	1	–	2	1	20
	0	–	–	–	–	–	–	–	–	–
	–	–	–	–	–	–	–	–	–	2
Denmark	+	4	1	–	–	–	–	4	–	9
	0	–	–	1	1	1	–	–	–	3
	–	–	–	–	–	–	–	–	–	–
Germany	+	20	37	–	–	2	–	–	–	59
	0	–	–	–	–	–	–	–	–	–
	–	5	–	–	–	–	–	–	–	5
Greece	+	7	–	–	2	–	–	–	–	9
	0	–	–	–	–	–	–	–	1	2
	–	–	8	–	–	–	–	–	–	8
France	+	–	9	–	–	14	2	–	–	26
	0	–	–	–	6	–	–	–	–	6
	–	18	–	–	–	–	–	–	–	18
Ireland	+	2	3	–	–	–	–	–	–	5
	0	1	–	–	–	1	–	–	–	2
	–	–	–	–	–	–	–	–	–	–

Table 9.4: continued

Political group Country	Voting	SOC (125)	EPP (117)	ED (63)	COM (45)	L (33)	DEP (22)	CDI (11)	NA (10)	Total
Italy	+	12	26	-	22	5	-	2	4	71
	-	-	-	-	-	-	-	-	-	-
	0	-	2	-	-	1	-	-	-	3
Luxembourg	+	-	2	-	-	1	-	-	-	3
	-	-	-	-	-	-	-	-	-	-
	0	-	-	-	-	-	-	-	-	-
Netherlands	+	7	7	-	-	3	-	-	2	19
	-	1	-	-	-	-	-	-	-	1
	0	-	-	-	-	-	-	-	-	-
United Kingdom	+	6	-	22	-	-	-	-	-	23
	-	3	-	6	-	-	-	-	-	12
	0	48	-	5	-	-	-	4	8	8
Total	+	48	103	22	22	28	2	4	8	237
	-	12	-	6	9	2	-	-	-	31
	0	34	-	6	1	2	-	-	-	43
Number of votes		94	103	34	32	30	2	8	88	311

Key: Voting: (+) = Yes; (-) = No; (0) = Abstention

Party groups: SOC = Socialists; EPP = European Peoples' Party (Christian Democrats); ED = European Democrats (Conservatives); COM = Communists; L = Liberals; DEP = European Progressive Democrats (Gaullists); CDI = Group for the technological coordination and defence of Independent Groups and Members; NA = Non-attached

Member States acting separately'.

The Union's areas of competence are divided into two parts in the Draft Treaty - common action, and cooperation between the member states. The first (Art. 102) includes all the decisions taken by the institutions of the Union within the framework of the powers and responsibilities conferred on them by the Treaty. By cooperation the Draft Treaty (Art. 10.3) means 'all the commitments undertaken by the member states in the framework of the European Council' - that is, on a purely intergovernmental basis. This distinction is politically of great significance because the Union's institutions normally act - with certain limitations (28) by majority decision, while it can be assumed that unanimity is required for a decision of the European Council on questions of co-operation. (29)

In the Draft Treaty the following competences are envisaged for European Union:

- Exclusive competences: Free movement of persons, free movement of services, goods and capital within the Union's territory, trade policy (Articles 47 and 64), competition policy (Article 48), and also, after a ten-year transitional period, development aid policy (Article 64.3).
- Concurrent (e.g. shared) competences: Conjunctural policy (Article 50), credit policy (Article 51), monetary policy (Article 52), sectoral policies - above all agriculture, fisheries, transport, telecommunications, research and development, industry and energy (Article 53), social and health policy, consumer policy, regional policy, the environment, education, research, culture and information (Articles 55-62).
- Cooperation: International relations (Article 66), and also - should the European Council so decide - armaments policy, the sale of arms to non-member states, defence policy and disarmament policy (Article 68).

In comparison with the powers of the European Community the authority of the Union would thus be very wide. In commentaries by academics the fear has been expressed that the Union could extend its sphere of activity too far. (30) The principle of subsidiarity as formulated in Article 12, paragraph 2 offers, they say, but little protection against any centralising tendencies of the Union and is in addition hardly capable of being enforced. Criticism has also made of Article 71, paragraph 2 of the Draft Treaty which would permit the Union to change the nature or the basis of assessment of existing revenue or to create new revenue. (31) Long-term financial planning by the member states would be made impossible, and in addition upper limits for revenue would have to be set to prevent the poorer states enjoying a majority voting position from forcing the richer ones to finance social measures. The inclusion of unnecessary details in the Draft Treaty was also criticised, for example in the articles on telecommunications and the free movement of goods and services. (32)

What changes would the Draft Treaty bring to the division of powers between the Union (or Community) and the member states? As the Draft Treaty builds explicitly on the 'acquis communautaire' few new powers would be added in the first instance to those the European Community already has. (33) On the basis both of the far-reaching concurrent competences of the Union and of the decision-making procedure envisaged, according to which a national government is unable to block an initial move by the Union in the area of a concurrent competence and national parliaments are not consulted on the matter at all, the warning about the Union possibly having too large a measure of competence appears to be justified. (34) The way the principle of subsidiarity was applied in practice would become a matter of central importance for the Union's areas of competence.

Institutional Arrangements

During the EP's deliberations on the decision-making process in a future European Union the differing principles and perspectives of the MEPs became particularly apparent. The members of the EPP proposed a clearly federalist-oriented model that was in many ways similar to the political system in the Federal Republic of Germany. (35) Socialist MEPs spoke in favour of a cautious further development of the existing institutional structures, since the Community – as one of their spokesmen stressed – was based on cooperation and its institutions similarly should be built on the idea of cooperation (36). British MEPs adopted a special stance in pressing for the retention at least for a while of the right of veto in the Council. (37)

The common aim of making the decision-making process at one and the same time more democratic and more efficient was for the most part undisputed. A majority was of the opinion that decisions which directly affect the citizens concerned can only be acceptable if they are given a parliamentary stamp of approval. To this extent fulfilling the demand for such legitimation could be a major contribution to the efficiency of the decision-making system. (38) By stressing the democratic requirement for a stamp of approval the EP at the same time justified its own claim for a greater degree of participation in the decision-making process. The guidelines for the Draft Treaty adopted on July 6, 1982 showed that the EP already then considered a regard for the principle of the division of powers to be a significant factor in the future decision-making process. Legitimation and democratic control as well as the active participation of the member states were to be guaranteed; at the same time attempts were made to make the system more efficient. (39) But ways had to be found to try to reconcile a number of conflicting demands: the directly-elected Parliament's wish for a right of decision on the same footing as the Council; the interest of the member states to maintain control over the decision-making process; and the need to find a way to make it impossible to block that process.

The procedure envisaged in the Draft Treaty goes a long way towards taking account of these demands. The EC institutions remain to a large extent the same but their powers, and in part also the way they are set up and constituted, are changed. For the sphere of common action it is proposed that there should be a system of co-decision, in which Council and Parliament would be given roughly equal political weight. This means that the EP would obtain a considerably increased significance by comparison with the present situation. Legislative power would be vested in it together with the Council; it would draw up the Budget together with the Council; and it would play a part in the conclusion of international agreements. The EP would also acquire the right to vote on the investiture of a new Commission on the basis of the latter's programme.

Particular importance is attached to the European Union's legislative procedure. The dual aim of the EP and Council working together on an equal footing and of an effective decision-making process led to a relatively complicated legislative procedure in which the Commission's role would be of great significance. The Council and Parliament would normally take decisions by a simple majority, but for particularly important pieces of legislation, known as 'Institutional Laws', larger majorities would be required. Deadlines are laid down for different stages of the legislative process: non-observance of these would be taken to indicate assent. The aim of such time limits would be to improve the efficiency of the decision-making process. However, a law could not be passed unless it had been given the express sanction of either Parliament or Council (Article 38.5). In the event of conflict a Conciliation Committee, consisting of a delegation from the Council of the Union and one from the EP, would be convened.

Article 23.3 of the Draft Treaty led to considerable controversy. Under pressure particular-ly from British and also from French MEPs agreement was reached in this context on a modified right of veto for the member states over a transitional period of ten years. If a national representation in the Council invokes a vital national interest that is recognised as such by the Commission, the vote has to be postponed and the reasons made public. These more stringent conditions were adopted as a way of ensuring that only in exceptional circumstances could a national veto block the decision-making process.

Implementation Procedure

There was considerable debate in the Institutional Committee and in plenary about the procedure for the implementation of the Treaty on European Union. With the decision to draw up a new treaty rather than amend the existing Treaties, the EP had already made clear its intention to avoid the amendment procedure envisaged under Article 236 of the EEC Treaty, requiring the unanimous agreement of all the member states. It had become clear at the time of the 1979 direct elections that there was considerable opposition in individual member states, particularly in Denmark, to the plans for the creation of a European Union. The proposed procedure was designed to permit progress by those member states determined on reform, but its aim was not to exclude individual member states but rather to apply pressure on all of them to sign the Treaty of European Union. To have the EC and European Union existing alongside one another seemed hardly feasible for both theoretical and practical considerations. (40)

Article 82 of the Draft Treaty proposes a procedure whereby implementation is possible as soon as the Treaty is ratified by a majority of EC states, provided these have at least two-thirds of the total population of the European Community. However, implementation would not be triggered automatically on fulfilment of these conditions and would not take place until an agreement had been reached among the signatory states on the procedure to be followed and on their relations to those states which had not yet ratified. Both in the EP itself and among academics this procedure has been criticised as being neither desirable nor practical (41), and yet it is only in this way - the authors of the Draft Treaty believed - that there would be a prospect of realising their project.

To summarise, it can be said that the Draft Treaty does not represent an utopian grand design for a European federal state but that it seeks acceptable developments of the 'acquis communautaire' which can satisfy the demands of an efficient and democratically based European Union. The adoption of long-term transitional arrangements and a temporary modified right of veto for member states in the Council ultimately also enabled many Socialists, some of the British Conservative MEPs and even some of the Gaullists to register their agreement.

THE CAMPAIGN FOR THE DRAFT TREATY

Altiero Spinelli had warned people early on not to think that with the adoption of the Draft Treaty in the EP the political battle for the creation of a European Union would be over. The opposite would be the case, and to this end the Parliament must work out a strategy that would aim '... to overcome the hesitations, uncertainty and opposition in each individual country'. (42)

In adopting this strategy, leading MEPs took close account of the experience and lessons of the history of the European unification. Above all the EP did not want to rely on the good will of national governments, as these, as had been amply shown in the past, would hardly be prepared to accept a voluntary surrender of power. Innumerable previous proposals for reform had come to nothing because of the opposition either of individual national governments or the Council. Such a fate for the EP's Draft Treaty was to be avoided at all costs. The hopes for a successful conclusion to the Parliament's plans were based in particular on three considerations:

- First, the general public was to be mobilised in favour of the Draft Treaty together with the support of the media, interest groups and national political parties. The second European elections in June 1984 were seen as a favourable opportunity for this.
- Secondly, the support of national parliaments was sought, as it should be in the interest of the 'national sister institutions' to see a change in the EP's weak institutional position so as to overcome the lack of democracy in the Community.
- Thirdly, it was hoped that sufficient political pressure could be exerted on the national governments so that it would become impossible for them to disregard or reject the Draft Treaty. At any event every effort had to be made to prevent a situation in which one dissenting government alone could block or destroy the whole plan for reform.

As has been shown in innumerable opinion polls, the population of the Community is mostly well-disposed towards the idea of European unification. Between 1952 and 1983 an average of 87% of those questioned in the member states showed that they were in favour of the attempts being made to bring about a unification of Western Europe. (43) It was a matter of turning this positive basic attitude to good use for the EP's aims. The EP and its Institutional Committee were concerned to place its plan for reform in a variety of ways before the public. The members of the Committee tried with varying degrees of success to establish close and continuous liaison with national parties, interest groups and media. While the Draft Treaty was being worked out the Institutional Committee conducted several hearings with representatives of public opinion and leading interest groups. The MEPs involved in the elaboration of the Draft Treaty organised an exchange of opinion with academics in the European field so that the EP's plans would also be ventilated in academic discussion. The four big debates were all scheduled for the best days for publicity – Tuesdays and Wednesdays – during the weeks when the Parliament was in session and were accompanied by an intensive press campaign.

With regard to mobilising the public for its reform plans, the EP pinned its hope on the opportunities provided by the campaign for the second European elections in June 1984. In an opinion poll in the run-up to the election the percentage of EC citizens who supported the goal of the political unification of the member states with a European government answerable to the EP was four times as high as those who rejected this aim (44). Only in Denmark was the proportion of opponents higher. Table 9.5 shows the way the MEPs (grouped according to nationality) voted on February 14, 1984 on the Draft Treaty, compared to the views of the general public in the various member countries. The high proportion in each case of those who expressed no opinion is striking. The way the MEPs voted, taken overall, reflects precisely the basic attitudes in their own countries.

In spite of these favourable conditions the candidates for the second directly-elected EP only partially succeeded in mobilising the citizens of Europe for the EP's plan for reform. In almost all the member states the 1984 European election campaign was governed by predominantly national matters. (45) The Draft Treaty was mentioned in many election manifestos (46) but it was hardly put across to the voters in a forceful way. The national parties, in part in the face of opposition from the EP candidates, placed the emphasis in the election campaign elsewhere, and the 'European elements' in the parties carried insufficient weight to prevent this happening. Consequently a favourable opportunity for mobilising the population was not exploited sufficiently. It is nevertheless worth noting that in the run-up to the election, and also after it, a number of interest groups – and especially the European Movement – persisted in their support of he EP's Draft Treaty. (47) In individual member states the Draft Treaty was supported by local committees and key figures by means of advertisements in leading daily newspapers. (48) In general, however, such signs of an active engagement on the part of the public remained the exception rather than the rule. The broad mass of the population took little notice of the EP's aims for the establishment of a European Union.

The EP's second plan of campaign, cooperation with the national parliaments, also turned out to be rather unrealistic. If Altiero Spinelli and his colleagues thought at first they could by-pass the governments and go straight to the national parliaments for ratification of their reform plans, they very soon had to recognise that each national constitution gives the government a position of prime importance when international treaties are

Table 9.5: The Draft Treaty on European Union in the EP and as reflected in EC Public Opinion (figures in per cent) (45)

Country	MEPs			General Public		
	For	Against	Abstentions/ Absent	For	Against	Don't know No opinion
Belgium	83.3	0	16.7	45	6	49
Denmark	12.5	56.3	31.2	12	35	53
Fed. Republic of Germany	72.8	0	27.2	48	8	44
France	32.1	7.4	60.5	40	11	49
Greece	37.5	8.3	54.2	41	9	50
Ireland	33.3	13.3	53.4	34	11	55
Italy	87.6	0	12.4	58	7	35
Luxembourg	50.0	0	50.0	55	12	33
Netherlands	76.0	0	24.0	63	9	28
United Kingdom	28.4	14.8	56.8	24	20	56
Average	54.6	7.1	38.3	43	11	46

formulated - and from the legal point of view this was technically the case with the Draft Treaty. Consequently, the EP's interest in a close association with the national parliaments receded noticeably. It had intended to establish first contacts with its sister institutions in May 1983, but owing to problems over dates in the Institutional Committee this did not happen. As a result the opportunity of involving the parliaments of the member states from the start of the work on the Draft Treaty was lost.

After the Draft Treaty had been adopted in plenary on February 14, 1984 an EP delegation presented the final text to all the national parliaments and governments. With the exception of the Italian parliament, which very quickly approved the Draft, the 'natural coalition of parliaments vis-à-vis the executive bodies', which various MEPs had hoped for, did not materialise. Indeed the contrary appeared to be the case, with individual national parliaments - notably the Danish parliament - jealously guarding their powers against the 'ambitious upstart EP'. (49) Even the German Bundestag, which is regarded as being comparatively well-disposed to the idea of integration, took a long time before responding, so that the opportunity was missed of influencing the intergovernmental deliberations which were going on at the same time. In a hearing in the Bundestag's Foreign Affairs Committee considerable criticism was made of the details of the Draft Treaty, although there was strong support in principle for the EP's aims. (50) In other member states the attitude that emerged in parliament was partly favourable and partly one of 'wait and see'. Clearly nearly all the parliaments were leaving the political initiative to their governments.

On April 17, 1985 the EP took stock of the current state of its consultations with national parliaments. At this point the importance of close cooperation was emphasised once again and the national parliaments were asked to lose no time in continuing their deliberations, so that influence could be exerted on national governments and the inter-parliamentary dialogue intensified. (51) But it was impossible for the strategy of a 'coalition of parliaments' to undermine the predominance of the governments in the move to bring about European Union. The EP supporters of the Draft Treaty knew from previous unsuccessful reform plans that it would be very difficult to obtain the agreement of the governments of the member states to a project of this scope. The EP attached the utmost importance to being directly and responsibly involved in the elaboration and realisation of the Draft Treaty. It repeatedly declared its willingness to review the Draft Treaty in the light of the different national views on how it should be amended, but it wanted to do any necessary revising itself, in order to retain its own leading political role in the matter and to prevent too much of the substance of the Draft from being lost. (52)

The various national governments were very sceptical in their reactions during the initial phase of the work on the Draft Treaty. The Belgian Foreign Minister, Leo Tindemans, recommended in the course of a hearing held by the Institutional Committee in April 1982 that the Parliament should not expect too much in view of the previous negative experience with the Genscher-Colombo proposals. With the second European elections drawing closer, however, the representatives of national governments began to display a greater interest in the EP's initiative – perhaps also for electoral reasons. The German Federal Chancellor, Helmut Kohl, publicly supported the idea of a European constitution and the establishment of a European Union on various occasions. (53)

The proponents of the Draft Treaty in the EP regarded the appearance of the French President, Francois Mitterrand, at the EP on May 24, 1984 as a decisive breakthrough. Three weeks before the date of the second European elections Mitterrand formulated France's readiness to 'examine and to support' the EP's draft, 'with the basic premise of which we agree'. (54) It is possible that a personal explanation of the main points by an EP delegation, consisting of Pieter Dankert, Mauro Ferri and Altiero Spinelli, shortly beforehand (on April 18, 1984) had contributed to this open-minded approach on his part. (55) Mitterrand's announcement was followed on June 25/26, 1984, at the Fontainebleau meeting of the European Council, by the decision to set up an Ad Hoc Committee composed of the personal representatives of the ten heads of state and government to work out proposals for institutional reform. That, in turn, was followed a year later by the European Council's further decision to convene an Intergovernmental Conference formally to negotiate amendments to the existing treaties as well as a treaty on political cooperation. (See Chapters 10 and 11 below).

A PROVISIONAL BALANCE SHEET

Although the eventual outcome, in the shape of the Single European Act, was to fall far short of the Parliament's own proposals, the elaboration and adoption of its Draft Treaty was a significant achievement for the first directly-elected European Parliament in at least four respects:

- First, it made a major contribution to defining and giving tangible form to the term 'European Union'.
- Secondly, it gave a powerful new thrust to the discussion on reform in the Community.
- Thirdly, its initiative led to the limited agreement of the European Council in Luxembourg on a revision of the Treaties.
- Fourthly, with its Draft Treaty the EP supplied long-term guidance and at the same time a yardstick against which future agreements for a reform among the member states will be measured.

An analysis of the deliberations on the Draft Treaty showed clearly that the pre-1979 expectations of a direct election bonus bringing a new legitimation to the EP, and thereby a rapid realisation of the Parliament's plans, were over-optimistic. The theory of the paramount significance of national governments in any progress towards European unification was thus reaffirmed.

Nevertheless the EP's contribution to Community reform should not be underestimated. It was able to make clear to the electors and other interested parties in the Community what it considered to be the main elements of European Union: and in particular that the European Union's sphere of action should not be limited to selected areas of policy drawn up on a list, as is to a large extent the case in the present European Community. While the Union should have an exclusive responsibility (as the EC does today) for certain sectors, such as agriculture and trade, it should in addition have a wide field of concurrent competences. Following the principle of subsidiarity, it should be given those tasks that can be tackled more effectively jointly than if this were done by the individual member states on their own. The current practice of allotting responsibility for certain areas is replaced by a general principle whereby responsibility is divided up between the Union and the member states according to the nature of the problems. Furthermore, the differentiation between common action and cooperation makes the incorporation in the Union of intergovernmental matters possible. In the institutional field the aim is co-decision with the Council. This takes into account the demand for a democratic legitimation of the exercise of power but at the same time the criteria of efficiency is also met by the introduction of time limits for decisions. A flexible procedure for the coming into force of the Union would also permit it to become a reality even in the face of opposition from individual EC states.

Even if political and academic circles consider some individual provisions in the Draft Treaty imprecise, impracticable and in need of revision, the Draft of February 14, 1984 is nevertheless a fully formulated treaty text for the establishment of European Union. This text appears, first, to be basically capable of being put into practice; secondly, it represents a compromise between the various political and regional trends in the Community; and thirdly, it was given the stamp of approval by a large majority of the MEPs.

This Draft Treaty already provided a focus for an intensive European political debate when it was still being worked out. All the Community institutions and the parliaments and governments of the member states had to take account of the document, even if they did so in varying ways and with varying results. The EP's strategy for implementing the Draft Treaty had three prongs but proved to be only partially successful. Only the beginnings of a substantial mobilization of public opinion for the EP's aims - above all during the second European election campaign - could be made. Cooperation with the national parliaments bore fruit for the most part, but because of their tendency to leave the political initiative to the governments this cooperation only played a supporting role in the central plank of the EP's strategy of exerting influence on the national governments. The latter could not shut themselves off entirely from the EP's demands for reform, but they did refuse to include the Draft Treaty among the subjects for discussion. Instead, procedural matters and pragmatic reforms in the direction of a 'policy of small steps' were agreed upon in various decisions taken by the European Council at Fontainebleau, Milan and Luxembourg. With the result of the Luxembourg negotiations, therefore, an intermediate stage on the road to a reform of the Community was reached. The struggle for European Union, however, continues.

Select Bibliography
Roland Bieber, Jean-Paul Jacqué and Joseph H.H. Weiler (eds), An ever-closer Union, A Critical Analysis of the Draft Treaty Establishing the European Union, Brussels 1975
Michael Burgess, 'Federal Ideas in the European Community: Altiero Spinelli and the European Union, 1981-1984', in: Government and Opposition, 1984, No. 3, pp. 339-347
Francesco Capotorti et al., Le Traité d'Union Européenne, Commentaire du projet adopté par le Parlement Europeen, Brussels 1985
Richard Corbett, &The European Parliament and its Initiatives', in: Contemporary Review 1984, No. 1421, pp. 292-298
Klaus Hänsch, 'The Reform Proposals, the Strategy of Small Steps Versus the General Reform' in: Rudolf Hrbek et al., Parlement Européen, Bilan et Perspectives 1979-1984, Bruges 1984, pp. 136-173
'Integration, Sonderheft zum Vertragsentwurf des Europäischen Parlaments' (including contributions by H. Schneider, U. Everling, W. Weidenfeld, H v.d. Groeben et al.), in: Integration, 1984, No. 1
Jean-Paul Jacqué, 'The Draft Treaty establishing the European Union', in: Common Market Law Review, 1985, No. 1, pp. 19-42
Juliet Lodge (ed), European Union. The European Community, in search of a future. London, 1986.
Juliet Lodge, 'European Union and the First Elected European Parliament: The Spinelli Initiative', in: Journal of Common Market Studies, 1984, No. 4, pp. 377-402
Dietmar Nickel, 'Der Entwurf des Europäischen Parlaments für einen Vertrag zur Gründung der Europäischen Union', in: Integration, 1985, No. 1, pp. 11-27
Dietmar Nickel and Richard Corbett, "The Draft Treaty Establishing European Union", in: Yearbook of European Law, 1985
Dietmar Nickel, "Le Projet de Traité instituant l'Union Européenne", in: Cahiers de droit Européen, 1984, Nos. 5-6, pp. 511-542
Ihgolf Pernice, "Verfassungsentwurf für eine Europäische Union", in: Europarecht, 1984, No. 2, pp. 126-142
Roy Pryce, Towards European Union, New Europe Papers, No. 8, A Federal Trust Study, October, 1983
Paul de Saint-Mittiel, "Le Projet de Traité instituant l'Union Européenne, in: Revue du Marché Commun, 1984, No. 276, pp. 149-152
Heinrich Schneider, Europäische Union durch das

Europäische Parlament - zur Initiative des Institutionellen Ausschusses", in: Integration, 1982, No. 4, pp. 150-163

Jürgen Schwarze and Roland Bieber (eds.), Eine Verfassung für Europa, Von der Europäische Gemeinschaft zur Europäischen Union, Baden-Baden, 1984

Hans-Joachim Seeler, "Vertrag zur Gründung der Europäischen Union", in: Europarecht, 1984, No. 1, pp. 41-53

Altiero Spinelli, Towards the European Union, Sixth Jean Monnet Lecture, European University Institute, Florence, 13 June 1984

Altiero Spinelli, "Die Parlamentarische Initiative zur Europäische Union", in Europa-Archiv, 1983, No. 24, pp. 739-746

G. de Thomasis, "Le Project d'Union Européenne à la veille de la campagne pour les deuxièmes élections Européennes", in: Revue du Marché Commun, 1984, No. 227, pp. 212-214

Wolfgang Wessels, "Der Vertragsentwurf des Europäischen Parlaments für eine Europäische Union, Kristallisationspunkt einer neuen Europa-Debatte", in: Europa-Archiv, 1984, No. 8, pp. 239-248

Notes

1. EC Official Journal, C.77, 19.3.84, p. 33 ff.

2. For the powers of the EP see Eberhard Grabitz and Thomas Läufer, Das Europäische Parlament, Bonn 1980; Michael Palmer, The European Parliament, What it is - What it does - How it works, Oxford etc. 1981; Jean-Paul Jacqué et al., Le Parlement Européen, Paris 1984

3. Ronald Inglehart et al., "Broader Powers for the European Parliament? The Attitudes of Candidates", in: European Journal of Political Research, 1980, No. 8, p. 122

4. "Resolution of the EP of 21 December 1961" (Pleven Resolution), in European Parliament, Committee on Institutional Affairs, Selection of texts concerning institutional matters of the Community from 1950 to 1982, Luxembourg 1982, pp. 116-118

5. "Resolution of the EP of 10 July 1975" (Bertrand Report), ibid. pp. 342-348

6. EP Doc. 148/78

7. EP session reports, EC Official Journal, Appendix No. 233, September 1978, p. 128

8. See manifesto of November 20, 1977, as

documented in: Martin Bangemann et al., <u>Programme für Europa</u>, Bonn 1978, p. 243 ff.

9. European People's Party, political programme of March 7, 1978, ibid. p. 213 f.

10. Confederation of Social Democrat and Socialist Parties in the European Community, Election manifesto of June 6, 1977, ibid., p. 148

11. Declaration by the leaders of the Social Democrat and Socialist Parties in the EC, dated 23 June, 1978

12. For example, statements distinctly favourable to the idea of integration were contained in the SPD's manifesto for the 1979 European elections

13. On the position of the British Conservatives see Richard Rose, "The British Conservative Party", in: Roger Morgan and Stefano Silvestri, <u>Moderates and Conservatives in Western Europe</u>, London 1982, pp. 94-116

14. See Jean Charlot, "The Gaullist Party", in: ibid. pp. 55-72.

15. The Folkebevaegelsen mod EF obtained 20.9% of the total votes in the 1979 European elections and 20.8% in the 1984 European elections, giving it 4 seats in the EP on each occasion - cf. Ole Borre, "Denmark", in: <u>Electoral Studies</u>, Vol. 3 (1984), No. 3, pp. 268-273.

16. The results of the first European elections are set out in <u>EC Bulletin</u>, No. 6/1979, 1.3.1.-1.3.4.

17. Altiero Spinelli described this very graphically in his lecture <u>Towards the European Union</u> (see Select Bibliography above).

18. For details of this see Klaus Hänsch, "The Reform Proposals, The Strategy of 'Small Steps' versus the General Reform", in: Rudolf Hrbek et al. (ed.), op.cit., pp. 136-173; Bruno Bengel et al., <u>Nur verpasste Chancen, Die Reformberichte der Europäischen Gemeinschaft</u>, Bonn 1983, pp. 64-72.

19. C.f. for example Focke's statements in the EP on July 9, 1981 in: <u>Proceedings of the European Parliament, EC Official Journal</u>, Appendix 1-273, p. 244.

20. EP Doc. 1-347/79.

21. On this see also Rita Cardozo and Richard Corbett "The Crocodile Initiative", in: Juliet Lodge (ed.), <u>European Union: The EC in Search of a Future</u>, London 1986.

22. See Extracts from the first issue of the <u>Crocodile</u>, in: <u>Towards European Union, From the Crocodile to the European Council in Milan (28-29 June 1985), Documents selected and introduced by</u>

<u>Marina Gazzo</u>, (Agence Europe), Brussels and Luxembourg 1985, pp. 11-17.

23. EP Doc. 1-889/80, 6.2.1981.

24. "Resolution setting up a committee on institutional affairs (9 July 1981)" in <u>EC Official Journal</u>, C234, 14 September 1981.

25. EP Doc. 1-940/81 rev. II ("Jonker Plan").

26. See among others, Altiero Spinelli, <u>Manifest der europäischen Föderalisten</u>, Frankfurt 1958.

27. Based on table in <u>The New Federalist</u>, No. 2, 1984, p.10.

28. Article 23.3 gives the representatives of the Member States in the Council a modified right of veto for a transitional period of 10 years.

29. According to Article 32.3 the European Council determines its own decision-making procedure; see also Article 68.2.

30. Cf. Ulrich Everling, "Zur Rechtsstruktur einer Europäischen Verfassung", in: <u>Integration</u>, Vol. 7, 1984, No. 1, p. 12 f.; and John Pinder in Roland Bieber et al., op.cit., pp. 103-126.

31. This was criticised above all in the German debate on the Draft Treaty; see for example the statements by Dieter Blumenwitz, an experts on the subject, at the hearing in the Foreign Affairs Committee of the German Bundestag on October 2, 1985 in: <u>Deutscher Bundestag, Auswärtiger Ausschuss</u>, 712-2450 (shorthand record of the 52nd session), pp. 70-73.

32. See John Pinder, ibid., p.125.

33. Claus Dieter Ehlermann, 1984, ibid., p.276.

34. Wolfgang Wessels 1984, ibid., p. 239 and p.242; Ulrich Everling, 1984, ibid., p.13.

35. EP Doc. 1-940/41 op.cit.

36. See the statements in the EP by K. Focke on September 19, 1983 in: <u>Proceedings of the EP, EC Official Journal</u>, Appendix 1-303, p. 242.

37. Article 23.3 was adopted under particular pressure from British Conservatives.

38. Cf. Dietmar Nickel 1985, in: Roland Bieber et al., op.cit., p.11.

39. EP decision of 6 July 1982, in: <u>EC Official Journal</u>, C238, dated 13 September 1982, p.27, (7).

40. cf. Joseph H.H. Weiler and James Modrall, "The Creation of the European Union and its Relation to the EEC Treaties", in Roland Bieber et al., op.cit., pp. 161-176.

41. Ulrich Everling 1984, op.cit., pp. 22 and 23.

42. Altiero Spinelli, <u>Towards European Union</u>, op.cit., pp. 23-25.

43. Commission of the European Communities, <u>Europe as seen by Europeans, 10 Years of European Polling - 1973-1983</u>, Luxembourg 1983, p.22.

44. Commission of the European Communities, <u>Eurobarometer</u> No. 21, Brussels 1984, p. 13.

45. Ibid.; in part the author's own evaluations.

45. On this see the detailed country-by-country reports in: <u>Electoral Studies</u>, Vol. 3, 1984, No. 3.

46. This was the case above all with the Liberals and the EPP.

47. For example, the European Movement put the Draft Treaty in the forefront of its Congress in March 1984 in Brussels.

48. cf. Agence Europe, 21.10.1983 and 6-7.2.1984.

49. See Klaus Pöhle, "Relations between the European Parliament and National Parliaments", in: Rudolf Hrbek et al. op.cit., pp. 508-517.

50. German Bundestag, 10th parliamentary term, Foreign Affairs Committee - 712-2450, shorthand record of the 52nd session - public session for the provision of information on Wednesday, October 2, 1985, Bonn.

51. See report by Seeler, EP. Doc. A2-16/85, April 9, 1985.

52. See for example the EP decision on the Ad Hoc Committee for European Union of July 27, 1984, para. 3, in: <u>EC Official Journal</u>, C239, 10.9.1984.

53. See "Élaborer en commun une constituion européenne", in: <u>Le Soir</u>, 9.1.1983; "Kohl fordert eine politische Union Europas", in: <u>Frankfurter Allgemeine Zeitung</u>, 5.4.1984.

54. <u>Bulletin of the European Communities</u>, 5/1984, 3.4.1.

55. See Agence Europe. No. 3835, 19.4.1984, p.3.

Chapter Ten

THE EUROPEAN COUNCIL'S AD HOC COMMITTEE ON INSTITUTIONAL AFFAIRS (1984-85)

Patrick Keatinge and Anna Murphy

THE FONTAINEBLEAU INITIATIVE

The conclusions of the European Council, meeting at Fontainebleau on 25-26 June 1984, referred to a decision to establish two committees to advance the concept of European Union. One, the Adonnino Committee, was instructed to make proposals to promote the image of a 'people's Europe' among the general public, but the purpose of the second group was more directly related to political change. It was described as 'an ad hoc Committee consisting of personal representatives of the Heads of State and of Government, on the lines of the Spaak Committee', created in order 'to make suggestions for the improvement of the operation of European cooperation in both the Community field and that of political, or any other, cooperation'. (1) For the following twelve months the deliberations of this group - variously called the 'Ad hoc Committee on/for Institutional Affairs', the 'Spaak II Committee', or the 'Dooge Committee' - served as the focus for the evolving debate on European Union. The multiciplicity of titles is itself an indication both of the purpose of the exercise and of some of the ambiguities and tensions it entailed; by the end of the period under review perhaps the most widespread usage was to refer to the chairman's name and this is the form adopted here.

The establishment of the new body must be seen in the context of the two attempts to define and implement European Union which had evolved in the very recent past, the Solemn Declaration on European Union, signed at Stuttgart in June 1983, and the European Parliament's Draft Treaty establishing the European Union, which had been adopted by the Parliament in February 1984. (2) President

Mitterrand, speaking at the European Parliament on 24 May 1984, had already suggested 'preparatory consultations' about a new treaty arrangement, to be based on both these initiatives, and the Stuttgart Declaration in any case committed its signatories to a 'review of progress towards European Union' by 1988 at latest. The task of the Dooge Committee, therefore, could be seen as an attempt to translate a wide range of existing views on the nature of European integration into politically acceptable terms which would lead to significant political reform. That this was an ambitious proposal was evident from the obvious gap between the minimalist and maximalist orientations of the Stuttgart and Parliament documents respectively.

The circumstances in which the initiative was taken combined to present a rare 'window of opportunity'. The Fountainebleau summit saw a resolution in principle of the long-standing dispute between the British government and its partners over the budget issue, and a resolve to expedite the accession of Spain and Portugal, planned to take place in eighteen months time. In effect the Community's first enlargement had been barely digested before the operational problems of further enlargement were to be faced. The brevity of the equilibrium so painfully achieved, particularly after the disastrous summit at Athens in December 1983, gave every incentive to act urgently. The newly elected members of the European Parliament, for their part, conscious of the apathy demonstrated in the poll the previous month, were anxious that reforms be achieved well before they had to face the electorate again.

Domestic considerations also amounted to an uneasy and transitory equilibrium. The governments of the major states were secure in the short term, and in the normal course of events would not have to face national elections before 1986. However, given the persistence of large-scale unemployment throughout the Community and sluggish performance in the leading economies no government could afford to be complacent. Both opinion polls and electoral tests indicated an awareness of the limitations of existing policies, and in so far as solutions were to be found at the European level a more decisive approach at that level might even offer electoral dividends.

The global environment in the summer of 1984 offered some room for manoeuvre. East-West relations, so far as Washington and Moscow were concerned were stalemated. There were no significant arms control negotiations following the 'Euro-missiles' deployment late in 1983 (though the Conference on Disarmament in Europe in Stockholm kept the lines open formally). Both superpowers were in the throes of a leadership hiatus; the brief interregnum of an ailing Chernenko was matched by Ronald Reagan's campaign for re-election. The latter's visit to western Europe at the beginning of June had perhaps been addressed as much to his domestic audience as to the immediate concerns of East-West diplomacy. The issues of western solidarity, both economic and political, did not disappear, but American preoccupation with the presidential election did serve to keep them in the 'pending' tray.

It can be argued that such an ambitious proposal as that made at Fontainebleau could only be plausibly advanced by one of the major member-states and with a visible and effective commitment at the highest political level. These conditions were certainly met in this case. France's Presidency of the Council in the first half of 1984 saw the crystallisation of Francois Mitterrand's European policy, itself elevated to a higher place in his government's priorities; nothing illustrated this more strikingly than the personal involvement of the President himself, 'véritable homme-orchestre.' (3) A major element of Mitterrand's political reputation was at stake, the more so given the increasing difficulties he was encountering elsewhere.

The strategy of the Fontainebleau initiative reflected an emphasis on 'high politics'. The Ad Hoc Committee was a creation of the European Council, brought into being by that body, composed of personal representatives of its members, and ultimately accountable to it. The explicit reference to the Spaak Committee seemed to add emphasis to this fact, and even to offer guidelines for the new group's procedures and function. However, a closer examination suggests that the analogy may have emerged more as a rhetorical device by the Presidency than as a serious attempt to ensure that history would repeat itself. (4) The Spaak model implied that the enterprise would be led from the outset by a political personality who, emerging from the consistory at Fontainebleau, would subsequently remain aloof from a national point of view. But given the notorious confusion surrounding proceedings of the European Council, it is not surprising that this did not occur; indeed, some participants had little recollection of the matter being discussed in detail.

In the event the implementation of the decision was simply left to the incoming President of the Council, the Irish premier, Dr Garret FitzGerald, and the latter appears to have received little further direction. It was generally assumed that the new committee was to operate, as the Spaak Committee had done, outside the routine administrative frameworks of either the Community or national levels. Spaak's brief had been daunting enough, but the outcome now being sought was so general as to be essentially ambiguous throughout the committee's existence and beyond. The invocation of Spaak and a 'new Messina', in conjunction with President Mitterrand's references to a new treaty, reflected expectations of significant political change, but the rest of the wording of the conclusions of Fontainebleau – where 'cooperation' prevails over 'union' by two to zero – suggested quite another ending.

PROCESS AND PROCEDURES

The chronology of the Dooge Committee consists of three phases, punctuated by successive meetings of the European Council. During the first phase, as the Committee was set up and produced an interim report to the Dublin Council (3–4 December 1984), the political environment did not change significantly from that prevailing at Fontainebleau. The Dublin Council, mainly preoccupied by the enlargement issue, merely noted this document and requested that the final report be submitted by the time of the Brussels Council (29–30 March 1985), although full consideration was to be held over until the Milan Council (28–29 June 1985).

By the second phase, between Dublin and Brussels, the interests of national administrations had been aroused and this was reflected in some of the differences between the interim and final reports. The third phase was more confused. After submitting the final report to the Brussels summit the Dooge Committee itself was disbanded, though its recommendations had not yet been decided on. The preparation for this part of the process was entrusted to the Italian Presidency, under Signor Craxi, a task complicated by the effects of significant changes in the environment which are examined below.

The procedures to be followed by any ad hoc deliberative body are in themselves the first questions to be agreed, and may reflect important substantive differences. The ambiguity surrounding the conclusions of Fontainebleau was not altogether surprisingly followed by a 'misunderstanding' over the composition of the Committee and the role of its chairman. In July Dr FitzGerald chose James Dooge, leader of the Irish Senate and a former foreign minister, as his representative and, in his capacity as President of the Council, he informed the other governments that the latter was 'available' to act as chairman. At this stage it seems that no alternative candidate for the chair was being promoted but at the beginning of September, just before the Committee was due to meet, it became public knowledge that Chancellor Kohl was dissatisfied with the status of some of the nominations, most of which had already been made. This criticism, associated with a German preference for their former President, Karl Carstens, as chairman, was also evident in the Belgian government, perhaps mindful for its part of the Spaak tradition and the experience of its foreign minister, Leo Tindemans. These reservations caused a delay in the Committee's establishment, though the Germans did not press the point further, even when the Irish Presidency ended at the New Year. The confusion did, however, represent the first manifestation of crossed lines within the German government, a phenomenon which was to recur over the following months.

Senator Dooge did not see himself as the reincarnation of Paul Henri Spaak. His first concern was that the Committee should respond to the urgency of the situation, and that its members should operate effectively as a unit. In this respect his role as chairman rested on an ability to develop informal contacts among the group rather than attempting to act as the primary source of substantive innovation. Coming from the one 'new' member-state which did not display marked objections in principle to further integration, he was perhaps in a favourable position to attempt to bridge the gap between these countries and the original six.

The composition of the Committee is summarised in the accompanying Table 10.1. Formerly the representatives of the national leaders, the members were a heterogeneous mix of political figures (with ministerial as well as parliamentary experience) and of senior officials. The latter generally had considerable acquaintance with the working of the Community, though their professional connections with national administrations raised doubts about their political weight. In terms of his background,

Table 10.1: Membership of the Dooge Committee

	Representing Head of Government of:	Background
Frans Andriessen (to end 1984)	EC Commission	Commissioner
Jean Dondelinger	Luxembourg	Diplomat, former Permanent Representative to the Community
James Dooge (Chair)	Ireland	Leader of Senate, former foreign minister
Maurice Faure	France	Signatory of Rome Treaties, former minister, member of Monnet Action Committee
Mauro Ferri	Italy	Former chairman of EP Committee on Institutional Affairs
Fernand Herman	Belgium	Member of EP Committee on Institutional Affairs, former minister
Otto Møller	Denmark	Senior official, foreign ministry
Ionnis Papantoniou	Greece	Advisor to prime minister, former MEP
Malcom Rifkind	United Kingdom	Junior minister, foreign ministry
Carlo Ripa di Meana (from beginning 1985)	EC Commission	Commissioner, former member of EP Committee on Institutional Affairs
Jurgen Ruhfus	Federal Republic of Germany	Senior official, foreign ministry
Wilhelm van Eekelen	Netherlands	Junior minister, former senior official, foreign ministry

particularly his reputation as a European of the formative years, Maurice Faure was undoubtedly the dominant personality. His close personal relation ship with his head of state, who appears to have allowed him a considerable freedom of expression, gave added authority to his contribution. Similar personal relationships with their 'patrons' were enjoyed by some other members of the Committee (for example, Ferri, Dooge) but in other cases the connection was much less intimate. In particular, the German member, Jürgen Ruhfus, was probably in closer contact with his foreign and finance ministers than with his head of government. While during the first phase of the Committee's work it seems that most participants did not feel compelled to refer back in detail to their nominators, this was less true after the publication of the interim report. There were signs, for example, that the British member, Malcom Rifkind, consulted with Mrs Thatcher very closely about his contributions, and in general members encountered a wide range of domestic interests. The most formally constrained throughout was the Danish representative, Otto Møller, given the unequivocal political mandate and close surveillance which normally characterises Danish involvement in Community affairs. The Greek member's position was less obviously constricted but he did on occasion consult Athens by phone during meetings.

Each member had an assistant and a note-taker; collectively these formed a de facto secretariat which was managed by a core group of three: a coordinator nominated by the chairman and officials seconded from the Council and the Commission. (5) This 'light' secretariat, which had to be created from scratch, demonstrated a determination to maintain flexibility and independence from the bureaucratic structures of the Community; in this respect it was assisted by the provision of accommodation by the Belgian government and basic services supplied by the Council. By the same token it indicated the Committee's view that its task was not to explore technical or legal questions in any detail, as the Spaak Committee had attempted in 1955.

The Committee met eleven times in all, generally over two days. Strictly speaking it was not engaged in negotiations. Its members were not the plenipotentaries of governments, but rather were involved in a preliminary exploration of the national leaders' positions, in order to clarify the extent of agreement which might be possible. Thus in spite of the presence of advocates of the European

Parliament's Draft Treaty, that document was not used as the main basis of this 'pre-negotiation' phase, since it was generally accepted that an elaboration of the Parliament's approach would not be endorsed by the heads of government. Another early decision led to a novel feature in the format adopted for the Committee's report. Although it was agreed to aim at unanimity, this was not to be an overriding principle; thus where views differed from the majority position they were expressed in the form of reservations appearing as footnotes to the main text.

The Committee's working method consisted of the submission by individual members of brief papers on specific topics; these were then discussed within the context of a general overview paper which had been presented by Maurice Faure at the second meeting (hence a predeliction in France to refer to the end-product as the Faure report). Contact with Community institutions was ensured by formal participation of a representative of the President of the Commission and, informally the inclusion of present and former members of the European Parliament's Institutional Affairs Committee (Ferri, Herman, Ripa di Meana). In addition the Parliament's President, Pierre Pflimlin, met the Committee twice, and the chairman of the Institutional Affairs Committee, Altiero Spinelli, was present at three meetings; the President of the Economic and Social Committee, Gerd Muhr, also appeared. The question of the involvement of the applicant states, Spain and Portugal, was met by an agreement to keep them informed and towards the end of the Committee's work the personal representatives of their heads of government met the Committee. The proceedings of the meetings were confidential, though <u>Agence Europe</u> took a keen interest editorially and seemed generally to have access to information on a day-to-day basis.

Notwithstanding the expectations raised - for some in vain - by the Spaak analogy, the procedures of the Dooge Committee appear to have operated reasonably well. The final report was produced within the deadlines laid down and went far to clarify the extent to which agreement existed on both the objectives and mechanisms of a European Union. In this respect the critical parts of the report proved to be the footnotes, which generally made visible the obstacles to the success of the Genscher-Colombo initiative. However, the Committee succeeded in keeping some distance from the predators of intergovernmentalism who had savaged that exercise, at least until the Brussels European Council at the end of March 1985.

In the third phase, from then until the Milan summit, the task of 'selling' the report to the heads of government was given to the Italian Presidency. This involved a different political process, in which, mainly through bilateral consultations and a meeting of foreign ministers at Stresa (8-9 June 1985), the Italians sought to preserve the Dooge report as the basis for decisions at Milan. Inevitably, perhaps, 'counter'-proposals (such as the 'Howe Plan' submitted at Stresa) and 'counter-counter-proposals' (the Franco-German draft revealed on the eve of Milan) muddied the waters at a European Council which was more than usually incoherent. (6) Nevertheless, the Italian Presidency's advocacy of its draft mandate was energetically pursued and the active chairmanship of Signor Craxi at Milan at least kept the project alive for a further round of political decision.

THE ISSUES

The conclusions of Fontainebleau were, as we have seen, virtually open-ended on the subject-matter of the Dooge Committee's deliberations, thus accommodating the wide range of issues which had already been quite extensively discussed ·in the Genscher-Colombo framework and in the European Parliament. Agenda-setting was, therefore, more a matter of synthesising existing issues than of introducing new material. The first attempt to do this was reflected in guidelines suggested by Dr FitzGerald to Senator Dooge before the Committee met:

(1) the functioning and decision-making arrangements of the institutions and inter-relationships between them;
(2) the effectiveness of the Community's action in the social-economic sphere (including the European Monetary System) and in that of technology;
(3) the possibility and modalities of common action in, for example, the fields of education, culture, health, justice and the fight against terrorism; and
(4) progress towards European Union. (7)

Both the preface and the first section of the final report in effect placed this bare list in its general political context, as 'a qualitative leap' or

demonstration of political will to create a 'genuine political entity'; these general statements of intent attracted Danish and Greek reserves. (8)
     The bulk of the report consists of three sections: the first ('priority objectives') deals with substantive policies, the second ('the means') covers the central concern of decision-making, and the third ('the method') recommends a procedure to implement the rest of the report. The broadly socio-economic issues were characterised by a very considerable degree of agreement, at least at the high level of generality in which they were stated. In particular the need for a 'genuine' internal market was stressed, though it must be said that many of the specific national difficulties which were later raised at the intergovernmental conference in the autumn of 1985 were not alluded to. Technological innovation was also emphasized, an increasing awareness of deficiencies in the latter respect being seen during the brief life of the Committee. (9) On the other hand, the development of the EMS drew a predictable German reservation on the promotion of the ECU. (10) More contentious was the reference to economic convergence, which was in effect an uncertain compromise between the quite different notions of 'convergence-as-levelling-up-of-living standards' or 'solidarity' (espoused explicitly by the Greek representative and sotto voce by the Irish) and 'convergence-of-economic-policy' (supported by German, Dutch and Belgian footnotes). (11) A series of measures relating to 'the common values of civilization' and 'cultural values' received a wide measure of support; they were not explored in detail, partly because of the overlap with the parallel Ad Hoc Committee on a People's Europe (the 'Adonnino Committee').
     A second broad category of objectives concerned 'the search for an external identity', that is a consolidation and strengthening of European Political Cooperation (EPC) and the introduction of new objectives relating to 'security and defence'. Though not referred to in the FitzGerald guidelines, these matters did not appear out of the blue. Veterans of the Genscher-Colombo process could not have been surprised by Danish and Greek reserves on the first of these questions, nor the addition of Senator Dooge himself on the second. By the same token the common ground between the United Kingdom and the original Six was evident. This solidarity must be seen against the background of the concurrent reactivation of the Western European Union (WEU). The

Rome Declaration of October 1984 committed the WEU governments to consult each other more regularly and intensively within the context of the Western Alliance. This forum, which conveniently does not include Denmark, Greece or Ireland, was seen by some observers as a potential rival to European Political Cooperation. (12)

The clarification of attitudes towards objectives was however secondary to the section on institutional reform ('the means'). This was clearly regarded by the Committee as 'its real task'. (13) The consolidation of the role of the Court of Justice was the only wholly non-controversial item; by contrast, the Committee's positions on the Commission, the Parliament and, above all, the Council demonstrated sharp divisions. As regards the Commission, two matters in particular were the subject of debate, the ability of a President-designate to influence the choice of his future colleagues and the reduction of the size of the Commission to correspond with the number of member-states. (14) The proposed changes were rejected by the British and German representatives respectively.

The section on the Parliament reflected the concern of that body to 'democratize' Community decision-making by giving it an effective legislative role, which had been spelled out fully in the Draft Treaty. The Dooge report proceeded more cautiously in that direction, though not cautiously enough to win British, Danish or Greek acceptance. (15) By far the most important institutional section, however, was that devoted to the Council, and here, embedded among various pragmatically framed admonitions to good behaviour and a modest acceptance of 'differentiated Community rules', lies the crux of the matter, the proposals concerning 'principles of voting'. (16)

From the outset three options were on the table. The first was a continuation of the status quo, a position which itself could be rationalised either as constructive pragmatism or a diehard rejection of change. A contrasting proposal urged a decisive move to majority voting, where very exceptional recourse to unanimity would on no account be justified by reference to 'vital national interests'. The text of the interim report, which attempted a compromise position, represented a third option. (17) The concept of 'vital interest' was acknowledged but alongside the Community interest; the footnotes indicated dissatisfaction, from either side of the argument, from all but the representatives from

227

France, Italy and Ireland. In the most important single change between the first and second phase of the Committee's deliberations, this three-way split was formally reduced to two in the final report. The French and Italian representatives were moved to support the maximalist position, and on the last day the Committee met, after lengthy discussions about the form of presentation, majority and minority positions were formulated. The majority proposal excluded the term 'vital national interest' and the minority (Britain, Denmark, Greece) held to the existing political practice, at first sight suggesting a clear division of the Committee. But even here the footnote left its mark. An Irish reserve re-introduced the contentious phrase 'vital interest' to the majority proposal and the Luxembourg representative added an 'explanation' which was ambiguous to say the least.

The last section of the report ('the method')` though brief, was second in its political significance only to the proposal on Council voting. It called for an intergovernmental conference to negotiate a draft treaty of European Union, based on the 'acquis communautaire', the Stuttgart Solemn Declaration and the Dooge Report itself, and to be 'guided by the spirit and method' of the Parliament's Draft Treaty. It agreed that the decision to call such a conference would be such an important political commitment as to 'represent the initial act of European Union'. (18) Again the British, Danish and Greek members of the Committee demurred.

Taken as a whole the Dooge Committee's reports identified and clarified but did not reduce the areas of disagreement between the member-states; it thus did not have the effect of the Spaak Report of 1956. Read without the footnotes and appendices, it could be described by the President of the European Parliament, Pierre Pflimlin, as 'very close to the spirit of Parliament's draft'. (19) With the reserves, however, it is clear that the report indicated the composition of a possible two 'camps', and in this light European Union seemed to be taking the shape of the majority camp, based primarily on the original Six. This division had even been symbolised prior to the formulation of the interim report, when the assistants of the representatives of the Six held a preliminary meeting prior to a full meeting with their colleagues, a procedure which apparently did not find favour with the chairman. (20) Although this was not repeated, and had little substantive importance, the message was plain. The

will to come to the point of decision, however, did
not depend on the Committee's internal manoeuvring or
final proposals, but rather on the meeting of the
European Council at Milan.

The Conclusions of Milan

The Milan summit meeting on 28-29 June 1985 was the
first occasion on which the European Council gave the
best of its attention to a general consideration of
the future of European integration. (21) The Italian
Presidency, through its draft mandate, ensured that
the Dooge Report was on the table, but by this time
it was not alone; British and Franco-German drafts
which were almost exclusively concerned with
political cooperation and security (but misleadingly
labelled as 'European Union') were also present,
alongside the French 'Eureka' project for a
technological community and a comprehensive
Commission white paper on the internal market.

The political environment had recently become
decidedly more unsettled. The superpowers had
completed their change of leadership and renewed
their confrontation over arms control at Geneva. Here
Washington's insistence on President Reagan's
Strategic Defence Initiative (SDI) emerged as the
unnegotiable basis of the West's position, thereby
starting to assume the role of 'virility test' for
the Alliance in a way reminiscent of the Euromissiles
decision of 1979. SDI also raised the issue of
western Europe's technological deficiences (thus
acting as a spur for Eureka), but in a manner which
was often divisive, particularly between Paris and
Bonn. At the summit meeting of the major
industrialised powers in Bonn in May, President
Mitterrand found little support from his German
colleague, who was in the throes of serious
embarrassment over President Reagan's handling of
the commemoration of the allied victory in the Second
World War. A further serious disruption came with
Bonn's invoking of the veto over cereal prices barely
two weeks before the European Council. This decision,
the first such act in the Federal Republic's history,
was largely explicable in terms of domestic politics,
but was widely seen as a fatal contradiction in the
government's European policy.

Given these circumstances, it was hardly
surprising if the Milan meeting was approached with
despair by the protagonists of reform and with some
complacency by their opponents, and that in the event
it proved to be marked by incoherence. Yet it did not

end in futility, but rather with a series of agreements in its conclusions which were susceptible to opposed interpretations. (22) Supporters of the 'majority-camp' in the Dooge Committee could point to the retention of the major elements in its Report. (23) The principle 'objectives' were present, including a further stage in the realisation of the Eureka project, but the critical element was that, with a good deal of assistance from the determined and creative chairmanship of Signor Craxi, the Intergovernmental Conference - the mechanism for Dooge's 'method' - would in fact be convened. This decision was, for the first time in the European Council, taken on a majority vote. If this result demonstrated the divisions on institutional reform proper, which had been evident in the Dooge Committee, its expression at the highest political level was evidence for many of real political will to accomplish change. Thus for President Mitterrand Milan represented 'a cleaning up' and a step towards 'the test of truth'; (24) it was seen as the pursuit of a 'core-area' strategy, in which the pace of reform would be forced, irrespective of the need for consensus implied in revision of the existing treaties.

A more sceptical assessment was also quite prevalent. (25) Agreement on objectives was still generalised and incomplete; for example, the mandate for the intergovernmental conference, as expressed in the conclusions, referred to both British and Franco-German drafts on political cooperation, which different in emphasis and, in the case of the latter, did not really expand the scope for cooperation in the field of security. Nor did the Milan conclusions refer, as the Dooge Report had done, to a single draft treaty of European Union as being the aim of the proposed intergovernmental conference. On the contrary, a formalisation of EPC in treaty terms plus piecemeal amendment of the EEC Treaty under Article 236 was implied, and this did not necessarily provide for a comprehensive and coherent framework for European Union. Above all, the holding of an intergovernmental conference was no guarantee of its success, a repeat of the divisions at Milan being more than likely to occur. And, at a deeper level, the question was raised whether a 'two-camp' Europe, even if achieved, was in the end desirable.

Actors and Interests
If the Milan summit did not prove to be the expected

'end game' to the initiative taken twelve months earlier, it did illustrate the proposition that in order to understand political change in European integration it is essential to look closely at national actors and their interests. The Dooge Committee, deliberately designed to clarify national positions, represents a fruitful case-study in this respect.

The political leadership of France and Germany is generally regarded as the most important single factor in explaining deliberate acts of political change. In the case of France during the period under review, as during other periods when the transfer of sovereignty was at issue, (26) there was an evident inclination to innovate in European policy. Mitterrand's personal involvement before and at Fontainebleau and Faure's position in the Dooge Committee have been referred to already; suffice it to say that it often seemed that the pace of events hung on the French President's most cryptic comment. His speech to the European Parliament in May 1984 had raised expectations of significant political leadership and his more pessimistic demeanour twelve months later suggested that he was having second thoughts about forcing the pace, with the possible loss of British involvement. In general Mitterrand's European policy seemed to be moving away from the tradition of l'Europe des Etats and even from that other fixed point in de Gaulle's constellation, an independent defence policy. (27) All of this occurred in spite - or perhaps, too, because of - the President's decline in popular opinion and the prospects of facing a hostile Assembly in 1986.

A similar disposition to lead was not, however, evident in the Federal Republic. The problems encountered in the German nomination to the Dooge Committee, and the question of the chairmanship, were largely self-inflicted. The centrifugal effects of bureaucratic competition, especially between the Chancellery and Foreign Ministry, were not compensated by political direction based on clear long term priorities. Chancellor Kohl did not fail to declare his support for European Union in general terms, but was more sensitive than his French counterpart to reverses in domestic politics, particularly in regional elections, for the implications of Community reforms for the rights of the Länder were emerging as issues early in 1985. Decisions taken in Bonn too often contradicted the Chancellor's rhetoric. At no time was this more destructive than during the crisis over cereal prices in May and June 1985; the insistence on the veto seemed to be a fatal blow to the credibility of the government's broad European policy.

This asymmetry in Franco-German relations was a marked feature of the third phase of the Dooge project. (28) At the summit of the major western powers at Bonn in May serious differences over SDI and the GATT were evident, and a bilateral meeting later that month failed to resolve doubts about the two leaders' unity of purpose. The presentation of the 'Draft Treaty of European Union' on the eve of the Milan summit, with its narrow focus on political cooperation, seemed to reflect a loss of interest in the main substance of the Dooge Report. Even in the manner of its presentation the political leadership of Paris and Bonn seemed disjointed and unconvincing. (29) Yet the potential for decisive direction lay not far underneath this record of rather indifferent collaboration; the emergence of wide support in France for a significantly more 'European' orientation in defence policy would seem to consolidate the two countries' common interests in the long term. (30)

Of the other members of the 'majority camp' which provided core support for the Fontainebleau initiative, Italy was especially prominent. This was no accident, given the extent of Italian interest and participation in both the European Parliament's Draft Treaty and the Genscher-Colombo initiative. The importance of the large issues, even the 'ideology', of European integration in the context of Italian party and parliamentary politics ensured that politicians had every incentive to place the Dooge Committee's activities high on their agendas. For some, such as Altero Spinelli, the main concern was that the report did not go far enough and could be used to deflect attention from the Draft Treaty, but in general there was a willingness to emphasise the similarities rather than the differences between the two projects. The coincidence of Italy's Presidency of the Council with the second and third phases provided the opportunity for the Italian government to play an important leadership role. The opportunity was seized energetically and often successfully. In this case, unlike the German one, competition within the government may even have had positive effects as the head of government, Bettino Craxi, and the foreign minister, Guilio Andreotti, sought to match each other's successes. Thus the former had a key part in extracting the intergovernmental conference from the confusion at

Milan, while the latter was responsible for promoting the Dooge report at a time when the Paris-Bonn axis was in some disarray.

Among the smaller states, the Benelux tradition was maintained, most noticeably by Belgium. From the outset it was only to be expected, given the references to Spaak at Fontainebleau, that the Belgian government would have definite ideas as to how the initiative should proceed. In the Dooge Committee Fernand Herman appears to have been particularly active in pressing the maximalist option on the key issue of majority voting which prevailed in the final report; hence his triumphal footnote drawing attention to the 'considerable progress' since the interim report. (31) After the publication of the report the Belgian government even considered taking the initiative in promoting it prior to the Milan summit. (32) Throughout the period under review the Belgians were moving beyond their traditional insistence on working within the orthodox framework of the Rome treaties, particularly with regard to the reactivation of the WEU. The Netherlands, on the other hand, appear to have played a more muted role, possibly with a view to maintaining links with the British rather than emphasising the division in the Committee. Luxembourg's general support was evident, though Jean Dondelinger's curious reservation on majority voting suggests a lack of precise instructions.

Ireland's approach was governed by a decision to enter a reserve 'only on matters of the most explicit and fundamental principle'. (33) Increased sensitivities about neutrality necessitated a blanket reserve on the section on 'security and defence', though the eventual emphasis on the WEU (e.g. in the Franco-German draft at Milan) afforded some relief in this regard. Otherwise the government seemed anxious to be on the side of the angels, but a second reserve was reluctantly placed on the final formulation of the veto issue, on the grounds that it disguised critical difficulties. (34) The fresh memory of Ireland's invocation of the veto in March 1984 may have diluted political will on this question; nevertheless in the unprecedented vote at Milan on the intergovernmental conference Ireland was in the majority camp.

This was not true of the other two 'new' small states. Denmark and Greece expressed their position in rather different styles. The Danish view, well-known in advance of the Fontainebleau initiative, could be described as that of a 'strict

constitutionalist'. Opposition to change was put in
the context of the treaties, which were regarded as
adequate as a legal basis but which had not been
implemented. This theme ran through Mr Møller's
individual footnotes as well as in his annex to the
report where, in effect, the footnote becomes the
report. Against a background of continuing
opposition to a deepening of European integration,
clearly articulated in the Danish parliament,
nothing was more predictable than this position,
softened only by the recognition for 'a new impetus'
and the need for new resources for technology. (35)
The Greek representative, Mr Papantoniou, was, if
anything, more generous with reserves and was equally
negative on institutional reform; he also repeatedly
persisted with the theme of the redistribution of
resources to the poorer regions. (36) At the European
Council his head of Government, Mr Papandreou, who
strengthened his domestic base in a snap general
election at the beginning of June 1985, continued to
play a spoiling role.

Of the three states in the minority camp, the
United Kingdom alone had the political weight to
offer a comprehensive alternative to the possibility
of a treaty-based European Union. This was consistent
with the orthodoxy of pragmatism which has generally
lain at the root of British attitudes to integration,
where 'Union' was often seen at worst as a form of
'creeping federalism' and at best as the expression
of an irrelevant and politically empty intellectual
fad. But so long as British governments, once in the
Community, felt it necessary to concentrate on a
series of 'renegotiations' of the terms of entry it
was difficult to mount a positive challenge to the
original members' insistence on 'structures',
'institutions' and legal formulations, and to
promote an alternative vision of the future.

The success of the European Council at
Fontainebleau marked a turning point in this respect;
indeed Mrs Thatcher arrived at the meeting with her
own paper entitled 'Europe – the future'. (37) This
document, apart from a brief citation of the preamble
to the EEC Treaty, did not contain the word 'union',
but, so far as institutional reform was concerned,
listed specific changes mainly of a procedural
nature. The government's reluctance to countenance
treaty amendment or a new treaty is explicable both
in terms of Mrs Thatcher's sensitivity towards
'sovereignty' and the existence in both the
Conservative and Labour Parties of large minorities
with a similar view. This minimalist approach was

supplemented, however, by a much greater emphasis on policy objectives. Mr Rifkind's position in the Dooge Committee followed this pattern. There was a remarkable degree of agreement with the majority on objectives (against a background in which it seemed that joining the EMS was only a matter of time), while the reserves on institutional reforms attempted to indicate the possibilities of procedural change within the existing treaty obligations. (38)

In the third phase of the negotiations, while Paris and Bonn faltered, the British government advanced the 'Howe Plan' at the foreign ministers' meeting in Stresa; this consisted mainly of a code of good behaviour in decision-taking and a 'draft agreement' on Political Cooperation. At the same time Mrs Thatcher made it clear that she regarded a future intergovernmental conference as superfluous. In the month proceding the Milan summit it seemd that this was what 'European Union' would amount to, and the unexpected last minute decision at Milan to procede to an inter-governmental conference was seen as a significant tactical reverse for the British.

Although the Milan vote demonstrated the divide between the United Kingdom, Denmark and Greece and their partners, it did not in itself offer an insuperable obstacle to the continued defence of the minimalist position. The mandate for the intergovernmental conference was sufficiently broad to permit the participation of both camps, each of which was to be fully represented in the next phase of the search for political reform.

Notes
1.   For the conclusions of the European Council at Fontainebleau, see Agence Europe, 28 June 1984.
2.   See chapters 8 and 9.
3.   Philippe Moreau Defarges, '"... J'ai fait un reve ..." le président Francois Mitterrand, artisan de l'union européenne', Politique Étrangère, Autumn, 1985, p. 368.
4.   For the Spaak Committee, see chapter 4.
5.   For the organization of the Committee, see Katherine Meenan, 'The Work of the Dooge Committee', Administration, Vol. 33, no. 4. Ms Meenan, an adviser to the Taoiseach, Dr Fitzgerald, acted as coordinator of the secretariat.
6.   For the 'Howe Plan', see Agence Europe, 22 June 1985; for the Franco-German draft, see Agence

Europe, 29 June 1985.
   7.   Quoted   in   Meenan,   op.cit.,   p.581.
Striking by its absence from item 3 is 'security and
defence', though this is hardly surprising given the
provenance of the Guidelines.
   8.   Ad Hoc Committee on Institutional Affairs:
Interim report to the European Council (Dublin, 3-4
December 1984); Report to the European Council
(Brussels, 29-30 March 1985).
   9.   See Report, Section II.A (a) 1 and (b); see
also Meenan, op.cit., p.584, p.587.
   10.   Report, Section II.A (c).
   11.   Report,   Section   II.A   (a)   3;   see   also
Meenan, op.cit., p.584.
   12.   For   attitudes   of   EC   states   to   the
reactivation of the WEU, see P. Tsakaloyannis (ed.),
The Reactivation of the Western European Union the
Effects on the EC and its Institutions, European
Institute   of   Public   Administration,   Maastricht,
1985.
   13.   Meenan, op.cit., p.585.
   14.   Report, Section III.B.
   15.   Report, Section III.C.
   16.   Report, Section III.A.
   17.   Interim report, Section III.A.
   18.   Report, Section II.
   19.   European   Parliament,   A   new   phase   in
European Union, May 1985. This document provides a
useful parallel text of the Draft Treaty and the
Dooge Report, but without the reserves contained in
the latter. For a comparison between the Dooge
reports and the European Parliament's Draft Treaty,
see Roland Bieber, Jean-Paul Jacqué, and Joseph H.H.
Weiler (eds.) An ever closer Union, Commission of the
European Communities, Brussels, 1985, pp.9-14; Otto
Schmuck,   'Integrationsschub   durch   neuen   Vertrag?
Reformperspektiven   im   Vorfeld   des   Mailander
Gipfels', Integration 2/85.
   20.   There   are   indications   that   the   Irish
assistant was invited, but was not permitted to
attend.
   21.   For the Milan summit, see Otto Schmuck and
Wolfgang   Wessels,   'Die   Mailänder   Tagung   des
Europäischen   Rates   -   Weder   Fehlschlag   noch
Durchbruck zur Europäischen Union', Integration
3/85.
   22.   For the full text of the conclusions of
Milan and some other texts submitted during the
meeting, see Agence Europe, 30 June, 1 July 1985.
   23.   See for example, the interview with James
Dooge himself in The Irish Times, 2 July 1985.

24. Agence Europe, 30 June 1985.
25. Among the more severe critics of the Milan summit was the British media; see, for example, The Financial Times, 1 July 1985.
26. Moreau Defarges, op.cit., p.363.
27. Ibid, pp.371-72.
28. See Schmuck and Wessels, op.cit., pp.99-100.
29. See Le Monde, 29 June 1985.
30. See The Financial Times, 22 July 1985. It must be said, however, that the dispute over the 'Eurofighter' project later in the summer demonstrated the limits of common interests at a more specific level.
31. Report, Seciton III.A. For Mr Herman's views, see 'L'Union européenne avant le Conseil européene de Milan'. Institut d'Études européennes, Université libre de Bruxelles, 1985.
32. Agence Europe, 13/14 May 1985.
33. Meenan, op.cit., p.583. For Ireland's position, see C.P. Fogarty, 'European Union: Implications for Ireland', Administration Vol. 33, No. 4. The author is Deputy Secretary of the Department of Foreign Affairs.
34. For Senator's Dooge's comments, see Community Report, (Dublin EC Office) Vol. 5, No. 5, May 1985, pp.14-15.
35. Report, Annex A; Section II.A.(a).
36. See especially, Report, Annex B.
37. See Journal of Common Market Studies, Vol. XXIII, No. 1, September, 1984.
38. See Rifkind's reserves on majority voting and the European Parliament: Report, Section III.A. and C.

Chapter Eleven

THE 1985 INTERGOVERNMENTAL CONFERENCE AND THE SINGLE EUROPEAN ACT

Richard Corbett

The Intergovernmental Conference (IGC) held at the end of 1985, which led to the adoption of the 'Single European Act' in 1986, was the culmination of the process launched initially by the European Parliament and described in the preceeding two chapters. This chapter will describe the IGC and the events surrouding it and attempt to evaluate its outcome (1).

PROCEDURE AND METHODS

The Convening of the Conference

The political momentum built up · in favour of Community reform was sufficient to induce a majority of Member States to convene an Intergovernmental Conference by a majority vote at the European Council meeting in Milan. However, within such a Conference, unanimity is required for the approval of treaty amendments. It was clear that much would depend on the reaction of the three minority States (UK, Greece and Denmark) which had opposed the convening of the IGC. Much would depend too on the cohesion of the majority, which had displayed different priorities and motivations in the run-up to the summit.

Not wishing to provide any excuse for procedural delays over the summer, the European Parliament (EP), in its last session before the recess, approved a resolution giving its formal opinion as required by Art. 236 for the convening of an IGC. (2) The EP, having had a full report from the Commission President, Jacques Delors, to its Institutional Committee the day after his return from Milan, approved a resolution expressing satisfaction at the convening of an IGC, calling for it to work in partnership with the EP, and reiterating its position that, should some States block all moves to Union, those wishing to establish one should do so by themselves.

The necessary formal proposal put forward by the new Luxembourg Presidency proposed that the revision of the EEC-Treaty 'should be undertaken with a view to improving Council's decision-making procedures, strengthening the Commission's executive power, increasing the powers of the European Parliament and extending common policies to new fields of activity' (3). In convening the IGC on this basis, Council broke with precedent. Previous revisions of the Treaty were negotiated within the Council, often in close association with the other institutions, and the IGC had merely provided formal assent (4). This time, the real negotiations were to take place in the IGC, the outcome of which was unknown when the other institutions gave their favourable opinions.

Council was able to convene the IGC on the 22 July without opposition from the recalcitrant States, who were willing to participate in the procedure whilst reserving their position on the outcome. There was some argument as to whether a separate IGC should be convened to draft a political cooperation treaty, but it was decided to deal with both matters in a single conference of the level of Foreign Ministers. This would not pre-empt the decision on having a single or two Acts, and each aspect would be prepared by a specific working group. The political directors (senior national officials dealing with EPC) prepared the drafts regarding political cooperation, and a group chaired by Jean Dondelinger (the Luxembourg Member of the Dooge Committee) and composed largely of the permanent representatives of the Member States dealt with revisions of the EEC-Treaty. This not only left open until the end the question of separating EPC and Community matters (which Greece and Denmark were keen on): it also left open the possibility of threatening to sign an EPC-Treaty among only a certain number of Member States should negotiations become blocked.

Work also began on the two other procedures launched in Milan. First, Eureka began to take shape as a separate intergovernmental framework that would nevertheless involve the Community (5). It served as a reminder that it was possible to set up alternative frameworks to deal with major policy initiatives on terms set by certain major States, not necessarily involving the same membership as the Community. Second, consideration was given to the European Council's request that the Council 'study the institutional conditions in which the completion of the internal market could be achieved within the desired time limit'. This referred to institutional improvements not requiring Treaty amendments. A document drafted by the Presidency (6) concerned four main subjects: (i) altering the Council's Rules of Procedure to provide for a vote when requested by the President, the Commission or a majority of delegations; (ii) an undertaking by Member States to abstain rather than vote against proposals requiring unanimity where the measures concern an objective laid down by the European Council; (iii) an undertaking by those States which believe that the 'Luxembourg compromise' allows them to block a decision by invoking a vital national interest that they would do so only if they could justify such an interest in writing to the European Council; and (iv) the possibility of exempting member states from certain obligations.

Although discussed twice in COREPER, Council decided to leave these matters until after the IGC, as their combination with Treaty changes could crucially affect the impact of the latter.

The European Parliament and the IGC

The EP was wary of what it saw as the inevitable tendency for national officials to water down European proposals into minimal compromises, as had so often happened in the past (7). Indeed, this was one of the reasons which led Parliament itself to draft a Treaty, thrashed out as a political compromise among the major political parties represented in the EP, and presented directly to national governments and Parliaments for consideration, hoping to gain enough political momentum to overcome bureaucratic inertia. It was aware that a phase of intergovernmental negotiation and signature was necessary for a new Treaty (be it a revision Treaty or a new Treaty) and had indeed called on the Milan summit to convene one. However, it was determined that the process should retain its political character and was also keen to balance the inevitable national perspective of Foreign Ministry officials with a determined European input. It therefore called for a new Treaty to be approved jointly by the Conference and the Parliament, with an appropriate conciliation procedure to settle differences of viewpoints (8).

Member States were divided on how to reply to the EP. Council was not able to settle the matter on

the 22 July and it was left to the initial
ministerial meeting of the IGC itself on the 9
September to agree to 'take account in its work of
the Draft Treaty adopted by the European Parliament'
as well as 'any further proposal which the European
Parliament may wish to submit' and to propose that
'during the meetings of the Conference its members
should meet with' President Pflimlin and other MEPs
(9). The Conference also agreed 'to submit the
results of its work to the European Parliament'. The
word 'submit' seemed to imply more than merely
'inform' and Parliament proposed a procedure whereby
it would consider the outcome of the Conference and,
if necessary, vote amendments (constituting the
'further proposals' the IGC had undertaken to
consider) which would be submitted to the Conference
and subject to a conciliation procedure (10). This
interpretation caused a long wrangle within the IGC,
the outcome of which was a statement that 'submit'
meant merely to inform the EP and give it the
opportunity to express an opinion, but without a
second reading in the IGC (11). Italy later tried to
strengthen Parliament's bargaining position by
stating that it would only ratify a new Treaty if it
were accepted by the EP.

Parliament monitored the work of the IGC through
its Committee on Institutional Affairs and debated
the matter twice in plenary. The Commission and the
Luxembourg Presidency answered questions and spoke
in the Parliamentary debate on 23 October, reporting
on progress made. Through a special procedure, the
President of Parliament forwarded to the IGC the
comments made by the Committee on Institutional
Affairs on the early drafts tabled at the Conference
(12). Although Parliament had received assurances
from the Luxembourg Presidency that the relevant
extracts of its Draft Treaty were systematically
included in the dossiers on each of the areas in
which Treaty amendments were being considered, and
President Delors, giving seven examples, stated that
Commission proposals were based on the Draft Treaty,
Parliament did not consider that the early drafts
were satisfactory (13).

The meetings between Parliament's delegation
and the IGC were of limited value (14). The
delegation consisted of Pflimlin and Spinelli (15).
Only at the last meeting did almost all of the
national delegations explain their position in
detail. On this occasion the discussion centered on
the powers of the EP. The compromise drafts on the
table prepared by the Luxembourg Presidency were felt

to be insufficient by the EP-delegation, which
received some support from the Belgian, Dutch, French
and especially Italian delegations. The Italian
threat to veto any package not acceptable to the EP
turned this into one of the trickiest points in the
final stages of the negotiations.

The fact that the summit left some matters over
to the Foreign Ministers' meeting on the 16 and 17
December, with Italy maintaining its general reserve
pending the EP's opinion, gave the latter a chance to
come back with a final attempt to strengthen the
package. It adopted a resolution on the 11 December
stating that the results were 'unsatisfactory and is
unable to accept in their present form the proposed
modifications to the EEC-Treaty, particularly as
regards the powers of the European Parliament' (16).
The resolution spelt out a number of criticisms of
the package and called for amendments on the
legislative 'cooperation procedure', monetary
cooperation, on having a Single Act and on the
executive powers of the Commission. The ministers
made small gestures towards the EP's position on
these points in their final meeting and declared the
negotiations closed - still with Italian and Danish
reserves and without attempting to deal with a number
of issues that were simply dropped. These events are
described below.

Governments and other Actors
Throughout the negotiations there were naturally
other attempts to influence the course of events.
Early on some governments sought to put pressure on
the reticent States: Italian, Belgian and Dutch
politicians all spoke of the possibility of some of
the Ten moving ahead without the others (17). Others
laid down ambitious markers on strengthening the EP
and the Commission, majority voting in the Council
and extending the scope of the Community (18). Sir
Geoffrey Howe felt obliged to reply in a major
speech, stating that 'Britain is not afraid of
European Union', but going on to define such a Union
as 'a process of deepening and broadening the scope
of European activities', claiming that in that sense
'such a Union exists now' (19). Nevertheless, the
speech did contain the first indications that Britain
would accept Treaty amendments on a pragmatic basis.
Similar noises coming from Denmark were immediately
the subject of internal political wrangles.

Some national parliaments adopted resolutions
during the negotiations. The Italian, Belgian,

Dutch, Irish and French parliaments had previously given favorable treatment to the EP's Draft Treaty (20). In mid-October, the Italian Senate Foreign Affairs Committee unanimously urged the Government to keep the EP's Draft Treaty at the centre of debate, to confer legislative powers on the EP and to support the EP's proposals for associating itself with the IGC (21). On the 29 November the Italian Chamber of Deputies, also unanimously, stated that the proposals then on the table were unacceptable, supporting instead EP/Council co-decision and generalised majority voting (22). The German Bundestag held a public hearing on the 3 October with Spinelli and others and later adopted a resolution calling on the Government to use the Draft Treaty as the basis of its negotiating position, stating that the absolute minimum was the introduction of EP/Council co-decision on legislation and generalised majority voting in the Council (23). However, the resolution was approved only on the 5 December, which was far too late to have an impact.

The trans-national party political groupings also sought to influence the negotiations. The EPP held a 'summit' of all the Christian-Democrat Heads of Governments, party leaders, Commissioners and Foreign Ministers on 12 November in Brussels. They adopted a declaration confirming their desire to pursue political union 'in accordance with the recommendations of the EP and the Dooge Committee' and that the EEC 'cannot be governed by structures which are less democratic than those of the Member States', calling for an increase in the powers of the EP (24). The Confederation of Socialist Parties was divided, but at their Madrid congress approved a five-page document binding all its member parties other than the British and Danish ones. It took up virtually all the proposals concerning the institutions contained in the EP's Draft Treaty, and was presented to the Chairman of the IGC by a CSP-delegation led by its President Den Uyl (25). The Liberals also adopted an appeal to extend majority voting and the powers of the EP and to add a monetary dimension to the treaties. The European Democratic Group of the EP (largely British Conservatives) supported Treaty revision, called for a right of initiative for the Commission in EPC matters, the restriction of the veto to cases when a Member State justifies it in writing and presents it to the EP in plenary session, and a number of other reforms (26). This too can be seen as an attempt to push a particular government further along the path of reform.

Numerous non-governmental organizations were also active. At European level, apart from the European Movement and Federalist organizations, it is worth noting statements from the ETUC giving general support to the EP's Draft Treaty, and a statement from the European Conference of Local and Regional Authorities supporting 'the EP's demand without reserve' (27).

THE NEGOTIATIONS

The two working parties met almost weekly from the beginning of September. The EPC Party based its work on proposals submitted to the Milan summit. The working party on the EEC-Treaty set an indicative deadline of the 15 October for proposals. It received over 30 from the Commission and every Member State except the UK (28). Together, they covered almost all the main areas of change proposed by the EP in its Draft Treaty except the budget, which Delors claimed the EP had not pushed actively. The EP could thus claim success in that it had at least brought the national governments to the point of negotiating on all the main areas in which it had proposed reforms.

The working parties reported to the Foreign Ministers who met on six occasions before the Luxembourg summit and held an additional 'conclave' immediately before it. Progress was slow, the main questions were only settled - and even then not fully - by the Heads of Government who discussed the issue for some 21 hours - 11 more than planned. The loose ends were then settled in a final meeting of the Foreign Ministers on 16 and 17 December.

The proposals tabled showed that Member States had varying priorities. The extension of the scope of the Community was broadly accepted, with proposals even from Denmark to extend Community competence to new areas. On the level of integration, there was general resistance from the countries that had opposed the convening of the IGC and specific resistance on certain points from others. It was clear that any strengthening of the institutions would only get through by stubborn insistence from its advocates and as part of a global package. However, trade-offs were not easy to construct. Let us examine the negotiations subject by subject, without forgetting the links between them.

244

A.   **Internal Market**

This was a centrepiece of the talks, for reasons both fundamental and tactical. It was an area in which the basic aim of the existing treaties was still not achieved. Its importance was generally recognised and it was an ·issue which could entice the UK. Discussions centred on a Commission draft, although France also submitted a text. The Commission's initial proposal provided for an internal market to be achieved by 1992 defined broadly as an area 'in which persons, goods and capital shall move freely under conditions identical to those obtaining within a Member State'. Council would act by a qualified majority except on the free movement of persons. Implementing measures could be adopted by the Commission except where the Council unanimously reserved such rights to itself. Insofar as common provisions were not adopted by 1992 there would be automatic mutual recognition of national regulations.

Discussions centred on the <u>definition</u> of the internal market (felt to be too broad by the UK, France and the FRG), the automatic <u>deadline</u> in 1992 (felt to be too rigid by France, Greece and Ireland), and <u>majority voting</u> (opposed outright by Denmark and Greece and for the field of taxation and fiscality by the UK, FRG, Netherlands and Ireland; for social security for migrant workers and the organization of the professions by the FRG; and for insurance and banking by Ireland). In addition, some countries sought <u>derogations</u> for particular field (e.g. the UK and Ireland on health controls su¬h as rabies), some countries, notably Greece, Ireland and Portugal, fearing the centipetal effects of an integrated market linked their position to the outcome of negotiations on <u>cohesion</u>, and Denmark and Germany were worried that <u>harmonization</u> measures could force them to lower their standards of environment and consumer protection. The Commission proposal was generally supported by Italy and the Benelux countries.

A compromise was reached only after many hours of discussion at the summit itself. The objective of a broadly defined internal market by 1992 was finally accepted (with France, Germany and finally Britain making concessions during the summit), but it was specified in a declaration that the deadline as such would not create any automatic legal effects. There would be no 'lex specialis' allowing Council to act by qualified majority throughout this field, but instead a series of detailed treaty changes.

Qualified majority voting was agreed for the common customs tariff, banking, medical and pharmaceutical professions, services of nationals of third countries, liberalization of exchange policies and movement of capital (but preserving unanimity for de-liberalizing measures: an interesting form of entrenchement!), and air and sea transport. A new Art. 100A allowed qualified majority voting for all the harmonization measures formerly covered by Art. 100 except those concerning fiscal policy, free movement of persons and the rights of employees. Unlike Art. 100, it would no longer be restricted to directives harmonizing national provisions: i.e. regulations, even where no previous national provisions existed, could be adopted without recourse to Art. 235.

These provisions were accompanied by others that met concerns expressed by Member States. It was laid down that Commission proposals on health, safety, environment and consumer protection should be based on a high level of protection (harmonizing upwards). Where harmonized measures have been adopted by a qualified majority, member states would be free to apply national provisions on grounds of major needs (cf. Art. 36 EEC) or relating to the protection of the environment or working conditions. Such measures would have to be notified to the Commission which would confirm them after verifying that they were not a means of arbitrary discrimination or a disguised restriction on trade. In such cases, the Commission or any Member State could bring the matter before the Court of Justice directly (i.e. without first going through the Commission's 'reasoned opinion' procedure laid down in Art. 169 and 170 EEC). Another new Article (8B) provided for the Commission to report in 1988 and 1990 on progress made and for Council, by a qualified majority on a Commission proposal, to determine guidelines to ensure balanced progress. Art. 100B provided for an inventory in 1992 of remaining national dispositions not yet harmonized. The recognition of their equivalence would not be automatic but would be possible by a qualified majority. Art. 99 (indirect taxation and excise) was re-written to place an obligation on the Council to act before the 1992 deadline and to consult the European Parliament. However, unanimity was maintained for decision-taking.

Other declarations were added to the Acts of the Conference interpreting the agreement in these areas. In this way the rights of Member States to

take measures concerning immigration from third
countries, terrorism, criminality and traffic in
drugs, works of art and antiques was safeguarded,
though they did undertake in a separate 'political
declaration' to cooperate in these fields. There were
also unilateral declarations by Greece, Portugal and
Ireland on sensitive economic sectors and by Denmark
emphasizing the right to take safeguard measures
under Art. 100A.

B. Monetary Capacity

The Finance Ministers of the member states expressed
concern that amendments might be drawn up in this
area without their involvement. President Delors
undertook to discuss Commission drafts with them
before they were submitted to the IGC. This was the
only case of a sectoral Council intervening.

The Commission proposed to modify Art. 107 EEC
in order to provide a treaty reference for the EMS,
in which member states would be required to cooperate
(though not necessarily joining the Exchange Rate
Mechanism), and the ECU. The EMCF would have a Board
of Directors composed of the governors of the Central
Bank and a Commission representative, with decisions
taken unanimously by the Member States participating
in the Exchange Rate Mechanism. A full Monetary Fund
would be set up by a unanimous decision and
ratification by Member States.

The proposal merely codified the existing
situation and provided a cumbersome procedure for
further development. It was felt to be too weak by
France, Belgium (which tabled a proposal to
strengthen it), Ireland and Italy. However, the UK,
Germany and the Netherlands opposed any inclusion of
monetary articles in the Treaty revision. Chancellor
Lawson's delegation was reported as stating that 'the
inclusion of economic and monetary union as a goal in
the Treaty is unacceptable and pointless' (29).
Anglo-German resistance was confirmed during the
Thatcher-Kohl meeting in London on 27 November.
However, on the eve of the summit, the French and
Italian governments announced measures liberalizing
their exchange control provisions, which had always
been a sticking point for Germany in EMS-
negotiations. This cleared the way for Kohl to
compromise, leaving Thatcher isolated. It was
finally agreed to insert three extra indents in the
preamble of the new Treaty which referred to the
objective of economic and monetary union and to add a
new chapter to the EEC Treaty laying down that Member

States shall cooperate to ensure the convergence of economic and monetary policies. It referred to the EMS and the ECU, but stated that they shall respect existing powers in this field. Any further development requiring institutional change would require Treaty amendment (Art. 236) after consulting the monetary committee and the governors of the Central Bank. Further developments were thus even more restrictive than the Commission proposal. This was strongly criticized after the summit, notably by the EP, and at the Foreign Ministers' meeting of 16 and 17 December the issue was re-opened. A declaration was added to the Acts of the Conference specifying that further (non-institutional) development is possible within the framework of existing powers (i.e. without a Treaty revision). However, even this was not approved by all and had to be incorporated as a declaration of the Presidency and the Commission.

C.   **Cohesion**

This topic was rendered more salient by the enlargement to Spain and Portugal and by fears of the effect of a single market on peripheral economies. The main arguments centered on the strength of the commitment to economic re-distribution to be written in the Treaties, with a clear divergence between those countries likely to benefit and some of those likely to have to contribute, the latter tending to argue that cohesion could best be obtained by providing the same economic conditions throughout the common market and that emphasis should therefore be on convergence of economic policies. Subsidiary arguments took place on codifying the Regional Fund in a Treaty, on revising the provisions for the other structural funds, on whether to have a new Community loan mechanism and on the degree of coordination among the three funds.

Proposals were tabled by the Commission, France, Ireland and Greece. The final compromise was based on a revised Commission proposal. It provided for Community action to promote economic cohesion and reduce regional diversity (a reference to social working and employment conditions proposed by the Commission was dropped). National and Community policies would further these objectives which the Community would assist through the structural funds, the EIB and the other existing financial instruments. There would be no new form of Community loan. The Regional Fund was specifically mentioned and defined. A unanimous decision would be taken within one year on the rationalization and coordination of the three funds, followed by the introduction of majority voting for the Regional Fund and its maintenance for the other funds. A Commission proposal to revise Social Fund Arts. 123 to 127 was not taken up, most Member States feeling that they were flexible enough in their current form. The question of the overall financial commitment was settled by a declaration referring to the conclusions of the European Council meeting of Brussels in 1984 that the funds would be 'significantly increased in real terms within the limits of financial possibilities'.

D. **Environment**
Negotiations were based on a Commission proposal for four articles providing the objectives and principles of Community policy, a long list of specific areas for Community intervention, a provision allowing more stringent national measures where these did not distort the common market, and for Council to act unanimously on the principles of Community intervention, but by a qualified majority for implementing measures. Denmark also proposed six new articles along similar, but more general, lines. Germany submitted a proposal to add animal protection to Community competences (30). Ireland and Greece wished to balance environmental considerations with those of economic development and Ireland introduced an amendment to the Commission proposal to this effect. The UK, at that time involved in controversy over the degree of the responsibility of British industries for acid rain and sea pollution, was anxious to avoid giving the Community too much leeway to impose rigorous standards upon it. Some countries disliked the long list of specific areas for Community intervention arguing that it was unnecessary to be so detailed. Denmark and Greece opposed majority decision taking.

The final text met these concerns by stating that Community action should 'take account of' scientific evidence, different regional situations, potential costs and economic development. It included the principle of subsidiarity: the Community should act to the extent which the objectives can be better attained at Community level than at the level of individual Member States (31). The issue of decision-taking was effectively postponed: it was agreed that Council could decide unanimously which areas can subsequently be decided by a qualified majority. A curious compromise emerged on agreements with third parties in this area: although this was provided for, a paragraph was inserted that stated that it would not prejudice member states' competences to negotiate international agreements. However, a declaration in the Acts of the Conference confirmed the existing jurisprudence of the Court of Justice to the effect that the Community is competent for the external aspects of its internal policies. A second declaration specified that the Community's environmental activities may not interfere with national policies regarding the exploitation of energy resources.

E.   Research and Technological Development

As the negotiations took place at the same time as the discussions on Eureka, the Commission and several Member States were anxious to give the Community a broad range of possible means of action in this field. The Commission, Belgium and Denmark all tabled proposals, and negotiations were based on a Presidency redraft of the Commission proposal. Agreement was reached quickly on the various types of Community action (Community programmes, coordination of national prorammes, Community participation in programmes of other bodies or of Member States, the possibility for third parties to participate in Community programmes, the establishment of joint undertakings or other structures). However, there was divergence on decision-taking. Germany was particularly anxious that decisions on finance should be unanimous. The compromise negotiated provided for unanimity in the adoption of the multi-annual framework programme laying down the general lines of Community action, and for the creation of joint undertakings and structures. Qualified majority voting would apply for the adoption of particular programmes and their implementation. However, the framework programme would go into considerable detail, including the amounts estimated necessary for the Community's financial participation as well as the division of this amount among the various activities. It was specified that Community expenditure in this field would be approved under the budgetary procedure, but that the total amount could not exceed that provided for in the framework programme, thus limiting the EP's budgetary powers in this field.

F.   **Social Policy**
The Danish government submitted some proposals in
this area which may have been aimed at drawing in the
opposition Social Democratic Party by putting
forward proposals that could appeal to them. They
proposed articles allowing Council to adopt
directives laying down minimal criteria for safety
and health at work whilst allowing member states to
adopt more advanced criteria. Art. 122 would be
modified to lay down that the Commission's annual
report should include a chapter on social and working
conditions. Finally, an article would provide that
should unemployment increase above Y% (figure to be
negotiated), Council, on the basis of a Commission
proposal, should examine the possibilities to modify
the economic policies of member states. The
Commission put forward similar proposals on the
laying down of minimal standards, and also proposed
an article providing for dialogue between management
and labour at European level which could lead to
contractual agreements.
        The IGC approved a new Art. 118A based on the
Danish proposal providing for directives to lay down
minimum criteria on the working environment and to
protect the safety and health of workers. Council
would act by a qualified majority, though the UK
(fearful of the Vredeling-directive?) insisted on
unanimity until the very end when it settled for an
extra paragraph and a declaration in the Acts that
the Community will not place unjustified burdens on
small undertakings. It was specified that Member
States could adopt stricter conditions compatible
with the Treaty. The Commission's proposal on social
dialogue was adopted but the other proposals were
dropped.

G.   **Political Cooperation**
Political Union has been a constant theme from as far
back as the Ad Hoc Assembly and was a major feature
in the Tindemans report. From 1970 onwards the
Foreign Ministries of the member states cooperated in
EPC. An attempt to formalize this in an Act proposed
by Genscher and Colombo in 1981 ended up with a mere
Declaration in 1983. Parliament's Draft Treaty again
pressed for its formalization and its linkage to
Community institutions.
        Negotiations were based on the UK and Franco-
German (F/G) proposals tabled before the Milan summit
and subsequent proposals by Italy and the
Netherlands. All four followed a similar structure,

the first eight articles coinciding in subject
matter. All sought essentially to codify the existing
structure of EPC whilst introducing some small
changes.

On the declared aims and objectives, the UK text
was subtly weaker than the others, referring to the
strengthening of existing commitments (the others
spoke of creating a European Union based on the
Communities and EPC) and 'consultations ... to secure
a broad identity of view' (rather than 'the gradual
implementation of a European foreign policy'). In the
end, the marginally stronger wording was preferred to
that of the UK.

On the structure, all texts placed overall
responsibility under the European Council (renamed
'Council of the European Union' in the F/G text),
with day-to-day work carried out by the Foreign
Ministers (the Council in the Italian text) and by
officials. The Presidency would have a coordinating
and representative role. Divergences emerged on the
nature of the secretariat envisaged. The F/G proposal
was for a Secretary General appointed for four years
by the European Council heading a secretariat
appointed for two years by the Foreign Ministers. The
UK text referred to a 'small' secretariat in its
annexes, with office space and services provided by
arrangement with the Council secretariat. It
provided a list of functions which remained
technical. The Italian and Dutch proposals broadly
supported the UK text, presumably fearing a large
intergovernmental political secretariat that could
rival the Commission. On decision-taking, the common
assumption was unanimity. The Italian text referred
to 'consensus respecting the majority opinion'. The
text finally agreed made no reference to the European
Council and provided simply that the Foreign
Ministers and a Member of the Commission should meet
at least four times a year and on the occasion of
Council meetings. Member states would refrain, as far
as possible, from impeding consensus or joint action.
Initiative, coordination, representation and management would be under the responsibility of the
Presidency, assisted by a secretariat based in
Brussels. A political committee, correspondence
groups and working parties of officials were provided
for. Emergency meetings could be called within 48
hours by three Member States. Coherence between
political cooperation and the external policies of
the Community would be the joint responsibility of
the Presidency and the Commission. On external
representation, existing practices were added to in

that Commission representations were included in cooperation among missions in third countries and EPC positions applied even in organizations where only some member states were represented.

On security, all the proposals provided for closer cooperation. For the UK, this was to contribute to NATO and WEU, whereas the other texts all referred to increase coordination of European positions on political and economic aspects of security. The F/G and Dutch texts provided for member states wishing to cooperate more closely to do so within WEU, whose composition and framework could be extended. The Italians proposed consultation between the Presidencies of EPC and WEU, joint meetings between the EP and WEU Assembly, and that a number of security matters could be taken up in EPC itself. All these proposals caused difficulties for Ireland (not a member of NATO), Denmark and Greece. Security was among the last points to be settled in the negotiations. The final text stated that closer cooperation on matters of European security would contribute to a European identity and that member states were ready to further develop their cooperation on political and economic aspects of security. A reference to technological and industrial cooperation was included. The question of NATO and WEU was settled by providing that this Treaty was not an obstacle to closer cooperation among some Member States in these frameworks.

On the EP, the UK text provided for it to be 'informed', the F/G and Dutch proposals provided for its 'association' and the Italian text referred to the 'essential role' of the EP and laid down provisions for informing the EP and taking account of its view. The text finally agreed laid down that the EP be 'closely associated' with EPC, charging the Presidency both with informing the EP and with ensuring that its views are 'duly taken into consideration'.

The Italian text provided for revision after five years to make further progress, charging the Foreign Ministers with producing a draft for the European Council, which would be submitted to the EP. The final text provided for an examination after five years as to the necessity of revising the Treaty, but no procedures were specified.

H.   **Single Act**
The question of whether to have a single or two separate Acts covering Treaty revision and EPC was

left until the end, but right from the beginning the Commission argued for a single treaty comprising a preamble and three sections (joint provisions, EEC revision, EPC). In the end, this structure was followed, based on a French proposal.

The preamble contained general considerations on the need to continue efforts towards European Union. It also became a hold-all for compromises on proposals initially put forward as new Treaty articles, such as fundamental rights and monetary affairs. Title I (Common provisions) defined the common structure, but was less far-reaching than the initial French proposal which had envisaged the whole system (revised EC plus EPC) being called 'European Union' with general policy guidelines defined by a 'Council of European Union' (former European Council) assisted by a secretariat (additional to that of EPC). In the end, the Act merely mentioned the European Council, its composition specified to include the President of the Commission, but did not attribute any functions or secretariat to it. Titles II and III contained the IGC's conclusions on revision of the EEC Treaty and on political cooperation respectively. Title IV (final and general dispositions) contained the usual technical articles but also specified that the Court of Justice would not be directly competent for political cooperation nor for matters contained in the preamble of Title I. This limited the import of these sections of the Act.

I.   **Executive and Management Powers of the Commission**

Although Art. 155 of the EEC treaty provides for the Commission to exercise the powers conferred on it by the Council, in practice the latter had frequently refrained from conferring such powers, or has only done so subject to strict control by committees of national officials. The Commission and the Netherlands both put forward proposals seeking to strengthen the Commission's position, by laying down that it should automatically exercise implementing powers, but accepting that the Council could impose certain specific and limited modalities in this respect. The Commission proposal also provided for Council, acting unanimously, to reserve such powers to itself in specific cases. The Commission proposed adding such provisions to Art. 155 (Commission), whereas the Dutch proposed to add it to Art. 154 (Council), arguing that what was lacking was an obligation on the Council, not a right for the Commission. The IGC preferred the Dutch method, but included the Commission's loophole allowing Council to reserve powers to itself. On the 'modalities' it was provided that a set of principles and rules would be laid down in advance by the Council, acting unanimously. A Declaration provided for these rules to be adopted before the Single Act entered into force, and also laid down that the Advisory Committee procedure should be given precedence for implementing powers connected to Art. 100A. This last point was added by the Foreign Ministers on 16 and 17 December, after the EP had expressed fears that Council would reserve implementing powers for itself.

Taking up a point in the EP's Draft Treaty, the Netherlands proposed that when nominating a new Commission, the Member States should first nominate the President after consulting the Parliament, that the other Members of the Commission be appointed on his proposal, and for the new Commission to present itself to Parliament for a vote of investiture. This issue was not settled, ostensibly through lack of time, but Delors confirmed the Commission's support for the current pragmatic procedure in which Parliament holds an investiture debate and a vote (32). A Dutch proposal, not requiring Treaty amendment, to limit the number of Commissioners to 12 was opposed by Germany, Italy and France.

J.   **Powers of the European Parliament**

With Denmark and Britain opposing any formal increase in Parliament's powers, it was clear from the beginning that this would be a difficult area. The first round of discussions was based on proposals submitted by Germany, followed by one, along similar lines, from the Commission (which had disliked aspects of the German proposal which would have weakened its position). Both proposals sought to approach the issue by putting forward different 'baskets' in which Parliament's powers would be adjusted to various degrees, rather than confronting the more reticent member states with a blanket change. The proposals explored the following possibilities, in ascending order of importance:

- changing the legal name of the EP from 'Assembly' to 'Parliament'
- extending Parliament's legal right to be consulted to some articles not currently

      providing for this;
- formalizing the existing 'conciliation proced-ure' in the Treaty and extending it to all major items of legislation (33);
- providing for the Council to deliberate on the Commission proposal as amended by the Parliament and should it depart from the EP's position for a conciliation committee composed of 12 members each from the EP and Council to adopt compromise texts by a three quarter's majority (which would then require approval by the EP and Council);
- providing for a second reading in which Parliament, by a majority of Members, could propose new amendments to Council's text or reject it entirely, in which case Council could adopt the EP's amendments by a qualified majority but could only override parliamentary rejection of a text by unanimity;
- providing for 'joint legislative action' on 'constitutional' matters in which Council could only adopt texts approved by the EP.

Negotiations were difficult, even among those supporting a strengthening of Parliament's powers. There was opposition to the 'conciliation committee' suggestion which would have weakened the Commission's position by removing its power to withdraw proposals. Some countries opposed writing the conciliation procedure into the Treaty feeling that this was better left to inter-institutional agreement. The proposal for a second reading met with some sympathy, but many countries felt either that it went too far or that it did not go far enough. As to full co-decision on constitutional matters, the principle was eventually accepted by all countries except Denmark, but there was disagreement as to the articles to which it should apply: each article proposed met with at least one reservation (e.g. Greece and France re 138, France, UK and Germany re 201, France and Ireland re 236, Greece re 237).

Putting forward compromises as a first proposal left little room for further compromise when these proposals met with opposition from more reticent countries. More ambitious countries were in a difficult tactical position of having to propose strengthening texts already labelled as too far-reaching. Italy nevertheless attempted this with a proposal referring specifically to the EP's Draft Treaty as its source. It amounted to full co-decision between Parliament and Council for all main items of

Community legislation. It enlarged the 'constitutional' basket and proposed granting the EP a formal role in receiving petitions and conducting enquiries. Most of the delegations appeared to have considered Italy's proposal as tactical, signalling its support for the maintenance or strengthening of the Commission's proposal.

In spite of a French attempt to put forward a compromise proposal, and a discussion with the EP delegation on 21 October, the Ministers were unable even to agree on a mandate for the preparatory group. The Luxembourg Presidency, on its own initiative, instructed it to continue to examine the matter and drafted a compromise taking up the proposal for a second reading, but applying it only to 9 articles and changing the procedure dealing with Parliament's amendments in the second reading to leave it entirely up to the Commission to accept or drop them when redrafting its proposal. It retained the 'constitutional' basket, but limited it to Arts. 237 and 238. The incorporation of the conciliation procedure in the Treaty was dropped. This proposal was sufficiently watered down that only Denmark felt it went too far. The Benelux countries, Germany and France considered it to be the bare minimum. It was discussed on 16 November with the EP delegation which considered it totally unacceptable. It was at this point that Andreotti stated that Italy would not ratify a text unacceptable to the EP. Although he received some support, notably from Belgium and France, for strengthening the text on the EP, subsequent discussions in the conclave and the European Council itself were unable to agree on changes to the Presidency compromise. Subject to Danish and Italian reserves (for opposite reasons) the European Council approved the text, but instructed the Foreign Ministers to clarify the issue of deadlines and what should happen should the EP, in its second reading, reject the common position of the Council.

In its resolution on the results of the summit, the EP asked the Foreign Ministers to change the text so that the new procedure should apply to all acts requiring a majority decision in Council, so that in the second reading, Parliament's text would stand unless modified by Council within three months (by a qualified majority where the Commission did not approve Parliament's decision or unanimously where it did) and to fix a deadline for Council to reach a common position in its first reading (34).

The Foreign Ministers failed to agree on an

extension of the new procedure to further articles.
They did agree to allow <u>all</u> of the EP's amendments to
be submitted to the Council, even where the
Commission did not incorporate them into its new
proposal. However, amendments not taken up by the
Commission could only be adopted by unanimity. It was
specified that should Council not take a decision by
the three months' deadline, the proposal would fall.
Whilst not as fargoing as Parliament's proposal –
supported by the Commission, Belgium and Italy – that
its position should stand if Council failed to
overrule it, this provision at least put some
pressure on Council to adopt the amended proposal
rather than lose it entirely. On the question of the
deadline in the first reading, a Declaration was
added to the Acts of the Conference referring to the
proposal to improve Council's decision-taking
procedure and expressing the intention to do so as
soon as possible. This returned to the question of
amending Council's Rules of Procedure. Finally, they
agreed the formal change of name from Assembly to
Parliament.

K. **Court of Justice**
The Court is burdened with being the labour Court for
Community officials. The EP had been pressing for a
subsidiary Court to be set up to deal with such
matters (35). The IGC was seized with the matter by a
letter from the President of the Court of Justice and
approved a new article enabling Council, acting
unanimously on a proposal of the Court of Justice and
after consulting the Commission and the EP, to set up
a subsidiary Court to deal with matters others than
those submitted by Member States, Community
institutions, or by national jurisdictions according
to Art. 177 EEC. A right of appeal to the full Court
of Justice would remain on points of law. The
internal rules of this Court would be drawn up in
agreement with the Court of Justice and subject to
unanimous Council approval. In addition, it was
agreed that revision of the Court statute would no
longer require treaty amendment but could be done by
unanimous Council agreement at the request of the
Court and after consulting the EP and Commission. The
Court was also affected by the provision for direct
appeal on the internal market (see above section A).

L. **Human Rights**
The lack of any formal provision in the Treaties

requiring Community institutions to respect fundamental rights and member states to be democratic has often been the subject of concern and was one of the issues addressed by Parliament's Draft Treaty. Belgium proposed to amend the preamble to the EEC Treaty to include a reference to parliamentary democracy, human rights and fundamental freedoms and to extend Art. 4 to place an obligation on the Community to respect the European Convention on Human Rights. This would formalize the April 1977 Joint Declaration of Parliament, Council and Commission. The IGC agreed to include this matter in the preamble to the Act, and added the European Social Charter to the list of references rather than only taking those mentioned in the joint declaration: in effect taking up the list in Parliament's Draft Treaty. However, merely adding the matter to the preamble, excluded from direct competence of the Court of Justice, limited the import of this inclusion in the Treaty.

M.   Subjects not Included in the Final Compromise

A number of proposals did not find their way into the final package. Once the European Council had settled a number of major points, there was a reluctance to continue negotiations into 1986, with the French elections looming, and some of the matters left open were ones on which agreement seemed difficult. They included proposals on cultural cooperation (Commission, Netherlands, Italy), development aid (Netherlands, Denmark), differentiation (France), energy and local voting rights (both Denmark).

THE OUTCOME: EVALUATING THE EUROPEAN ACT

The European Act clearly fell far short of the EP's objective of a major transformation of the Community system. Nevertheless, it represented the first major overhaul of the Treaties (other than budgetary) and introduced a number of extensions and modifications to the Community system which deserve analysis.

The Act extended the formal competence of the Community to new areas. Community action in the fields of research (in virtual competition with Eureka), the environment, regional policy and some aspects of social policy would have a stronger legal base in the Treaties rather than relying on the cumbersome procedure of Art. 235. Community competence in these areas and its potential to act was therefore extended.

This was scarcely the case, however, for monetary cooperation. It was perhaps worth mentioning the EMS and the ECU in the Treaties, thus linking them formally to the Community, but the terms used in the relevant articles were so restrictive as to make subsequent development of the EMS more difficult than at present. The need for Treaty revision (Art. 236) with national ratification for each and every institutional development of the EMS effectively shut the door for many years on the transition of the second phase of the EMS, originally envisaged by the governments for 1980.

On extending the formal competences of the Community it is equally notable that this was not done in a number of areas. The most important of these were development policy (where there is a considerable 'acquis'), energy policy, culture and education. There is a danger that, in leaving these areas 'out in the cold', whilst allowing other policies to come in, they will be in a more vulnerable position.

The formalization of political cooperation was a major objective of Parliament's Draft Treaty. This was achieved through the Act. However, although its incorporation within the Single Act links it to the Community, as do the provisions for Commission participation in EPC, it retains a separate structure and method of working with no possibility, even gradual, laid down for the transfer of matters from the intergovernmental method of political cooperation to the more integrated Community method, which the EP's Draft Treaty had envisaged. Furthermore, the establishment of a secretariat for political cooperation, whilst possibly contributing to its effectiveness, could reinforce its separation from the Community. The provision that it be based in Brussels at least guaranteed its links to the Community system. Curiously, it would be the only body to have its seat formally fixed on a permanent basis, a fact that led Luxembourg to insist on a declaration that this would not affect the status quo of the Community seats.

There were other adjustments to existing EPC practices. References to security were a little more explicit, but did not go beyond economic, political and technological aspects. The procedures for cooperation among embassies in third countries were tightened up and extended to include the Commission's representations. It was also laid down that Member States should cooperate within international organizations, and that even where only some of them are represented, they should take account of joint positions developed in EPC. Coordination of Community and EPC would become the joint responsibility of the EPC President and the Commission, and not only a matter for the former as before. The undertaking to refrain, as far as possible, from blocking consensus and joint actions was new, but merely an exhortation. Revision after five years is to be considered. None of these novelties change the character of the cooperation. It remains a statement of intent, especially as the competence of the Court of Justice is not enlarged to include EPC.

Another major objective was to increase the effectiveness of the Community's decision-taking procedures, mainly by increasing the possibilities for majority voting in the Council. This was done for a limited number of articles. Most of these concerned the internal market: Arts. 28, 59.2, 70.1, 84, 100A, 100B, the provisions concerning pharmacists, doctors and bankers formerly in Art. 57.2, and, potentially, environmental matters. In addition, some majority decisions became possible through the 'cooperation procedure' with Parliament: Arts. 56, parts of 118, and the new articles on the regional fund and implementing measures on research. This extension of qualified majority voting is certainly significant, representing the legal surrender by member states of their supremacy in the fields concerned. However, its implementation in practice will depend crucially on the interpretation now given to the so-called Luxembourg compromise. This was not discussed in the IGC, not being a matter enshrined in the treaties. Some heads of government emphasized that this was not affected where vital national interests were at stake. A question-mark thus hung over these results, although the Presidency announced that Council would now discuss the proposals to change its Rules of Procedure. Equally significant was the number of areas in which member states, notwithstanding their interpretations of their right of veto, were unwilling to shift to majority voting. This included fiscal matters, taxation, free movement of persons, workers' rights, environment, the framework programme and overall level of finance for research and development, monetary cooperation, coordination of the structural funds and amendment of the statute of the Court.

The other provisions on the internal market were less significant than they appear at first sight. The 1992 deadline is merely declaratory, adding little to traditional European Council statements of intent concerning an objective planned for 1970 in the EEC Treaty! The possibility to adopt regulations (and not only directives) on the matters listed in Art. 100A, whether or not national norms previously existed, would give the Community more flexibility in these areas, but again a declaration stated that the Commission would give preference to the use of the instrument of a directive where harmonization involved the amendment of legislative provisions in one or more Member States. Allowing member states to derogate from harmonization measures constitutes a major new loop-hole, partly redeemed by the provisions requiring the Commission to confirm them and allowing the Commission or any member state to appeal directly to the Court on these matters.

Another way to improve the efficiency of the Community was to strengthen the Commission. The Commission and the Parliament have contradictory interpretations of the results of the IGC in this field. The Commission feels that the obligation placed on the Council to delegate implementing powers to the Commission will lead it to do so more frequently. The EP, however, considers that the provisions laid down (for the first time in the Treaty) allowing Council to keep such powers in its own hands, and in any case to specify the modalities of any delegation to the Commission, took away any progress made. The real impact will depend on the rules to be adopted by Council, in principle before the Act comes into force.

One of the most tricky areas to assess is the change brought to the powers of the EP. On one point there is no doubt: the provisions requiring the assent of the EP for further enlargement of the Community and Association Agreements would give the EP a real right of veto. However, it is a negative power; it gives the EP only a chance to accept or reject a package negotiated by others; and it concerns events not likely to occur frequently in future years.

The 'cooperation procedure' – limited to ten articles – is in essence a second consultation of the EP in more difficult conditions (needing an absolute majority to propose amendments and unable to use delaying tactics) than current practice in its single reading. Certainly the EP and the Commission, if supported by at least one member state, could put the other member states (or a qualified majority of them) in a position of either having to accept amendments or losing the proposal entirely, but this is already

possible where Council acts by a qualified majority
and where the Commission incorporates in its proposal
the 'amendments' Parliament proposes in its opinion
(sometimes pressing the Commission to accept its
amendments by threatening to delay its opinion). This
procedure would no doubt still continue and Council
would already face in its first reading a proposal
that incorporated EP amendments accepted by the
Commission, and which it could only depart from by
unanimity, or by a qualified majority persuading the
Commission to change it. It is difficult to see how
EP proposals not accepted in the first reading would
have a better chance in a second reading. The time
pressure put on Council in its second reading might
help, but the prospect of a proposal's non-adoption
is as likely to put pressure on the Commission as on
Member States. The novelty is the possibility for the
EP to reject a proposal entirely, in which case one
ally in Council would suffice for the measure to
fall. This would give Parliament a real chance to
kill proposals it doesn't like, but in practice the
EP, like the Commission, normally seeks to promote
Community measures and is rarely opposed to them
outright.

The procedure has some crumbs of comfort for the
EP. A second consultation, allowing the EP to react
once it knows Council's position, could give it some
scope to use public opinion. There could be some
pressure on Council - or at least some of its members
- not to systematically refuse all EP amendments. The
second reading provides for a more publicly visible
way of dealing with its amendments. In view of future
reforms, it might be useful for the ritual of two
'readings' to become entrenched in the public mind,
and at first sight gives the impression of classic
legislative procedures being followed at European
level. Parliament might also be able to use to its
advantage the new legal obligation placed on the
Commission and Council to 'inform the Parliament
fully of the reasons which led the Council to adopt
its common position', in order to extract information
from them on the position of the various members of
Council.

There is one way in which the EP could try to
develop the new procedure beyond what the Member
States had intended. This would be to combine the two
aspects of rejection and amendment. If in its first
reading it were to signal that it would reject a
proposal outright in its second reading, unless
certain amendments are adopted, it would give itself
a good bargaining position (notably in the

263

conciliation procedure which has not been abolished by the new cooperation procedure and could be combined with it in some areas). It would need only one ally in Council to force effective bargaining. On most issues, the EP should be able to find one ally for its amendments. Within Council, a delegation arguing for a position supported by Parliament in this way would be the only one to exercise a potential veto, as Parliamentary rejection is the only legal way to impose unanimity rather than qualified majority voting. The Commission too would be anxious to take up the EP's amendments so that its proposal can be adopted by a qualified majority. In this way, Parliament could achieve de facto co-decision in this limited area, especially if it can persuade one or more member states to make a general declaration that they would in principle not approve proposals rejected by Parliament. The EP could approach sympathetic national parliaments on this.

The Act also provides for the EP to be consulted in the traditional way in areas where this was previously not formally the case: air and sea transport, taxation (Art. 99), environment, the revision of the structural funds and the framework programme for research. These areas are now subject to Parliament's possibility to hold up decisions by delaying its opinion until it is satisfied with the Commission proposal. Lastly, legal recognition of the name 'Parliament' rather than 'Assembly' was achieved.

On the Court of Justice, the proposed subsidiary Court would be useful in divesting the main Court of minor matters, allowing it to act more speedily. Assuming the opportunity provided by this treaty amendment is taken, a useful improvement to the efficiency of the Court would result. The change in the method of revising Court procedures laid down in Title III of its statute so as no longer to require national ratification would also be a useful simplification, though unanimity would still be required in the Council.

Overall, then, the Act although couched in elaborate language, amounted mainly to a limited extension of the scope of the Community, codification of political cooperation formally linking it to the Community system, and some adjustments to institutional provisions that were more symbolic than substantial, but have some potential for creative interpretation. Given that negotiations had started with three countries opposing any change to the treaties, it could be argued that the Act represented an important re-affirmation of the validity of the Community method, keeping the EC at the centre of new areas of European cooperation and integration. On the other hand, given the aspirations of the EP and a number of member states, the reform fell far short of their hopes and what they considered to be necessary.

TOWARDS RATIFICATION

The IGC closed with Danish and Italian reserves and each government putting a different gloss on the result (36). Thatcher called them 'clear and decisive' whilst assuring the House of Commons that the veto remained intact (37). Mitterrand stated that 'some countries, including France, wanted more and will continue to demand it'. Kohl stated that his country would have been prepared to go further, particularly as regards the Parliament's powers. Schlüter said that he was satisfied with the results because ultimately they did not signify 'the slightest loss of sovereignty'. Martens expressed satisfaction, but was strongly criticised in Belgium for having accepted such a weak package and for not having taken the same position as Italy (38). The Portuguese government stated that it would have preferred more progress in conferring new powers on the EP (39).

The reserve of the Italian government implied that the EP's position would determine its acceptance by Italy, though unlike the 11 December, there was little scope to use this constructively. Although it was very far from the overall reform Parliament sought, most MEPs wished to avoid jeopardizing the package now that it was clear that negotiations were at an end, either because they felt that there were some positive elements, or because they felt the prospects of launching a future reform process would be weakened by its failure, or even, in the case of MEPs from governing parties, a desire to avoid embarrassing their heads of government. A minority wished to reject the package entirely as inadequate (though not all were convinced that this really would lead to its non-ratification), and the anti-marketeers opposed the package for the opposite reason. The Commission, the Council President and a number of national governments exhorted MEPs to accept the package. President-in-office Van Eekelen travelled to Brussels to 'sell' the package to the Committee on Institutional Affairs (40). In the end,

Parliament reiterated its negative assessment of the
package, but did so in such a way as to make it
understood that it was not calling for non-
ratification (41). Although there were misgivings
about the ambiguity of the resolution, mirrored in
the support for some of the amendments that were
tabled to it, the text reflected the dilemma in which
MEPs found themselves.

This, then, cleared the way for Italy to ratify.
What, then, of Denmark? The minority centre-right
coalition was willing to accept the Act. However, it
needed support in the Folketing from the Radicals
(Radikale Venstre) or the Socialdemocrats. Both
opposed the Act. The Socialdemocrats were divided on
the EC, with the leadership supporting Danish
membership but with a large minority opposed. The
party as a whole felt pressure from the growing
strength of the anti-EC Socialist Peoples Party. In
this situation, there was little incentive to go out
of its way to support the government, especially when
it thought it could bring the government down on the
issue. After intense internal discussion, it decided
to vote against the measures in the Folketing, which
rejected the package by a majority of five. Schlüter,
however, called a referendum, for which he had
support from the Radicals. The Foreign Minister made
a lightening tour of national capitals to establish
that the other member states were unwilling to re-
open negotiations, as the Folketing requested.
Indeed the Dutch Presidency emphasized this by
calling a signing ceremony for the Act on 17 February
– ten days before the referendum – which it hoped
would be the occasion for the eleven to show their
determination to the Danes. In fact, Greece refused
to put such pressure, and Italy saw no reason to lift
its reserve before Denmark, so the Act was signed by
nine. Both the Commission and the EP were represented
only by Vice-Presidents, showing their dissatisfaction with the Act.

The campaign in Denmark centred on its continued
membership of the Community. The government thought
it could win by presenting the rejection of the Act
as a first step down the path to withdrawal. Many
anti-marketeers were happy to campaign for
withdrawal, thus making the governments tactic
easier. Although the Socialdemocrats tried to
present the issue as the Act alone, with no further
implications, they had little success in this.
Furthermore, many prominent party members and trade
unions disagreed publicly with the party line,
calling for a 'Yes' vote. The referendum gave a 56%

majority for the reforms, a result few would have believed possible a few months before. Denmark, Greece and Italy then added their signatures to the Act on 28 February. In signing Italy recorded a lengthy declaration in which it spelled out the reasons for its dissatisfaction with the Act, supported the revision of Council's rules of procedure, and called for a review before 1988 to extend the Act, particularly with regard to the EP's participation in the legislative process. This was followed by a joint Italo-Belgian communiqué in which they announced their intention to coordinate their action in this direction.

CONCLUSIONS

A feature that distinguished this particular episode of reform from previous ones was its initiation by an elected Parliament. The reasons that led Parliament to take such an initiative itself have been described earlier. Parliament aimed to set in motion a political process, leaving the stage of intergovernmental negotiation until such time as sufficient political momentum had developed. In this respect, it was quite successful. Six national parliaments gave highly favourable treatment to the Draft Treaty, two even calling on their governments to ratify it as such. Political parties, trade unions, employers organizations and non-governmental organizations all gave support to Parliament. Certainly, there was no mass-mobilisation of the general public (notwithstanding the demonstration at the Milan Summit): the issue was confined to political elites. Nevertheless, the political elites in all member states became aware of Parliament's proposal and the issues it raised. In a sufficient number of member states it generated enough support for it to become either opportune or necessary for the government to take it seriously and push for reform, in turn obliging other governments to agree to discuss the issues.

It is unlikely that even the European Act would have resulted from a classic governmental initiative alone, as illustrated so often in recent years. The Treaty itself was no longer taboo and amendments were discussed on virtually the whole range of Community activities and on the powers of its institutions. In 1981, few people thought that Parliament would get so far, or even that it could draw up proposals that would gain the backing of its main political groups. When it did so few expected national governments to take the matter seriously and when Mitterrand welcomed the Draft Treaty, many felt that this was a ploy for the European elections. When the European Council established the Dooge committee on his proposal, and when it also concluded that a new Treaty on European Union was necessary, it was easy to point to the opposition of three Member States. When the European Council overrode this opposition there were doubts as to whether these States would participate in the IGC. When they did it was not at all clear that a Treaty revision would be approved. Yet, the momentum was sufficient to go through all of these stages though not to achieve as far-reaching a reform as the EP would have liked.

If the result was disappointing, this was partly due to two reasons which the EP had itself pinpointed at the outset of the process. The first of these was the need for unanimity. Parliament's Draft Treaty had envisaged the possible establishment of a European Union without all the member states of the Community joining. The precedent for this was the creation of the ECSC by only six member states of the Council of Europe at that time. Although the legal situation would be more complicated if such a maneouvre were attempted vis-à-vis the Community, Parliament had hoped that by avoiding Art. 236 EEC and conducting negotiations for a new, separate treaty it would create an entirely different dynamic (42). Reticent member states would be faced with a choice between joining in or staying out of the process: they could not simply sit back and block it. Although there was speculation at various times as to the possibility of such a conference being convened (43), notably before the Fontainebleau Summit, it did not happen. The last chance for this would have been if the reticent Members had refused to participate in the IGC called by the Milan Summit: it was perhaps because of this danger that the UK, Denmark and Greece agreed to participate. It is, of course, open to speculation as to how far the other Member States would have gone without them. Many matters in the IGC were blocked by other countries too. Nevertheless, the lowest common denominator would have been at a somewhat higher level, and such an operation would only be worthwhile if the results were significant.

The second reason advanced to explain the meagre result was the involvement of national officials. There the essence of Parliament's analysis was, perhaps, simplistic. Pointing to the repeated declarations of heads of governments in favour of European Union, and the opinion polls which consistently showed public support for the concept, it was easy to conclude that the blockage was taking place somewhere in between. Reality is of course somewhat more complex. Nevertheless, it is not unreasonable to suspect that national officials do have a vested interest in the status quo, or at least in the minimal change necessary to secure their objectives. On a number of occasions in the process, indications emerged that this was a factor. In France, for example, Maurice Faure's first draft of the conclusions of the Dooge committee was rumoured to have been approved by Mitterrand against the wishes of the Quai d'Orsay. French MEPs bemoaned the slowness with which foreign ministry officials took up instructions (44). Statements by French leaders often seemed to contradict those of officials in negotiations (45). Examples could be given for other countries, but it is clear that this is not a negligible factor.

Parliament was not able to overcome these obstacles, though the threat of a majority move to European Union and the political momentum generated before the negotiations were no doubt useful in ensuring that the first overhaul of the treaties since they were signed was actually carried through. Parliament was unsuccessful in ensuring much substance to the reforms. It will, however, have gained from the experience and one can expect new initiatives from the Parliament before the 1989 elections.

Select Bibliography

Primary sources:
Single European Act. EC Bulletin, Supplement 2/1986
Single European Act and Parliamentary scrutiny. House of Lords Select Committee on the European Communities. 6 May 1986. (HL 149)
Towards European Union II. From the European Council in Milan to the signing of the Single European Act. Documents selected and introduced by Marina Gazzo. Agence Europe, Brussels-Luxembourg 1986.

Secondary sources:
Juliet Lodge, 'The Single European Act: Towards a new Euro-Dynamism?' Journal of Common Market Studies, March 1986.

Notes
1.   For a more detailed account of these events

see Occasional Research Paper No 1, European Community Research Unit, R. Corbett; The 1985 Intergovernmental Conference University of Hull 1986.

2.   Minutes EP of July 1985 Official Journal (OJ) C 229 (9.9.85) p.29.

3.   EC Bulletin 7/8-1985, point 1.1.10.

4.   The 1965 'Merger Treaty', the 1970 and 1975 'Budget Treaties' and the 1975 revision of the EIB structure.

5.   See 'Declaration of Principles Relating to Eureka' adopted by the Hannover Ministerial Conference (5/6 November 1985); see Europe Documents No. 1380 (20.11.85).

6.   Agence Europe No. 4135 (19.7.85), p.4.

7.   See Explanatory Statement, Doc. 1-575/83/B p.4.

8.   See EP Minutes 17.4.85, OJ C 122 (20.5.85), p.88; other resolutions 12.6.85 in OJ C 175 (15.7.85), p.109, and 9.7.85 (supra note 2).

9.   EP Bulletin No. 39 (special edition 26.9.85), p.6.

10.   Press Release issued by Croux, acting chairman of the Institutional Committee (19.9.85) EP INFO-MEMO Br. 11/85 UP.

11.   EC Bulletin 10-1985, point 1.1.3.

12.   EP Bulletin No.39/Add.4 (5.12.85).

13.   Debates EP (23.10.85), OJ 2-331, p.92.

14.   See e.g. Press Release EP INFO-MEMO 117 (22.10.85) and Bull. EC 10-1985 point 4.1.3 and Debates of the EP (23.10.85), OJ 2-331.

15.   Accompanied on one occasion by Formigoni, chairman of the EP's Political Affairs Committee.

16.   Minutes EP (11.12.85), OJ C 352 (31.12.85) p.60. Adopted by 249 votes to 47 with 8 abstentions.

17.   See, for example, Dutch Foreign Minister to Dutch Parliament (Agence Europe No. 4156 (6.9.85) p.3, Italian Chief Official to Financial Times (F.T. 10 July 85, p.2), Croux letter to The Times (10 July 85).

18.   See, for example, Benelux summit 19 November 85 (Agence Europe 4208, p.5), Andreotti VIIIe Jean Monnet Lecture, 19 November 85 E.U.I.

19.   Information service of the UK Permanent Representation to the EEC No. 89 (5.10.85).

20.   See A New Phase in European Union (EP 1985) which includes the reaction of national parliaments. The Italian and Belgian Parliaments called unanimously for the ratification of the draft Treaty.

21.   Agence Europe No. 4189 (21/22.10.85).

22.   Camera di Deputati 29.11.85; unified text

of resolutions 7-00240 and 7-00242.
    23. Bundestag - 10 Wahlperiode - 181 Sitzung 5.12.85 Drucksache 10/4088.
    24. As translated by <u>Agence Europe</u> No. 4202 (12/13.11.85) p.4.
    25. PS/CE/139/85.
    26. Resolution TB/arch 21.11.85 and Press Conference (30.11.85) Agence Europe 4215, p.5.
    27. <u>ETUC statement on European Union</u> FS/AS/CL ETUC Brussels. Conference, see <u>Agence Europe</u> 4191 (25.10.85), p.5.
    28. The information used here on the proposals tabled and the reaction to them in the IGC derives from EP Bulletin No. 39 (26.9.85) and its addendum 1 (7.10.85), 2(10.10.85), 3(25.10.85), 4(5.12.85), 5(6.12.85), EC <u>Bulletin</u> 9-1985 (ch. 1), EC Bull. 10-1985 (ch. 1), EC Bull. 11-1985 (ch. 1), the Dossier di Documentazione No. 13 (12.2.86) of the Camera di Deputati (Rel. Com. and Int.), and the press, notably <u>Agence Europe</u>.
    29. <u>Agence Europe</u> No 4194 (30.10.85) p.5.
    30. Also taken from the EP Draft Treaty (Art. 59).
    31. See EP's Draft Treaty (preamble, last indent and Art. 12.2).
    32. Delors' press conference, Brussels 4.12.85.
    33. For existing procedure see EP-Council Joint Declaration of 4.3.75, European Treaties (Official Publication Office) p.900.
    34. Minutes EP (idem note 16 above).
    35. In the 1986 budget the EP had voted a new budget chapter 102 for the creation of a first instance chamber for certain cases.
    36. EC <u>Bulletin</u> 11.1985 point 1.1.2.
    37. Hansard 5 Dec. 85, Vol. 88, No 22, Col. 429.
    38. Criticism in "Interpellation" in Belgian Parliament by Dierickx, Van Miert and others, and in TV debate on 22.12.85 with members of EP's Institutional Committee (see <u>De Morgen</u> 24.12.85).
    39. <u>Agence Europe</u> No 4257 (10/11.2.1986).
    40. <u>Agence Europe</u> No 4234 (9.1.86) p.3.
    41. Minutes EP 16 Jan. 86 OJ C 36 (17.2.86) p.144. Approved by 209 to 61 with 42 abstentions.
    42. See R. Corbett: "Spaak II or Schuman II: the implications of Art. 82 of the Draft Treaty on European Union" in <u>The Federalist</u> (year XXVII No. 2, Oct. 1985) Pavia, Italy.
    43. Mitterrand had referred in his speech to the EP on 24 May 1985 to a 'conference of Member

States concerned' (Debates of the EP OJ 1-314 p.263) a hint repeated a number of times by French Ministers.

    44.   See e.g. Sutra Debates of the EP 23 October 85 (OJ No 2-331 p.99).

    45.   E.g. P.M. Fabius' speech to Congress of the Parti Socialiste, Toulouse Oct. 1985. Extracts quoted in <u>30 jours d'Europe</u> December 85 No. 329, p.2.

Chapter Twelve

PAST EXPERIENCE AND LESSONS FOR THE FUTURE

Roy Pryce (1)

As the preceding chapters have shown, since 1973 the search for 'an ever closer union' has been taking place in circumstances which in several crucial respects have been very different from those which prevailed when the Community consisted of only six member states. The most important changes are those which have occurred in the nature of the Community itself. Above all, it has been those resulting from the doubling of the number of its members, and its transformation from a relatively homogeneous group to one characterised by marked diversity which have proved decisive. Coupled with this has been a much more difficult set of economic circumstances. So although pressures on the member states to work more closely together have continued to increase, their capacity to respond effectively has been very limited. What has been achieved is a series of limited piecemeal advances. The outcome of the most recent negotiations, the Single European Act, belongs firmly to that category. And, whatever interpretation is put on it, it quite clearly does not constitute that transformation of the Community into a European Union which the members long ago pledged themselves to achieve.

The critical difference between the enlarged Community and that of the original Six has been that the former did not have some members persistently hostile towards its development towards 'an ever closer union'. The Six had the problem of coping with a very wobbly France in the 'fifties which acted successively as prime mover and then as prime obstacle to the development of the Community. But in that country there were always powerful friends of the Community manoeuvering in the background and waiting in the wings. And when de Gaulle came to power although his attitudes and policies were to create serious tensions with his partners, there was

never any doubt about French commitment to a closer
union among the states of western Europe. Since 1973
that common commitment has been lacking. This period
may prove to have been merely a deviant interlude in
the history of the process of integration, but it has
made progress towards European Union very difficult
during these last years.

RECENT EXPERIENCE

Given the unfavourable circumstances, we should be
surprised not so much by the failure to achieve this
goal as by the fact that, in spite of all the
difficulties, some forward movement has nevertheless
continued. The most successful strategies have been
those which have focussed on limited goals: for
instance, the creation of the European Council, the
introduction of direct elections, the establishment
of the European Monetary System, the pragmatic
development of Political Cooperation, and - most
recently - the Single European Act. All these are in
marked contrast to the much more ambitious aims of
European Union. Some indeed argue that the commitment
to this objective has been at best an irrelevance and
at worst a positive hindrance. In support of this
thesis they point to the continuing uncertainty about
the meaning of the concept, the hostile response it
has evoked in Britain and Denmark, and the way it has
generated far more rhetoric than positive action.

Role of Rhetoric
Such arguments, however, fail to take account of the
complex reality of Community politics. Part of that
reality is the important function performed by
rhetoric, as has been recognised by Christopher
Tugendhat, who served as a Member and subsequently
Vice-President of the EC Commission from 1979 to
1984:

> Rhetoric, accompanied by imaginative proposals
> and gestures, has a vital role to play in all
> political systems. It appeals to the emotions
> and instincts, raises men's and women's eyes
> from their immediate and parochial concerns to
> more distant horizons and generates the ground-
> swell and ultimately the popular demand that are
> necessary for the attainment of all great
> objectives. In a multinational system, lacking
> the cohesion of a nation state, its role is

particularly important. (2)

That role, Tugendhat adds, is essentially to 'expand the frontiers of the possible', and to realise the potential inherent in a given situation: in this case, in the Community. The role played by rhetoric varies from country to country, as does its style: both are heavily conditioned by historical and cultural factors. But for the members of the Community, most of whom have had to face changes of political regime in the last 30-40 years and three of whom have only recently emerged from dictatorial regimes, it plays a very important role, justifying the changes which have been made, underpinning current democratic and parliamentary regimes, and providing beacons for their future development. The rhetoric of European Union is part of the same political context. And it not only expresses deeply-held convictions but also provides the rationale, justification and incentive for political action.

Reiterated rhetoric has itself also generated and maintained pressure for action. The formal adoption by the leaders of the Community in 1972 of European Union as their future goal had a series of important political consequences. In the first place, it meant that the issue was placed firmly on the Community's agenda: it was a collective commitment undertaken at the highest level by the member states. Once undertaken, it could not simply be filed and forgotten. So even in the midst of a great weight of more immediate issues, space had to be found for it on the agenda – and not once, but on repeated occasions. And each time the issue returned it had to be treated, even by those who derided the idea, by at least a semblance of seriousness: it could not simply be discarded. And although the differences were such that it was impossible for several years to do more than simply repeat, and in exactly the same terms, the original commitment, the mere fact of repetition itself also had political consequences. Gradually it became more and more difficult to continue to do nothing. Devices were found by those who hoped the issue would go away, or collapse under the weight of reiterated opposition, to delay action as long as possible. So reports were called for, and – once received – committees were set up to study them and report again. This game was played successfully for a number of years. But at the same time a price was extracted by those who wanted something to come out of it. At first it seemed a very modest price: the Solemn Declaration of 1983 could be accepted because it was heavy only on rhetoric and empty of any substantive action. But by now the ·leaders of the Community were beginning to lose credibility: the cumulative effect of repeated rhetorical commitments was to make some form of action eventually inescapable.

From Exhortation to Action

Repetition also had the effect of building up other pressures in favour of eventual action. It provided, in the first place, both the justification and the occasion for continued concern and reflection about the longer term future of the Community even at a time when its day-to-day concerns were heavily dominated by immediate and pressing problems. Indeed, the more heavily these weighed on the agenda of the Community, to the point in the early 'eighties when they led to an apparent impasse and growing sense of crisis about its affairs, accompanied by a pervasive and growing pessimism about the capacity of western Europe to respond to the many challenges crowding in upon it, (3) the stronger the arguments became that such problems could only find a solution in the context of a major act of will and a transformation of the relations between the member states and the way they tackled common problems.

At the same time the commitment to European Union also acted as a stimulus to reflection about how this could be achieved. It was this thinking that was canalised, developed, and given more political immediacy by the action of Spinelli and his colleagues in the European Parliament. In the process, a significant new factor was introduced into the discussion of the future of the Community. Previously the European Parliament had played only a minor and subsidiary role in this respect: now it was able to seize the initiative, harness its own institutional ambitions to the achievement of European Union, and give a new thrust to the pressures for action.

This is another example of the way in which the commitment to European Union generated a momentum which, over time, became increasingly difficult to resist. Once this particular Pandora's box had been opened it was impossible wholly to lock it up again. Without the prior commitment of the leaders of the member states to the goal of European Union it would have been far more difficult for Spinelli and his colleagues to persuade the European Parliament to support their proposals. And subsequently it was difficult for the other leaders to oppose the initiative taken by Mitterrand at Fontainebleau in June 1984. That initiative itself had been solicited by Spinelli who appealed to Mitterrand to use the opportunity offered by the French presidency to resume its leadership of the Community. Even if other factors also prompted Mitterrand's action - some tactical considerations related to putting pressure on Mrs Thatcher to settle the budgetary dispute may also have been involved - the President's speech in May that year to the European Parliament showed that there was certainly a close connection with its own Draft Treaty. Whatever his precise motivation, his intervention again showed that both propulsive elites and national leaders have a crucial role to play if closer union is to be achieved, and that a combined and concerted effort is required if goals are not only to be defined but action taken to achieve them.

At the same time recent experience has also underlined several other conditions which need to be fulfilled if such action is to succeed. One is the need for persistence and patience. Several of the forward steps taken during the 'seventies, for instance, were conceived and proposed many years earlier. Provision was made in the 1952 Treaty of Paris for the introduction of direct elections to the Coal and Steel Community's Common Assembly, but it took more than 25 years before it was finally achieved. The moves towards closer political cooperation in the 'seventies were also a belated and very partial realisation of much more ambitious plans put forward at the time of the discussion of the project for a Political Community, and subsequently in the context of de Gaulle's project for a Political Union. Similarly, the creation of the European Monetary System can be traced back to ideas generated well before the Rome treaties, and given more precision in the discussions on Economic and Monetary Union in the late 'sixties and early 'seventies. So what at first sight might appear to be wholly discrete and pragmatic developments were in fact the delayed implementation of earlier and more ambitious plans. None of them would have come about had such plans not been enunciated in the first place, or subsequently pursued in spite of repeated setbacks.

The substantive changes brought about by these developments concerned different aspects of the work of the Communities: their scope, the intensity of forms of common action, and institutional arrangements. In their different ways they were all

277

intended to improve their functioning, their utility, and their acceptability. But each had to wait until sufficient support had been mobilised among the member states to persuade the more reluctant among them to agree. The process by which this was achieved was heavily contingent on the play of personalities and chance. The decision to hold direct elections, for instance, was only achieved as part of a deal concluded in 1974 to set up the European Council: it was the quid pro quo demanded by those member states which had always supported the original and more supranational institutional blueprint. The EMS, while being suggested by Roy Jenkins early in his spell as President of the Commission, only entered the realm of practical politics when it was taken up and pushed hard by Giscard and Schmidt. And in the development of EPC the common interest of the larger member states (including Britain) in acquiring more collective clout on the international scene was equally decisive. The common feature in all these cases was the harnessing of significant national interests to a particular project designed to strengthen the Community.

National Attitudes and Initiatives

So far in the case of European Union such linkages have operated only to a very limited extent. Italy and the Benelux countries have given their sustained support, but it has not been sufficiently high on the agenda of French and German leaders for them to give either systematic individual support or to take a major joint initiative to push it through. Giscard and Schmidt for their part were much more interested in achieving a significant advance in the field of monetary integration where the economic benefits even in the relatively short term were expected to be tangible and significant, and where there would be no need of side payments to the European Parliament or changes in the ways the Community conducted its business. Their successors, Mitterrand and Kohl, appeared at one point ready to take a joint initiative to rescue the Community from the crisis which overtook it in the early 'eighties, but this failed to materialise except for a belated, hastily-conceived and limp proposal for a treaty on political cooperation presented at a very late stage of the preparations for the June 1985 Milan meeting of the European Council. Its main effect then was to enrage Mrs Thatcher and endanger the outcome of the meeting.

Chancellor Kohl has given sustained and enthusiastic verbal support for the idea of European Union, but has not been able to deliver a significant initiative or a consistent policy: party rivalries within the coalition as well as the strength of ministerial bureaucracies and their political champions have proved too strong for his style of leadership. And while Mitterrand did take an important initiative at Fontainebleau in June 1984, his interest visibly diminished thereafter, not least no doubt because of his increasing preoccupation with domestic politics.

That initiative was nevertheless carried forward by a common conviction that something had to be done to make the Community a more effective instrument, and in particular by a convergence of pressures to concentrate on the achievement of a more effective internal market. It was a modest objective compared with the ambitions nurtured for the Community in the early 'fifties, and a very partial response to the challenges with which it is now confronted. It nevertheless had the advantage of being severely practical, strongly supported by powerful economic interests, and also - and not least - by Mrs Thatcher. So it was around this theme that a convergence of the longer- and shorter-range interests took place, and around it too that the bargains were constructed which led to the Single European Act. It was not at all what the protagonists of European Union had aimed for, but it at least had the merit of providing, if not without many difficulties, a <u>terrain d'entente</u> for the member states.

As the analysis presented in the last chapter has shown, the resulting agreement very clearly reflected the nature of the Community on the eve of its enlargement to include Spain and Portugal, and the uneasy balance of forces within it. In the absence of strong Franco-German leadership its original six member states proved incapable of acting as a compact group with a clearly defined and agreed set of objectives and strategy to achieve them; and while three of its newer members were reluctant to agree on moves towards a closer union, they pursued individual policies rather than forming a collective bloc. The outcome was a series of uneasy compromises, lacking any overall coherence, and shot through with ambiguities, reservations, and unresolved issues.

It is not surprising that the Single European Act has subsequently given rise to very varying interpretations. Opponents in Denmark and Britain have denounced it as another major 'surrender' of national sovereignty, while supporters of the Parliament's own proposals, including the Italian government, have strongly criticised the Act as being far too weak and feeble. Some even consider it to mark a retreat in certain respects from the 'acquis communautaire', and to have created new obstacles in the way of closer union, (4) while others on the contrary see significant possibilities of exploiting its provisions to extend, for instance, the use of majority voting in the Council and to expand the legislative role of the European Parliament. (5) Only time will tell which of these various interpretations is the more accurate - and that is likely to depend much more on the future balance of political forces within the Community than on the niceties of rival legal interpretations of its various provisions.

FUTURE PERSPECTIVES

Short-term Prospects

In the immediate future - that is, in the coming three to four years - the interest of many concerned with the achievement of a closer union will be focussed primarily on how the Single European Act will be implemented. It is unlikely that further significant initiatives will be taken during this period. The 'window of opportunity' that opened up after Fontainebleau has been exploited, if with disappointing results: both Mitterrand and Kohl are now preoccupied with their own political future and a general election also looms for Mrs Thatcher in 1987 or 1988. At the same time more immediate issues are again crowding in on the Community's agenda. It has to cope with the consequences of the entry of Spain and Portugal; face up to another impending budgetary crisis with the exhaustion of its (recently increased) funds and the threat of a reopening of the dispute about the British budgetary contribution; continue to grapple with the reform of the CAP; and also deal with a series of major external policy issues. In the forefront of attention are those concerned with relations with the United States, with persistent friction on trade issues running in parallel with tensions within the Atlantic Alliance on a whole range of issues arising from East-West relations.

The major goal which the member governments have set themselves is the achievement of a barrier-free internal market by the end of 1992. It is in the context of their efforts to achieve this that the

main test of the Single European Act will take place.
A first indication of the attitudes and policies of
the member governments will be given in the course of
the negotiation of a new set of internal rules of
procedure for the Council of Ministers providing,
inter alia, for the procedure to be used for the
calling and holding of votes. But a more important
test will be the actual use of the new articles
providing for majority decisions on specified
issues. It is by no means certain that regular use
will be made of these new rules, any more than has
been the case where the original treaties laid down
that qualified or simple majorities were to be used
to take decisions. (6) Member states may well
hesitate to press for a vote, even on an issue which
they wish to see settled and for which a majority
could be mobilised, for fear of being obliged to
accept similar treatment on issues on which they
anticipate being in a minority. Similarly, a member
state exercising the Presidency may be reluctant to
have recourse to majority voting, especially if it
happens to be one which opposed the introduction of
the new rules. And the Commission, for its part, will
have to make careful calculations about its need for,
and the availability of, allies among the member
states on a range of issues before pressing for a
vote in a particular case. The pressures to prolong
discussion until a consensus emerges will certainly
continue to operate strongly, and the governments
were careful, when laying down time limits for the
second phase of the new procedure of cooperation with
the Parliament, to leave themselves plenty of
loopholes - including an open-ended timetable (as at
present) for the first stage of the legislative
procedure, and the absence of any sanctions should
time limits not be observed.

There are many other uncertainties about how the
SEA will be implemented by the governments. Whether
or not, for instance, more use will be made of
existing majority vote provisions; to what extent the
threat or use of the veto in cases where a member
states argues that a very important national interest
is at stake will in any way be curbed or modified,
either formally or in practice; and to what extent
the various national reservations built into the SEA
will operate to defeat its original objectives of
more rapid decision-making and a more effective
common market.

Alongside these questions are others, of equal
importance, relating to patterns of interest within
the 12-member Community. It remains to be seen, for

instance, whether there will be a stable and substantial majority in favour of using the SEA to speed up decision making, or whether coalitions will be formed on a more ad hoc and temporary basis. Much will also depend on the exercise of leadership within the group, and whether this will prove to be even more fragmented and uncertain than in the past or whether - given the positive attitudes being displayed by Spain and Portugal - a decisive shift will take place in favour of a more dynamic approach to the building of the Community.

There are equal uncertainties as far as the European Parliament is concerned. It, too, has first to revise its own Standing Orders to equip it to operate the new system: a process which in the past has - as its own members confess - proved 'long and arduous'. (7) Having done this, it then faces the task of working out strategies to maximise the advantages it can draw from the SEA: some of these have been outlined in the last chapter. But it will only be able to reject or propose amendments to the 'common position' of the Council if a majority of its members can be mobilised. In an assembly of 518 members divided both by national considerations and a wide gamut of different party affiliations, this may prove to be difficult, other than on exceptional occasions. At all events, the construction of such majorities will require leadership, skill and diplomacy, as well as complex bargaining among the party groups. The new system of cooperation could in fact prove to be a poisoned chalice, offering the appearance of some greater influence on decisions but in practice offering fewer real possibilities than existing practice.

Those involved in working out a strategy for the European Parliament in the new situation have already shown more than a little concern about the balance sheet it will be able to present to the citizens of the Community countries when the next elections to it are held in June 1989. In advance of these elections the Parliament needs a clear strategy with regard to its own Draft Treaty for European Union. Shortly before his death in May 1986 Spinelli had made his own views known: true to the line he had regularly taken, he argued that Parliament should aim to fulfil the role of a Constituent Assembly, and be mandated by the governments to draw up a definitive Treaty for European Union which would then be submitted for ratification direct to the appropriate constitutional authorities in each member state. He also suggested that at least in certain countries (and in

Italy in particular) that mandate should be conferred by a popular referendum. But others were sceptical about such an approach, arguing that it was unrealistic to expect most member governments to agree to such a procedure. The issue can be expected to remain controversial throughout the remaining life of the present Parliament. But if there are no major changes in the overall configuration of the political forces in the Community countries in the remaining years of the present decade, the prospects for any major new leap forward during this period appear slight. By the same token it remains doubtful whether the Community will be able to reach even the more modest goal of a genuine internal market by the end of 1992. At the current rate of progress, its slow shuffle forward will leave it still some way from its target by that date.

Longer term Prospects
Looking further forward to the end of the century and beyond, the central questions to be posed are the extent to which the pressures and forces which have shaped the Community over the past fifteen years are likely to be modified; whether the resultant changes are likely to make it easier or more difficult for its members to move towards a closer union; and the most appropriate strategies for making progress towards that goal. In seeking answers to these questions we need to pay particular attention to the factors likely to affect the two major constraints which have so far impeded progress in that direction: on the one hand, the strength of the loyalties felt towards the nation state and the resistance offered by national economic and political structures to closer integration; and on the other, the concern felt strongly in some member countries that a closer European Union might disrupt the Atlantic Alliance and weaken or remove the strategic protection of the United States.

National and Community Environments. As far as the general economic, social and political environment in western Europe itself is concerned, there is little reason to expect any major upheavals. However pessimistically the Europeans may sometimes judge their own situation, the region is likely to remain one of the more prosperous, peaceful and stable parts of the world. Current political regimes, including those parliamentary systems which have recently replaced authoritarian rule, face fewer threats than at the end of the 'sixties, in spite of continuing high levels of unemployment. Opposition parties, including the Communists, accept the rules of the democratic political game, and there is only a small minority of groups which favour violence. The political swings that will certainly take place can be expected to remain within much the same parameters as in recent years, and this means a continuation of a broad consensus of political support for the Community.

But this scenario also implies a continuation of the current strength of national structures and the loyalties that go with them. There will be little chance in such circumstances for a European Union to be constructed which is regarded as being hostile to, or likely to undermine, the identity of the individual member states. Strategies designed to achieve such a Union have to demonstrate that it would not be a New Leviathan, either by design or accident; (8) that it would only have powers in those matters where the individual states are no longer able to act effectively on their own; and that it would preserve and enhance, rather than diminish, the diversity which all Europeans prize.

As far as the Community environment itself is concerned, this is likely to be more stable than in the past fifteen years at least as far as the number of members is concerned: the period of rapid successive enlargements is now over. Turkey is the only sizeable country which appears to be interested in the possibility of membership, and that remains an uncertain and long-term prospect. (9) The members of the Community should therefore have more time and energy to devote to its own development. The spread of interests of its 12 members will, however, not make it easy to arrive at common policies, and the entry of Spain and Portugal has exacerbated such problems as the balance to be struck between the interests of the richer and poorer members of the club, the size and use of the Community's budgetary resources, and a range of sectorial issues including agriculture and fisheries. Existing policies will have to be adjusted to accommodate this increased diversity of interests, and this means more extensive use of the panoply of devices the Community has already developed to meet such needs, ranging from various kinds of temporary or semi-permanent waivers, extended timetables for the implementation of common policies, and specific measures to deal with particularly intractable problems in a

particular region or country. The development of a
12-member Community also means that it is unrealistic
to expect that all its members can move forward over
a whole wide front and at the same speed towards
closer union. Any strategy aiming at European Union
will have to make proper provision for this.

The International Environment

By far the biggest challenge to the Community will,
however, be posed by pressure from its international
environment. The members of the Community, both
individually and collectively, are very heavily
dependent on this environment and extremely
vulnerable to changes in it. This is true both for
their welfare and their security. Over the years the
degree of their dependence and vulnerability has
steadily increased. This is likely to continue in the
future in part as a reflection of the growing
interdependence of the world as a whole but also
because of the heavy dependence of the Community on
international trade and its position in a region
where the two Super Powers confront each other. At
the same time the Community has also emerged as an
actor of some consequence in world affairs and the
level of its involvement continues to grow through
the extensive network of trade and other
relationships which it has developed with other
countries and parts of the world.

   Taken together these factors are likly to have
two main effects on the Community. This first will be
to increase the pressures on its members to take up
common positions on issues of the Community's
external relations, and to develop their internal
cohesion to enable them to do so. Part of this
pressure is likely to arise from the need to take up
a collective position in the face of particular
events or crises. The first six months of 1986
provided three examples of the type of situation of
which there will be many more in the future: the US
demand that the members of the Community should take
common action against the terrorist activity being
promoted and supported by the Libyan leader Colonel
Gadaffi; the need to take collective action to
protect Community citizens against the effects of the
radioactive fallout following the Chernobyl disaster
in the Soviet Union; and the need to formulate a
collective stance to put pressure on the South
African government to end apartheid following its
introduction of a state of emergency. In addition to
responding to such immediate events, there will also

be steady pressure to maintain and develop common policies over the whole range of the Community's external relations, and to develop the instruments necessary to enable it to take effective action. Such considerations will give added force to the pressures to ensure that an effective internal market is achieved; to develop complementary policies to sustain the Community's industrial base, especially in fields of high technology; and to increase its internal and external monetary cohesion.

But alongside these pressures impelling the members of the Community towards closer union, sharp divergencies are likely to remain about the content of the policies needed to provide a response to them. The difficulties experienced in the first half of 1986 in arriving at common positions on the three major issues mentioned above illustrate the type of problems which are certain to persist. The various members of the Community - and not least its more important members - continue to differ on such major issues as its posture towards the United States and the Soviet Union, as well as key aspects of international trade policy. The result is greatly to diminish its capacity to take rapid and concerted action, and frequently to confine its response to an external challenge to the line of least resistance or a weak policy based on the lowest common denominator of agreement. Conflicts over such issues can also feed back into other policy areas and have a negative impact on the overall performance of the Community.

In the coming years the ability of the members of the Community to develop common responses to external challenges will be of even greater importance than in the past in the context of their capacity to move towards a closer union. It will be severely tested in many areas, and especially with regard to relations with the United States and the Soviet Union. Important structural shifts are currently taking place in those relationships, and not simply cyclical changes due to the personalities and policies of the leaders of the two Super Powers. On the surface many familiar features remain: the division of Europe, the rival alliances, and Soviet and US troops and bases encamped in their respective spheres of influence. Western Europe also continues to be dependent on the US for its strategic defence. But the strains and stresses are now more than ever apparent. Some of these arise from the growing impatience in the US with the continued stationing of their troops in Europe to defend a group of countries whose contribution to their own defence many now consider far too small. On the European side there are doubts about US strategic and nuclear policies and its posture towards the Soviet Union. Recent shifts in the tone and content of Soviet policy are another important factor in some significant changes in European perceptions of the two Super Powers and future relations with them.

In western Europe these new developments have so far produced far more discussion than agreement on their implications and the policy response that should be made to them. They have encouraged those already critical of NATO policies and membership to develop a number of possible alternative strategies, ranging from proposals that the US should remove its nuclear bases from western Europe, through various types of non-nuclear policies, to projects for the disengagement of European countries from the two rival alliances. But those opposition parties, like the SPD in Germany and the Labour and Alliance parties in Britain which have in varying degrees challenged conventional wisdom have not found it easy to agree on alternative strategies. And while most of the member governments, for their part, have responded very cautiously to these new factors and have stressed both their commitment to the Alliance and the extent of agreement on its aims and policies, this has not disguised the extent of the uncertainties and disagreements on their part too. But at the same time they have had difficulty in establishing common European positions on a range of important issues. The costs of their inability to work more effectively together are becoming steadily higher, and sapping efforts to give a clearer and sharper expression to their own specific interests within the Alliance.

The capacity of the members of the Community to overcome their differences and move towards a common defence and security policy will provide a critical test in the coming years of their commitment to closer union. The prospects for this depend very much on the willingness (or otherwise) of a core group among them - and in particular France, Germany and Britain - to concert policies and action. More than anything else it is the path they take on this set of issues which will determine whether or not a real European Union emerges, for without substantial progress towards a defence union it will remain seriously incomplete.

Past Experience and Lessons for the Future

Conditions for Moving Towards Closer Union
There is no doubt of the extent and nature of the
challenges which the members of the Community will
face in the coming years: what is uncertain is their
ability to respond to them. It is not the task of
this study to attempt to make predictions about this:
what our analysis can do, however, is to suggest the
conditions which need to be fulfilled if the
Community is to advance towards a closer union, and
the most promising types of strategy to achieve this.

A Renewed Motivation. One condition is that the
promotional elites should maintain their commitment
to, and enthusiasm for, the Community and be capable
of attracting the support of a younger generation for
its further development. Now that it has become so
much an established feature of the scene a good deal
of the idealism intially associated with it has
evaporated, to be replaced by more mundane arguments
about the costs of 'non-Europe' and the material
benefits which a more effective internal market would
bring. (10) There are many to whom such arguments are
the crucial ones, and it would be quite impossible to
pursue the aim of a closer union successfully unless
there were strong expectations of significant
economic gains. But the enthusiasm of a younger
generation will not be captured by such arguments
which lack the element of idealism which was so
marked a feature of the goals originally set for the
Community. In this context the opening sentences of
the Schuman Plan declaration deserve to be recalled:

> World peace cannot be safeguarded without
> constructive efforts proportionate to the
> dangers which threaten it.

> The contribution which an organised and living
> Europe can bring to civilisation is
> indispensable to the maintenance of peaceful
> relations.

The need to recapture this original vision of a
Community serving not only the interests of its own
citizens, but those of mankind as a whole through its
contribution to securing a more peaceful world has
been strongly argued by Christopher Layton in a
recent report which also explores how Europe's
potential contribution to a better world order could
be made. (11) Starting from the premiss that if
humanity is to survive a new and urgent phase of

288

international cooperation and action is necessary,
and a remainder that the founding fathers of the
Community intended that it should play a role in this
context, the report argues that it is now more than
ever in Europe's own interest that it should do so.
As the region with the largest share in world trade
it has an obvious interest in a stable and developing
world economy. As a front-line region between the two
Super Powers it has a fundamental interest in detente
and disarmament. Its historical relationships,
trading interests and humanitarian concern already
make it the largest giver of aid and development
assistance to the third world and it has a major
interest in assisting poor countries to achieve
sustainable development. Having pioneered the first
international legislation to protect the environment, it is also well placed to contribute to the
world-wide agreements which are now needed, for
instance, to protect forests from acid rain and
people from industrial poisons of the sort released
by the accidents at Seveso and Bhopal, and from the
nuclear fallout from Chernobyl. More generally, too,
the example of the Community as an evolving regional
union which has found ways of reconciling the
interests of former enemies in a voluntary process
which preserves the identity of its component nations
can both encourage other regional groupings and
suggest some of the strategies and techniques best
calculated to succeed. The Community's experience
provides evidence that progress towards peaceful
relations between nations can be made more swiftly at
the regional than at the world level. It also
suggests very strongly that a multi-polar world
consisting of several such groupings alongside the
Super Powers is a desirable objective and an
important way of preventing global polarisation.

If such perspectives on the wider tasks and
objectives of the Community were to be more widely
recognised and accepted, and a vigorous debate
stimulated on how it should set about their
achievement, this could harness powerful new
energies, not least those of young people. They have
already shown their readiness to respond generously
to appeals such as Live Aid to rescue the starving of
the world, but are impatient and often disgusted by
the state of the world and the threats which hang
over it. Unless the Community is seen to be relevant
in the context of these global concerns and at least
potentially capable of playing a positive role in the
construction of a safer and more equitable world it
will fail to gain their support. And without that not

only will the prospects of its further development sharply diminish: it could quite easily be relegated to a marginal and declining role in the future.

A Clear Goal: Sustained Pressure. A second important condition for progress towards closer union is that those in the vanguard of moves towards this goal should have a clear objective around which to mobilise support. By now European Union has established itself both as that objective and also as a rallying cry. It has the formal and reiterated support not only of the heads of government, but of the majority of the political parties in the member states, and of the European Parliament. The latter's Draft Treaty provides a comprehensive proposal setting out what it should consist of and how it should be organised. At the same time as a battle cry 'European Union' has the great virtue of simplicity: with imagination and effort it could become a powerful popular slogan.

In maintaining and building up pressure for the achievement of European Union among both elites and the general public the European Parliament has a crucial role to play. By virtue of the initiatives it has already taken the Parliament now occupies a potentially strategic position. It is able, if it so chooses, to take up a leadership role with respect to the promotional elites, both encouraging their further reflections and providing a forum where pressure can be maintained on the member governments. At the same time, through the direct contact its members can have with the general public, and in particular on the occasion of the next European parliamentary elections in 1989, it can keep the issue of European Union alive in the media and in the mind of the general public. It can lead a campaign for another round of negotiations, and seek to influence the parameters, substance, and outcome of such negotiations.

Some of its members, following the position taken by Spinelli shortly before his death, aim to persuade it to be even more ambitious. They argue that the Parliament should be given a mandate from the governments to act as a Constituent Assembly and negotiate the terms of a treaty to usher in European Union. Some also propose that the outcome should then be submitted without alteration for ratification by the member states, so avoiding an intergovernmental conference. It may be worth pursuing such a line to establish a bargaining position to make sure that the

Parliament would have an opportunity for genuine influence over the contents of such a treaty. But the governments are most unlikely to allow the Parliament to monopolise the process of negotiation and dictate the terms of European Union. Both the experience of the Ad Hoc Assembly in 1952-54 (in a much more favourable environment than today) as well as the recent experience of the European Parliament in the negotiations leading up to the Single European Act underline the strength of the resistance it can expect from national governments and their respective administrations.

Harnessing National Interests

More generally, the experience of the Community as a whole since 1973 also provides a number of warnings about the strength of the obstacles to be overcome and the additional conditions which need to be fulfilled if genuine progress towards European Union is to be made.

In the first place, much stronger suport will be required from the member governments accompanied by more positive and concerted action particularly on the part of French and German leaders than has so far been available. Verbal commitment has not been lacking, but the willingness of the governments to accept an outcome as modest as the Single European Act clearly demonstrates the limits of that commitment.

Further progress will not be made unless the ambitions to achieve closer union are harnessed to the resolution of serious and immediate problems perceived by the member states and the expectation on their part of palpable benefits in the short or medium term. To satisfy this condition something more than the proposals set out in the Parliament's Draft Treaty will be needed. While it provides a constitutional framework to bring together in an organic relationship both the activities covered by the Community treaties and those being conducted through the system of political cooperation, and sketches in the further objectives to be sought – together in some cases with the means for their achievement – its provisions do not, as they stand, provide a sufficient incentive for governments to subscribe to them. As far as its institutional proposals are concerned, for instance, the proposed package of measures imply a major shift of authority in favour of the European Parliament largely at the expense of the member governments. Strong though the case certainly is to ensure more effective parliamentary supervision of the Community, and participation in its legislative processes, (functions which national parliaments are unable to perform), the package proposed by the Parliament is hardly calculated to attract the enthusiastic support of the governments to which it is addressed.

Long experience of previous attempts at institutional reform, including that leading up to the Single European Act, also teaches that such attempts - and in particular those of the European Parliament to increase its own powers - are only likely to succeed if they are related to the achievement of policy goals sought by the member states. The pursuit of European Union must necessarily include, therefore, the identification of such goals and the building of coalitions among the member states for their achievement. The same is also true of attempts to increase the Community's budgetary resources, which remains another crucial aspect of moving towards closer union.

The most promising area for progress in this direction appears to lie at present in a further development of economic integration. The central thrust of policy-making is currently focussed on the internal market, and there is resistance in some capitals to moving towards closer monetary integration. But in the coming years the need to go beyond the present first stage of the European Monetary System is likely to emerge both as a necessary support for the maintenance and development of the internal market, and also as a desirable complement to it. This, together with measures to strengthen the Community's industrial base, and further reform the CAP, could provide the basis for a new package, including institutional reform, leading closer towards European Union.

It cannot be ruled out, however, that developments in the international environment may provide an incentive for a new thrust towards a defence union, alongside measures designed to achieve a more effective range of concerted actions in the field of foreign policy. Were such pressures to develop, they should be harnessed to the same objective of European Union. As in 1952-54 there would a need to provide a strong institutional framework to ensure the political guidelines and supervision required to control the policies and military apparatus of such a union.

A Flexible Strategy

A flexible strategy is required to take advantage of whichever route emerges as the most promising one to take. The strategy also has to be flexible in terms of a willingness to seize opportunities either for incremental advances or, if circumstances allow, for a major leap forward. As our analysis of past experience has shown, both types of advance have been made at different periods and it is very difficult to forsee the circumstances in which one or the other may be feasible. It is important that those in the vanguard should aim high and have their proposals ready to take advantage of favourable circumstances: the governments can be relied on to provide their usual quota of shorter-term considerations. And in any case, a long haul still lies ahead. Even the most ambitious leap forward on the lines envisaged by the Draft Treaty, while offering the prospect of the achievement of European Union in name, would leave much of its substance still to be achieved.

Flexibility is also required in a Community of Twelve to take account of the difficulties of all advancing at the same pace, in all sectors, towards the desired objective. Within those spheres covered by the Community treaties this has already been recognised by a variety of devices, and that need will persist for the forseeable future. The same considerations also apply to those areas covered by political co-operation and - with even greater force - in defence and security matters. Two principles should be followed: first, that no individual member state or minority group of states should be able to prevent the majority from moving forward; and, second, that no individual member state should be obliged to subscribe to objectives with which it disagrees, or to implement decisions in conflict with its basic interests. (12) The application of these principles would imply a continued degree of 'differentiated integration' and its possible extension to new domains. It has been suggested, for instance, (13) that in addition to providing greater flexibility with regard to the rules to be applied to individual policy sectors (particularly those relating to processes of harmonisation), and to the implementation of such rules, the same principles should also apply to decisions regarding the extension of Community powers and competences ('organic laws' in the language of the Parliament's Draft Treaty). One way of providing for this would be to allow a majority of member states representing two-thirds of the Community's population to take such decisions. Those states in the dissenting minority would then have the option of rallying to the majority position, negotiating a waiver, or - as a last resort - of leaving the Community.

The introduction of such a system under the Community's present rules would, however, itself require unanimity, and that is unlikely to be forthcoming. Other means will have to be found of dealing with the problem of a reluctant minority. Some regard the persistence of such a minority as the crucial problem for the whole future development of the Community. But even in recent years it has been far from a consistent or compact bloc, and both its composition and behaviour may well change in the future as national governments change and their policies evolve. The greater problem in fact, as it has been throughout the history of the Community, is the building and sustaining of a majority of member states committed to, and determined to achieve, closer union. This has to be built around a core group of countries sharing such a commitment, and that core has to include both France and Germany. A heavy responsibility continues to rest on the shoulders of the leaders of these two countries, as it has done from the beginning of the process to which they gave birth.

Select Bibliography

Karl Kaiser, Cesare Merlini, Thierry de Montbrial, Edmund Wellenstein and William Wallace, The European Community: Progress or decline? Eng. ed. London, Royal Institute of International Affairs, 1983.
Philippe Moreau Defarges, Quel avenir pour quelle Communauté? Paris, 1986.
John Pinder, 'European Union: gradualism and constitution', The Federalist (Pavia) December 1985.
Loukas Tsoukalis (ed), The European Community: past, present and future, Special issue of Journal of Common Market Studies, September/December 1982.
Wolfgang Wessels, 'Die Einheitliche Europäische Akte - Zementierung des Status quo oder Einstieg in die Europäiche Union?' Integration (Bonn), April 1986; 'Zu den Ergebnissen der Luxemburger Vertragskonferenz vom Herbst 1985: 39 Thesen'. Institut für Europäische Politik, Bonn, February 1986

Notes

1. The views expressed in this chapter are based on a collective reflection to which several

TEPSA institutes and associations have contributed. See in particular the articles and papers cited by John Pinder, Robert Touleman, Jacques Vandamme and Wolfgang Wessels.
2.   Christopher Tugendhat, <u>Making sense of Europe</u>, London, 1986, p.22.
3.   See, for instance, <u>Newsweek</u>, April 9, 1984. Cover story on 'The decline of Europe'. 'Economic stagnation and political malaise', it wrote, 'darken the future of a once-proud continent'.
4.   For a negative judgement on the SEA, see in particular the remarks of Pierre Pescatore, a former judge of the Communities' Court of Justice. Text published by <u>Agence Europe</u> in its series <u>Europe Documents</u>, no 1397, 27 March 1986.
5.   See John Pinder, 'The Single European Act as a federal increment: A critique from a neo-federalist perspective'. Federal Trust, London 1986.
6.   See Wolfgang Wessels, <u>39 Thesen</u>, op.cit., pp.6-7.
7.   Working Document on the strategy of the Committee on Institutional Affairs, European Parliament, 7 March 1986. Doc PE 103.892/rev. p.7.
8.   John Pinder, 'Economic and social powers of the European Union and the Member States: subordinate or coordinate relationship?' in Bieber, Jacqué and Weiler (eds), <u>An ever closer union</u>, Luxembourg, 1975; and 'Economic union and the Draft Treaty' in Juliet Lodge (ed), <u>European Union</u>, London 1986.
9.   For a recent study, see <u>Turkey and the European Community</u>, a summary report prepared by the Deutsches Orient-Institut and the Federal Trust for Education and Research of an international study group. Hamburg/London, December 1984.
10.   For an influential statement of these arguments, see <u>Towards European economic recovery in the 1980s</u>. Report presented to the European Parliament by Mr M. Albert and Professor R.J. Ball, August 1983.
11.   Christopher Layton, <u>One Europe: One World</u>. Report of a study group jointly sponsored by the Federal Trust for Education and Research, the Wyndham Place Trust and the One World Trust, London, 1986.
12.   For a first statement of these ideas see Robert Toulemon and Jacques Vandamme, 'L'Union Européenne: Perspectives du Sommet de Milan à la lumière des travaux du Comité Spaak No 2 et des positions des états de la Communauté'. Paper of the Trans European Policy Studies Association (TEPSA) presented at a conference organised by it, the

Istituto Affari Internazionali, and the Banca Nazionale dell'Agricultura, Rome June 1985.

13. Robert Toulemon, L'Union Européenne après l'accord du Luxembourg: intégration et flexibilité', TEPSA, February, 1986.